The Encyclopedia of
HOME WIRING
& ELECTRICITY

Martin Clifford

Drake Publishers Inc
New York · London

Published in 1974 by
Drake Publishers Inc.
381 Park Avenue South
New York, New York 10016

Library of Congress Cataloging in Publication Data

Clifford, Martin, 1910-
　The encyclopedia of home wiring and electricity.

　1. Electric wiring, Interior — Amateur's manuals.
2. Household appliances, Electric — Maintenance
and repair. I. Title.
TK9901.C62　　　621.319'24　　　74-6034
ISBN 0-87749-680-3

Printed in the United States of America.

CONTENTS

INTRODUCTION

This book is a "home electric-wiring smorgasbord," which is just another way of saying that you do not have to start with the first chapter and then pick your way, word by word, to the very end. That is what you should do if you want to become more expert in home electrical repairs, but if you have a specific wiring problem for which you want immediate help, there is no need for you to hold yourself back with additional information you may not want.

There are a number of good reasons for learning about electricity and the work it does, all of them economic. With some information and self-acquired know-how, you can extend the life of your appliances beyond the inevitable day when they must be replaced; you are less at the mercy of electricians; you can shop for electrical parts, paying much less than the full list price; and you can avoid many, if not all, charges for in-house labor. There is still another advantage: the intangible, but still very real satisfaction of being independent, of not being forced to rely wholly on the possible whims of some outside electrical contractor.

This does not mean you must immediately cast off your life line to your local electrician. Home wiring and home electrical repairs are matters of interest to the government, for wiring and electrical repairs do involve your health and safety and that of your neighbors. Therefore, what you may or may not do can be hedged in by local ordinances. Further, if you rent an apartment or house, your lease may include some very specific clauses about what you may install or change. You may learn that all of your new wiring becomes the property of the owner when you move, assuming you were legally permitted to do the wiring in the first place. Finally, your apartment or home insurance policy may contain restrictive clauses, written in legalese, stating that your insurance company will gladly accept regular payment of your premiums but is under no obligation to pay if

wiring, or changes in wiring, is not done by a licensed electrical contractor.

This sounds discouraging but it still does not mean that in-house electrical wiring and repair is outside your province. It does mean that if you want to become your own apartment or home electrician you should proceed with due legal caution.

Your insurance broker can interpret your home-owner's policy for you; your municipal government should be able to supply you with information concerning local laws; and The Encyclopedia of Electricity and Home Wiring will help you do a large amount of home electrical wiring and repairs with safety and reliability in mind.

MARTIN CLIFFORD

Lakewood, New Jersey
July, 1974

Chapter 1

BASIC FACTS ABOUT ELECTRICITY

Electricity is an in-depth subject and is so because every home, with few exceptions, makes use of it. That use may be nothing more than a flashlight, or may consist of every conceivable appliance. The extent to which you want to become involved in home electrical repairs depends entirely on your own wishes and your own needs. However, if you want to be more than a dilettante you should do two things: You should learn the language of electricity and some of its arithmetic.

Although the language of electricity is technical, the widespread use of electricity has made some of the terms part of our daily language. They are, however, often bandied about incorrectly. And so, as a start, it is important to assign more precise meanings to various electrical terms. The advantage to you in learning electrical definitions is that you will be able to make your electrical purchases knowing as much if not more than the man behind the counter, removing once and for all that feeling of helplessness and idiocy we all have when we talk to someone who has a better command of technical language. You will know precisely what you want to buy, the specific reasons for buying a particular item, and you will no longer be palmed off with a more expensive, but possibly inferior substitute.

These technical words and phrases will be defined and explained as they are used, but some of them do require repeated emphasis to become part of your everyday vocabulary. And, some electrical words will not even find their way into these chapters because of their limited application. To instantly find the language you want when you need it, turn to the glossary of electrical words at the end of the book.

Many people suffer a mental block at the mention of mathematics. For all your electrical wiring problems, however, all you will need will be elementary arithmetic, the sort of arithmetic taught to children in the fourth grade involving nothing more than simple multiplication and division, addition and subtraction. Understanding such arithmetic and being able to use it can save you time and money, and will result in a better electrical installation. The arithmetic can be done in lieu of using an expensive test meter, and since it will become part of your personal mental memory bank, you will never be without it or lose it.

VOLTAGE

The basic unit of electrical pressure is the volt. You will hear phrases such as "This line carries 120 volts" with its implication that the 120 volts are gliding smoothly and without effort along a line. That's just so much nonsense. Voltage is a pressure. It is an electrical pressure but a pressure nonetheless. The battery in your car supplies an electrical pressure, and so do the electrical generators of your local power utility.

Voltage is often compared to water pressure. The water that flows out of a faucet doesn't fall out; it is pushed out. The device that does the

1

pushing is a pump. The pump does not move out of its position, and if properly designed, supplies constant pressure. If its pressure increases, the water may come pouring out of your faucet with unexpected and surprising strength. If the pressure drops substantially, what may come out of the faucet may be just a trickle.

Voltage works similarly. To operate properly, an appliance requires the correct amount of voltage or electrical pressure. Too much, and the appliance will "overreact," or may become damaged. Too little, and the appliance will either not work at all, or do so poorly.

Power utilities are able to control the amount of electrical pressure available at the various outlets in your home or apartment. Generally, the pressure remains remarkably constant, but during periods of heavy power usage, as in the summer when many air conditioners are functioning at the same time, your utility may decrease the electrical pressure by a few percentage points. This can lower, slightly, the operating efficiency of some of your in-home electrical devices. A television picture may start rolling or may become slightly smaller; your air conditioner may not pump out cool air with its usual enthusiasm. These are temporary faults, automatically corrected when the power-line voltage is increased to its normal value.

UNITS OF VOLTAGE

Home electrical appliances are rated in terms of electrical pressure, that is, voltage. The most common are 110 volts and 220 volts. Therefore, the first step when buying an appliance is to make sure there is a common meeting ground between the voltage available at the various outlets in your home and the voltage requirements established by the manufacturer of the appliance. If, for example, you connect a 110-volt appliance to a 220-volt line, you have an excellent chance of destroying the appliance, plus the possibility of a fire, if

protective devices such as fuses do not open fast enough. If you connect a 220-volt appliance to a 110-volt line, the appliance will either not work properly or may not work at all.

The amount of electrical pressure demanded by electrical components varies. A flashlight may call for a few volts; your in-home radios and television receiver will require 110 volts; while a dust precipitator in your workshop may demand several thousand volts.

The microvolt is a millionth of 1 volt. To make up an electrical pressure of just 1 volt, you would need to gather together a million microvolts. If you think that a microvolt must be a mighty small amount of electrical pressure you are right. Still, the signal on your television receiver antenna is just a few microvolts, or may be 50 or 100 microvolts. The electrical pressure in some of the circuits of your transistor receiver can be just a few microvolts.

The millivolt is a thousandth of a volt. Gather a thousand microvolts and you might be able to join them into a single millivolt. The reason why electrical pressures are designated in terms of millivolts is that it is much easier to talk about millivolts than thousands and thousands of microvolts.

Like the microvolt the millivolt is also related to the volt. It takes a thousand millivolts to make up or constitute a single volt. Five volts are the same as 5,000 millivolts and this, in turn, is the same as 5,000,000 microvolts. The microvolt and the millivolt aren't used in connection with home wiring or home appliances, but you should know about them for they are used extensively in connection with home-entertainment electronic products: television receivers, radio receivers, and the various components of high-fidelity sound systems.

The kilovolt is still another multiple of the volt. A kilovolt is a thousand volts. If you can accumulate a thousand volts—and you can—you will have a kilovolt. Walk across a rug on a rather dry day and you will accumulate an electrical pressure, distributed across your body surface, of several kilovolts or more. Touch a doorknob and the spark you may see will be physical evidence of what those few kilovolts can do. If your hair is dry, and you have enough of it, combing it vigorously can also result in an electrical pressure of several kilovolts.

These are very high electrical pressures and yet the only effect on you will be a momentary shock when you touch the doorknob, or mild annoyance at not being able to comb your hair properly. And so, very high electrical pressures, under certain circumstances, are absolutely safe and notable only for their nuisance value. Quite often you may not even be aware of the tremendous electrical pressure being built up on your body surface. That's what happens when you walk along a street, but the electrical pressure can disappear as quickly as it is produced. Automobiles and trucks can develop very high volts. In the case of gasoline trucks the voltage may become high enough to produce a spark discharge—the same type of spark you produce when you walk across a rug or touch a doorknob. For gasoline trucks this is a potential source of disaster, and so they are equipped with electrical discharge devices.

The megavolt is the last of our multiples of a volt. A megavolt is a million volts. If you are interested in numbers, a megavolt is a million million times as strong as a microvolt. For the home owner, a megavolt is only of passing interest except when a storm is about to test the strength of lightning arresters.

For the home owner and the apartment dweller, the basic unit of electrical pressure, the volt, is of greatest interest. But you should be aware that we can have smaller electrical pressures such as the microvolt and the millivolt, and much larger ones such as the kilovolt and the megavolt.

ABBREVIATIONS

One of the bits of information you should have before buying any appliance is its voltage rating. This is often printed or engraved on a metal plate positioned in some inconspicuous area of the appliance. Look for it. The word "voltage" will be abbreviated as V or v. Thus, a unit rated for 115 volts may have this down as 115v or 115V. You should, of course, know the amount of voltage being supplied to your home by your local utility. The voltage rating not only applies to appliances, but to radio receivers, television sets, air-conditioning units, and electric-light bulbs.

SOURCE VOLTAGE

There are three basic ways by means of which you can get the voltage you will need. Two of these you pay for directly; the third is free. The most common is the voltage made available to you by your power company. Often referred to as power-line voltage, or more usually the line voltage, it has a nominal value of 115 volts, but is often called 110 volts, 115 volts, or 121 volts. Since these three different designations refer to the same voltage, any appliance marked 110V will work from any outlet that your utility has informed you is 121V. The same applies to 115V.

Another common voltage is that supplied by batteries. This is the voltage your car battery furnishes, or the batteries in your portable transistor radio, or the battery in your powered grass trimmer, or electrical scissors. Batteries and their voltages are described in the separate chapter on that subject.

The "free" voltage mentioned earlier is that supplied by your radio or television station and is the voltage produced across your antennas by these stations.

In each instance, voltage supplied—whether by your power company, or by batteries, or your radio or television stations—is sometimes called source voltage. In your home, the source voltage is that which is available at the various outlets, also referred to as the line voltage.

VOLTAGE UNDER OTHER NAMES

Voltage has a number of synonyms, and since these may be used by electricians, electrical contractors, salesmen in electrical-parts stores, or in electrical-parts catalogs, it is just as well to become familiar with them. Voltage is sometimes called electromotive force, abbreviated as EMF or alternatively as emf. Voltage is also known as potential, abbreviated as P or p; and sometimes as potential difference, shortened to PD or pd. A 12-volt source can be said to have a PD of 12, or an EMF of 12, or may simply be described as 12V or 12v. These various designations may appear in the same written description of an electrical appliance. The attitude of many electrical manufacturers is that it is the obligation of the user to become familiar with the terminology, an optimistic belief at best.

PRODUCING VOLTAGES

There are many ways of producing voltages. We can do so by friction: Just the act of rubbing one object against another will result in a voltage. We can do so chemically: A battery is an example. We can also develop voltages by using light, heat, pressure, or by magnetism. Some of these techniques are interesting, but not too practical. Others are of enormous importance and will be discussed in detail in appropriate sections in this book.

POLARITY

There are two basic types of voltages. The one in which the electrical pressure remains fairly constant is called DC. The other, in which the electrical pressure keeps changing, is called AC.

A new, freshly charged battery is a prime example of a DC voltage. A battery, rated at 12

volts DC, often written as 12 VDC, will maintain an electrical pressure of 12 volts whether it is at work or not. Your power-line voltage, the voltage available at the various outlets in your home, varies between zero and a maximum value of about 161. The change between zero and 161 takes place regularly and rapidly, so much so, in fact, that your appliances receive an effective voltage of about 115.

Every auto battery has a terminal with a plus (+) symbol marked or stamped into one of its lead terminals. The other post is sometimes marked with a minus (-) symbol. These symbols represent the polarity of the battery. Plus polarity means the plus (also called positive) terminal. Minus polarity means the minus (also called negative) terminal. The polarity of a battery does not change: The plus terminal is always plus; the minus terminal is always minus. For this reason, a battery or similar voltage-producing source, is called "direct." A direct voltage, abbreviated as DC, is the voltage produced by a source whose polarity does not change.

Your local power company uses huge rotating generators to produce the voltage for your outlets. Unlike the battery, the voltage at the output of the generator changes its polarity on a regular basis. The plus terminal becomes minus, then plus again, then minus, and so on. Similarly, the minus terminal becomes plus, then minus, then plus, and so on. This sort of voltage, in which the polarity keeps changing, is called alternating voltage, and is abbreviated as AC. For the most part, electrical devices designed for AC should not be used on DC voltage, and vice versa. An electrical appliance tagged as 115 VAC is designed for use with an alternating voltage having an electrical pressure of approximately 115 volts.

A DC voltage isn't inferior or superior to AC. They are simply two different types. Each has its applications and uses, and both are needed and used in the home. Some appliances are designed to work from either kind of voltage, but you can assume this is not the case unless the manufacturer's tag on the appliance indicates otherwise.

CURRENT

While an electrical pressure does not move, and while, hopefully, the effective amount of pressure remains fairly constant, the pressure or EMF does result in the movement of extremely tiny particles called electrons. The sum movement of these electrons is called a current of electricity, more commonly referred to as current.

We can make a comparison between the water-pressure pump at a reservoir station, supplying water pressure, with possible resulting water flow through a pipe, to a voltage source such as a battery and the resulting flow of electrons or current through a medium such as a copper wire. Like all analogies, this one isn't rigorously correct, for electrons and water are different, and there is also a considerable difference between a water-pressure pump and a battery.

In the case of a water pump, a pipe, and a faucet, you can have water flow or not, just as you please. As long as you keep the faucet closed, and assuming it is in good condition, with no dripping, no water will move out of the faucet into your sink. The pressure, though, remains unchanged. In other words, you can have pressure without water movement. A voltage source operates similarly. You can have electrical pressure without the movement of an electrical current. The storage battery in your car supplies an electrical pressure whether you use the car or not. That electrical pressure is approximately 12 volts (for most cars) whether your car is parked or out on the road.

Similarly, in your home, there is electrical pressure at the various outlets. Current does not begin to flow until you connect some sort of electrical appliance into the outlet. The electrical pressure is there on a 24-hour basis. Current flows only when you decide that it should.

DIRECT CURRENT

The abbreviation DC, used earlier, is actually an abbreviation for direct current. Direct current is the kind of current produced by a DC voltage source, such as a battery. However, regardless of the kind of voltage source, current always flows from the negative or minus terminal, through the device or appliance, back to the plus or positive terminal. Since the movement of the current is always in one direction, it is called direct. And while DC is an abbreviation for direct current, it is also used in connection with voltage. Thus, a DC voltage means a voltage source, such as a battery. The abbreviation is nonsensical, for a DC voltage means a direct-current voltage, a neat bit of double-talk, but it is in common usage.

ALTERNATING CURRENT

The rule in current flow is that current always moves from minus to plus. This is applicable, regardless of the kind of voltage source used. For a battery, the flow of current is quite simple. If we select the minus terminal of the battery as a starting point, we can consider the current moving out of the minus terminal, through the device, back to the plus terminal of the battery, and then through the battery to the minus terminal. But this is our starting point and so the process continues. Actually, there is no precise starting point for a direct current any more than one part of a wheel can start turning before some other part. All portions of a wheel move simultaneously. In a direct-current connection, current flows simultaneously through the battery, wires, and appliance.

Matters are quite different in an alternating-current setup. Not only does the polarity keep changing, but the electrical pressure as well.

The rule that current must move from the minus to the plus terminal still holds. If you could freeze the action of the voltage source, current would move from the minus terminal of the generator (using that as our starting point) through the appliance, back to the plus terminal of the generator, and then through the generator to its minus terminal. However, if we unfreeze the action, the minus terminal will become plus, and the plus terminal minus. Current will now move from the opposite terminal, through the appliance, back to the positive terminal of the generator, and then through the generator. The result of this behavior is that the current circulates back and forth at a rate depending on how fast the polarity of the voltage source is changing. Because the current keeps changing its direction of flow, surging back and forth, it is called alternating. An alternating current is abbreviated as AC. An alternating voltage is called an AC voltage, written out as an alternating-current voltage, also a bit of nonsense as far as abbreviations go, but there it is. That is what is used in electrical work.

Both types of current, direct and alternating, have their uses and both are desirable. They are supplementary, not competitive. There are times when an alternating voltage (AC) and an alternating current (AC) are needed, while at other times a direct voltage (DC) and a direct current (DC) are essential. Your portable transistor radio works on DC, your home television receiver on AC. DC for the home television receiver would be impractical; AC for the portable transistor radio would be equally undesirable.

UNITS OF CURRENT

Just as the volt is the basic unit of electrical pressure, the ampere is the basic unit of electrical current. Some appliances require "heavy" currents—that is, currents that are a few amperes or more—while other appliances are more modest in their demands. Generally, heat-producing components have strong current demands. Electric ovens, for example, electric heaters, toasters, and irons are all "transducing" units—that is, they convert electrical energy to heat energy. In so doing, they gulp huge amperes and therefore require very special treatment.

Not all units are designed for heavy current use, and so it is helpful to have a submultiple of the ampere known as the milliampere. That prefix, mille—means a thousandth part of, and so a millivolt is a thousandth of a volt and a milliampere is a thousandth part of an ampere. Divide an ampere into a thousand equal parts and each will be a milliampere. A milliampere is a rather small current unit; most household devices demand much more current than this. However, Christmas-tree bulbs, flashlight bulbs, transistor radio receivers, and certain circuits in television receivers are quite content with milliamperes of current.

Small though a milliampere may be, there is still a much smaller unit called the microampere. Micro-is a prefix meaning a "millionth," and just as a microvolt is a millionth of a volt, a microampere is a millionth of an ampere. Arithmetically speaking, a microampere is also a thousandth of a milliampere. Solid-state devices often have currents in the order of microamperes and milliamperes.

MORE ABBREVIATIONS

The abbreviation for ampere is the letter A, usually capitalized, but sometimes appearing in lower-case form. The term 6A is for 6 amperes and so is 6a. The letter M, either capitalized or in lower case, is the abbreviation for milli-. Thus, a millivolt might be written as MV or as mV, or as Mv, or as mv. There is no standardization and the user is left to his own devices when a manufacturer marks Mv or MV on a product. The letter M or m is also used for milliampere-current designations. MA is a milliampere. So is Ma or ma or mA. A device marked 115V, 65 MA requires an

6

electrical pressure of 115 volts, and if properly connected to the voltage source, will take 65 milliamperes of current from the source. Unless the component very obviously requires an AC voltage, it may carry a plate reading, "115 VAC, 65 MA." This is your indication that it is to be connected to a 115-volt AC source and that it will then take 65 milliamperes of current from the line.

The abbreviation for micro-is the Greek letter mu, written as μ. 120 μDC means the component is to be connected to a DC voltage source and that the current taken by the component from the source will then be 120 microamperes. The Greek letter mu is used to represent either microamperes or microvolts. For microamperes it may be written as ua, or uA. For microvolts it can be written as uv or as uV.

While the prefix kilo-, meaning a thousand, and the prefix mega,-meaning a million, are used in connection with volts, an ampere is a rather substantial current unit and so you will not see the terms kiloampere or megampere, except in very special, non-household applications.

THE LOAD

Any device, or component, or electrical appliance connected to a source of voltage is called a load. You have 115 volts at each of your outlets in your home, but until you connect an appliance, such as a lamp, radio, or iron, to any one of them, your power line is unloaded. To you, a radio set is just that. To an electrician and to the power line, that radio set is a load. A load is any device that takes or "draws" current from the voltage source. When you use a flashlight, the battery or batteries inside the case are "unloaded" until you push the ON button; when you do, you connect the bulb to the batteries. You thus complete a circuit and current flows from the batteries through the bulb. The bulb is said to be a load and to draw current from the batteries.

A heavy load is one that requires a large amount of current; a light load demands much less. An electric oven is a heavy load; with one or more of its burners turned on, it takes or "draws" a current of many amperes from the power line. A toaster is also a heavy load but does not require as much current as an electric stove and is therefore a lighter load. An electric fan or a home radio receiver could be a still lighter load. Turn on an electric light bulb and you "load" your power line. Turn on another, identical bulb and you double the load—that is, you now require twice as much current.

RELATIONSHIP BETWEEN CURRENT AND VOLTAGE

Let's start right off by saying there is no relationship. A high-voltage source does not necessarily mean a large amount of current. Your car storage battery is probably somewhere around 12 volts, but when starting the car it may be required to deliver several hundred amperes. Meantime, back in your house, Junior has just turned on a radio whose current requirements are less than one ampere, but which gets its voltage and current from the 115-volt AC outlet.

As a general rule, very high voltage often means a very low current, while a very low voltage is often associated with large currents. But there are so many exceptions you should consider the statement rather less as a rule and more as a possibility.

AMOUNT OF LOADING

Your local utility alternating-current generator has a very high current capability. This means that this generator can deliver as much current as you want, or your neighbors or your entire community insist on. At night, with all appliances and lights turned off, your current requirements are very small and could easily total less than an ampere. You might have one or more electric clocks that are never turned off, a small night lamp in a doorway near a nursery, or a small light inside your door nameplate. But when you get up, you may turn on a light and at once the current being delivered to your home increases. As the toaster is turned on for breakfast, as you use your electric shaver, and turn on the radio to hear the news, you make a greater and greater demand for current. Note that the voltage available at the outlets remains constant. What does change is the amount of current your household "draws" from the voltage line. You impose a lighter or heavier load on the line, depending on how many and which appliances you decide to use.

RESISTANCE

A certain amount of friction exists between the tires of your car and the road. This friction produces heat, which in turn increases the wear on your tires. And because friction is a sort of rubbing action, you must use some of your gasoline to overcome it. While it does seem as though friction is an unnecessary waste, anyone who has ever skidded on a relatively friction-free icy road is appreciative of the benefits of friction.

The current available from a battery or utility generator and from these sources to your appliances is delivered by wires, usually made of copper or aluminum, or some other metallic substance. Silver can be used and is used for certain special conditions, but copper and aluminum are more common for home and apartment use. The current, then, flows through connecting wires to the load and from it. The combination of voltage source, such as a battery or generator, connecting wires, and the load (an appliance, for example) is called a circuit. A circuit represents a complete path for the flow of current—that is, current can flow from the voltage source to the load, through the load, and then back to the voltage source again. As long as this process continues, the circuit is a continuous, unbroken one and is known as a closed circuit. A closed circuit is one through

which current can flow. The circuit can be interrupted or broken by a switch and so a switch, in its basic form, is simply a device for opening or closing a circuit. With the help of the switch, the current flow or no-current flow condition is under your control.

However, the entire circuit consisting of a voltage source, connecting wires, and the load does offer some opposition to the flow of current. In effect, what we have is electrical friction. When current flows through electrical friction, two things happen as a result: The amount of voltage available across the terminals of the load may be reduced, and the amount of current flow may diminish. Thus, your car battery may measure 12 volts, but because of electrical friction in the connecting wires, the voltage measured across your horn may be only 11.5 volts. Your horn may require 2 amperes, but because of electrical friction, the actual amount of current delivered may be only 1.9 amperes. These are small differences, and so when you depress the horn button, it will shriek and pedestrians will scoot out of your way.

Like voltage and current, electrical friction has its basic unit. This unit is known as the ohm, but there are two multiples you should know about, since they can appear in connection with home wiring and its problems. One of these is the kilohm. The prefix kilo-means a thousand, and so a kilohm is a thousand ohms. You will recall that the prefix mega-means a million; a megohm is therefore a million ohms. It takes a thousand ohms of resistance to constitute one kilohm. It also takes a thousand kilohms to make up one megohm.

VOLTAGE, CURRENT, AND RESISTANCE

Voltage, current, and resistance—these are the three important factors in any home wiring installation and they affect the purchase of any home appliance. Every electrical item you buy for your home or apartment is a problem in voltage, current, and resistance—a problem that is perhaps more involved than you may realize. However, this does not mean it will not be possible for you to solve it. All you need to know is the relationship existing between voltage, current, and resistance, and some facts about home wiring, and you'll be ready to approach home wiring, installation, and appliances with a good measure of confidence.

OHM'S LAW

There is a definite, arithmetic relationship between voltage, current, and resistance. As a general rule, if you increase the voltage of the source, the current flowing to the load will also increase. The source voltage may be out of your control, or it may not be. If your local power company decides to raise the line voltage in your home, the current flowing to the load will also increase. The source voltage may be out of your control, or it may not be. If your local power company decides to raise the line voltage in your home, the current flowing to your various appliances will increase. Your lamps may burn a bit brighter; your radio may sound slightly louder; and your toaster may work just a little faster. Conversely, the reverse will happen if for some reason your local power company decides to lower the voltage.

A similar situation exists in your car. If your battery is past its prime, if it has not recharged, the voltage across its terminals when you apply a load (such as trying to start the car) may result in nothing more than a few weak grunts. Because the voltage of the battery has dropped, not enough current reaches your starter motor, and as a result it may barely work at all. In both of these examples we have a direct relationship between voltage and current. As voltage goes up, so does current. As voltage goes down, so does current. Whether or not this is desirable depends entirely on the load. In the case of the auto, a substantial decrease in voltage means not enough current to start the car. In the home, a slight decrease in line voltage means less current to your television receiver. The receiver may be affected, or may not be, depending on the receiver and the amount of voltage decrease. In extreme cases the picture may become smaller, it may roll or tear, and the brightness may diminish. All of these things may happen, or none.

We can express the relationship between voltage and current by a very simple equation. We can let the letter E represent electromotive force or electrical pressure, also known as voltage, and the letter I represent current. Then:

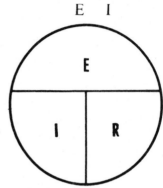

Aid for remembering Ohm's law: I is equal to E over R; R is equal to E over I (or E divided by I). E is equal to I times R.

Do be careful. That symbol between E and I is not an equals sign. It is a proportionality symbol. All it means is that if you increase E, the amount of I will go up, just a shorthand way of saying that raising the voltage also raises the current proportionately. And if you lower the value of E, the value of I is also lowered proportionately. Raise the voltage by 10 percent and the current will also go up by 10 percent. If the voltage is 10 volts, a 10 percent increase is 1 volt and so the voltage will rise to 10 plus 1 equals 11 volts. If the current is initially 1 ampere, a 10 percent increase is 0.1 ampere: 1 ampere plus 0.1 ampere equals 1.1 ampere. And so, when the voltage rises from 10 to 11 volts, the current will rise from 1 ampere to 1.1 amperes. E, then, is directly proportional to I.

The current I, however, is inversely proportional to resistance, R. This isn't mathematical double talk, for it is easily explained. We can write it as:

$$I = E/R$$

I and R are like children on the opposite ends of a seesaw. When one goes up, the other comes down. That is exactly what we mean by inversely proportional, but stated somewhat less elegantly. In practical terms, it means that you can control the amount of current flow by means of resistance. If you increase the resistance in a circuit, and there are devices available which can do just that, the flow of current decreases. Conversely, if you decrease the resistance in a circuit, the flow of current will increase.

This may sound difficult, but you do it all the time. If you have an electric-light dimmer, you can make your lamps glow more or less brightly. All you are doing, actually, is increasing or decreasing the amount of current flowing to a lamp by varying the amount of circuit resistance. And that is also what you do when you adjust the volume control on your radio or television receiver.

We now have two ways of controlling the current: by increasing or decreasing the voltage; and by increasing or decreasing the resistance. To simplify matters, we can combine all our efforts into one simple equation known as Ohm's law:

$$I = E / R$$

This is probably the simplest and most practical formula in electrical work, and is so valuable that it merits memorizing. The current I is in amperes, the voltage E is in volts, the resistance R is in ohms. If, for example, you want to double the amount of current flowing in a circuit, you can either double the amount of voltage, or reduce the resistance to half its original amount. Use either way, whichever is more convenient or better for you. Current control is very important, for in your house or apartment and particularly in wiring, it will be necessary for you to decide just how much current will go where. This isn't a hypothetical situation, for the amount of current flow will decide the size of the wire you will use, and the size of the wire you use will decide how much you will pay for it.

VARIATIONS OF OHM'S LAW

There are two other ways of writing Ohm's law. One of these is:

$$R = E / I$$

If you know the voltage (in volts) and the amount of current (in amperes), you can calculate the resistance by dividing the voltage by the current. If, for example, you measure the voltage across a battery and you read 12 volts, and a meter in the circuit indicates a current of 2 amperes, then the circuit resistance will be E/I equals 12/2 equals 6 ohms. While there are instruments for measuring resistance, it is often helpful to have some idea of the approximate value of resistance before measuring. Of course, if you do not have a resistance-measuring meter, you can easily calculate it by knowing the amount of voltage and current.

Another form of Ohm's law is:

$$E = I \times R$$

This very useful form of Ohm's law tells us that if we know the amount of current flowing in a circuit or through a component, and if we know the value of resistance, we can calculate the amount of voltage. Thus, if an appliance has a resistance of 115 ohms and requires 1 ampere of current to function properly, the voltage required by that appliance will be 1 x 115 equals 115 volts.

The three different forms of Ohm's law are easy to remember, and are as useful in home electrical wiring as any tool. The important feature to remember about Ohm's law is that the units should all be basic ones—that is, in terms of volts, amperes, and ohms. If multiples are available, convert them to basic units. If you know a current is 500 milliamperes, for example, convert it to amperes by dividing by 1,000: 500/1,000 equals ½ ampere equals 0.5 ampere; 2 kilovolts equals 2 x 1,000 equals 2,000 volts; 25 kilohms equals 25 x 1,000 equals 25,000 ohms.

POWER

Every appliance requires four fundamental considerations: (1) When buying the appliance, you must decide whether it will do the job you have in mind; (2) installation of the appliance; (3) maintenance and repair; and (4) cost of upkeep. This last factor, cost of upkeep, is generally given little, if any, thought, and yet the daily operation of an appliance may ultimately cost more than the original price.

There are three factors that govern the cost of using any appliance: the amount of voltage needed by the appliance; the amount of current load; and the length of time the appliance is used. The product of two of these, current and voltage, results in a new unit known as the watt. Thus, to determine the wattage of an appliance, multiply the amount of current it draws from the line by the voltage of the line. A toaster that uses 10 amperes of current when connected to the 115-volt line has a wattage rating of 10 x 115 equals 1150 watts. The wattage rating is often marked on the data plate of the appliance.

WATTAGE UNITS

The prefix kilo-can be applied to watts, just as it is to volts. Since the prefix kilo-means 1,000, a kilovolt is a thousand volts. A kilowatt is 1,000 watts. There are some appliances that do have kilowatt ratings. To convert kilowatts to watts, divide kilowatts by 1,000.

Another multiple of the watt is the megawatt or million watts, but this is such a large amount that it doesn't find application in home wiring or repair.

TOTAL POWER

Since the voltage delivered to your home is quite constant, you can calculate the total power in watts used by adding all the currents taken by your various appliances and then multiplying this sum by 115, your approximate power-line voltage.

If your toaster takes 6 amperes, your color tv 3 amperes, and your air conditioner 8 amperes, then the total current demand is 6 plus 3 plus 8 equals 17 amperes; 17 x 115 equals 1955 watts, rather close to 2 kilowatts. If you want to learn just how much power each of your appliances uses, look at the data plate on the units, or else consult the instruction manuals you may have received with them or write to the manufacturer. The information is available; it's just a question of digging it out. In some instances the information plate will just have the amount of current required by the unit. Fair enough. Multiply the figure supplied by 115 and you will have an approximation of the power requirement.

WHAT YOU PAY FOR

Wattage is simply an indication of the requirements of an electrical device. An electric iron may have a rating of 1 kilowatt. You can calculate just how much current the unit needs by using a simple formula. To calculate power in watts, we start with:

$$W = E \times I$$

W is in watts, E is in volts and I is the current in amperes. However, we can take the same formula, turn it around a bit, and come up with:

$$I = W / E$$

It isn't as difficult as it looks. Divide the power rating of the appliance by the line voltage and you'll have the current in amperes. In the case of the 1-kilowatt iron, 1 kilowatt is equal to 1,000 watts:

$$I = (1,000/115) - 8.7 \; amperes \; approximately$$

Your electric company not only counts the total watts you use, but the amount of time of such usage. The basic unit for measuring cost is the kilowatt hour. This charge varies from one utility to the next, and is also sometimes measured on a sliding scale—that is, the more electrical power you use, the less it begins to cost. The basic charge might be 10¢ per kilowatt hour for the first 10 kilowatt hours; 9¢ per kilowatt hour for the next 20 kilowatt hours; 8¢ per kilowatt hour for the next 15 kilowatt hours.

If you use an electric iron having a 1-kilowatt rating for one hour, your cost, exclusive of taxes, will be 10¢, assuming you are paying at the rate of 10¢ per kilowatt hour. If you use that iron for only half an hour, then the rate of 10¢ per kilowatt hour remains the same, but your cost for the half-hour will be only 5¢.

While costs per kilowatt hour are usually measured in pennies, a monthly electric bill can sometimes be staggering. There are two reasons for this: The first is that there are 24 hours in a day and nearly always 30 or 31 days in a month. Multiply 24 by 31 and you get 744 hours during which you use smaller or larger amounts of current. If you have an average of twenty 60-watt bulbs in your home, their total power consumption if all are turned on at the same time would be 60 x 20 equals 1,200 watts equals 1.2 kilowatts. This may not seem like much, but consider that you do have some bulbs rated at 75 or 100 watts, that you may have one or more heat lamps, that you may have outdoor flood lamps rated at about 500 or more watts. Lamps, though, are economical compared to an electric toaster, a heater, a console television set with a large screen, or electric radiators. Now add to this your radio receiver, your electric mixer, blender, electric shaver, electric toothbrush, sun lamp, electric grinder, electric hair dryer, electric hairbrush, electric clocks, and you will soon have a most impressive total. The criterion for cost depends on two factors: how much current the unit requires, and the length of time it remains turned on. You save very little money by disconnecting your electric clock. It is rated at about 3 watts and so in a 744-hour month it will require 2232 watts. at 10¢ per kilowatt hour the clock will cost 2.232 x 0.10 equals 22.3 cents to operate. The convenience and accuracy of the clock is certainly worth that much!

Consider your electric baseboard heaters. They

may be rated at about 3 kilowatts. If you have five of them then 5 x 3 equals 15 kilowatts. If these heaters remain turned on for an average of 300 hours, then the total power consumption is 4500 kilowatt hours. At 10 cents per kilowatt hour, you will be paying $45 per month for electric heat. The obvious thing to do is to switch to a more economical form of heating, or to insulate your house as thoroughly as possible, and to do anything you can possibly do to keep cold air drafts from sweeping into your home.

The big expense in your electric bill, then, is any appliance that is "current hungry" and that must operate for extended periods of time. If you insist on the convenience of a self-cleaning oven, consider also that it requires a large amount of current. Against this, you may wish to weigh the fact that you do not "self-clean" that often and that you are willing to pay for the convenience. The following table supplies the approximate wattage ratings of home appliances, approximate because there are substantial variations even among similar types. Thus, one television receiver might be rated at 150 watts, such as a small-screen black-and-white unit, or more than 300 watts for a large-screen color set. One electric fan might call for 40 watts, a larger one for 80 watts. But the table will give you a general idea of how the "electrical dollar" is spent.

Appliance	Average Wattage for 115-Volt Line
Air conditioner, room type	1,000
Blanket	250
Clock	3
Coffee maker	1,000
Dryer	4,000
Fan, 8-inch	30
Fan, 10-inch	35
Fan, 12-inch	50
Fan, attic type	400

Food mixer	200
Freezer	500
Fryer	1,200
Garbage-disposal unit	500
Hair dryer	300
Heater (radiant)	1,200
Hot plate	1,000
Humidifier	500
Infrared heating lamp	350
Iron (clothing)	1,000
Iron (soldering)	100
Lamps	60
Mixer	200
Motors	300
Radio	75
Record player	50
Refrigerator	300
Roaster	1,200
Rotisserie	1,300
Sun lamp	400
Television receiver	300
Toaster	1,200
Vacuum cleaner	350
Washing machine	1,300
Water heater	4,500

This isn't a complete list nor will every home have every one of these appliances. But from this list you can see which are more expensive to operate than others. A quick look at the data plate on an appliance should give you a rough idea of what it will cost for in-home use. If you know your cost per kilowatt hour, the number of kilowatts the appliance will use when turned on, and the number of hours of expected use, you should be able to make a fairly accurate prediction. Remember, also, that the operating cost of any new appliance must be added to your existing electric bill and not considered by itself.

HOW TO READ A KILOWATT-HOUR METER

Most people do not check their electric bills, accepting them on faith, correctly reasoning that power companies are not in business to cheat them. But your electric-power bill is based on a reading of a kilowatt-hour meter somewhere inside or outside your home. The meter reader is a professional, is experienced, but he is also human, and so can make mistakes.

The meter that measures your use of electric power is called a kilowatt-hour meter. It makes two measurements: power used in watts, and elapsed time of usage.

There are two types of watt-hour meters. The newer is a cyclometer type and looks like a small box with rectangular openings through which numbers can be seen. The cyclometer supplies a direct reading in kilowatt hours and is as easy to read as a digital clock. When the meter reaches 9,999, it begins once again with 0,000.

How to read a kilowatt-hour meter: Upper drawing shows meter at start; lower drawing, one month later. The reading of the meter starts with 6019 kilowatt hours. The reading a month later is 6289 kilowatt hours. 6289 - 6019 is 270, and so the consumption is 270 kilowatt hours.

You can make your own readings in two different ways. Select a particular hour of a certain day and take a reading. Then, one month later, at the same hour and on the same day, take your next reading. Subtract the first reading from the second and you will have your power usage for that month. If you do this month after month, two facts will emerge. You will learn that during certain months of the year your power use may rise drastically. The second is that you will now have a yardstick for comparing your results with that on your electric bill. To make a more accurate check, take a reading immediately after that taken by the meter reader working for your local power utility. If, for example, on March 1, your kilowatt-hour meter reads 1,657 and a month later reads 5,003, then your power consumption is 5,003 - 1,657 equals 3,346 kilowatt hours. Multiply this number by the prevailing rate per kilowatt hour, add taxes, and the result should be very close to that shown on your bill.

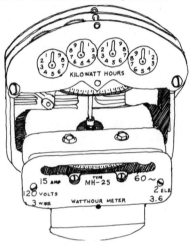

The watt-hour meter uses four dials. The first dial at the left measures thousands; the next dial measures hundreds; the third dial measures tens; and the last dial, the one at the right, measures units or ones.

An older type of kilowatt-hour meter, but one that is still widely used, has four dials, somewhat like miniature clocks, as shown in the illustration. If you will examine dials marked 1 and 3, you will see they are numbered in reverse order, while dials 2 and 4 follow a clockwise numbering system.

Reading such a meter is easy. Start with the first dial on the left and read the number the meter pointer has just passed. If, for example, the pointer is between 4 and 5, write the number 4. Then read the second dial in the same way, followed by the third and finally the fourth or last dial. This reading, for example, could be 4 3 7 8. This is *not* the number of kilowatt hours used, but is your starting reference. At approximately the same time on the

following month, take another reading. Subtract the first reading from the second and the difference will be the kilowatt-hour usage.

CALCULATING YOUR ELECTRIC BILL

What you pay for electricity depends on where you live. In some areas the rate may be flat—that is, you pay the same amount per kilowatt hour regardless of how much electricity is used. You may also pay on a sliding scale, more for the first few kilowatt hours and less and less as you use more and more. In some areas there may be special rates for appliances that use large amounts of current, such as electric water heaters, ranges, or baseboard heaters. If you do not understand just how your electric bill is calculated, visit the offices of your local power company. If you have a prior understanding of the difference between a kilowatt and a kilowatt hour, if you have learned how to read an electric meter, and if you know which of your appliances consume power at an enormous rate, you will be in a much better position to understand and use, for your benefit, information supplied to you by your electric company. Electrical economy in the home is like thrift; to be useful it must be developed as a habit. It's easy to leave lights on as you walk from room to room; it's economical to turn them off.

MEANING OF FREQUENCY

The first block diagram in the illustration shows a battery connected to a load, such as a lamp. As indicated by the arrows, the current always moves in the same direction. The current may be called steady, or direct, or unidirectional. All these words apply. The abbreviation for direct current, as indicated earlier, is DC.

An alternating voltage behaves as though being supplied by a battery whose terminals are constantly being reversed. We could generate an alternating current by mounting a battery on some sort of rotating table. More practically, we use an

AC generator, a rotating device for producing or generating an alternating voltage. The number of times per second that the polarity of the generator is reversed is called its frequency. If there are 60 reversals per second, then the current will reverse its direction of flow this many times. The current reversal is produced by the constantly changing polarity at the terminals of the generator. A single backward and forward motion of the current in one second is called a cycle per second. The cycle per second is now becoming known as a Hertz. Sixty Hertz means 60 cycles or 60 complete reversals of current per second. Hertz is abbreviated as Hz and cycles per second as cps.

The frequency, or number of complete changes of current flow per second of a current is another bit of information often supplied on the data plates of appliances. An appliance marked 200W, 115V, 60 Hz, means that the unit must be connected to a 115-volt outlet in your home. Sixty Hz indicates that the voltage must be AC, and further, must have a frequency of 60 cycles per second. And, when these instructions are followed, the unit will take 200 watts of electrical power from the line, as long as the appliance is in use. For each hour that the appliance is operated, you will be charged for 200 watt hours. In five hours you will be billed for 200 x 5 equals 1,000 watt hours equals 1 kilowatt hour, abbreviated as 1 kw hr or as 1 kwhr.

Many electric-power companies supply AC to their customers with the AC having a frequency of 60 Hz. However, there are some that do operate with a lower frequency, such as 50 Hz, while others may go as low as 25 Hz. Whether an appliance marked as 60 Hz will work well on 50 Hz or 25 Hz depends on the type of appliance. That is why, when you plan to move from one part of the country to another, you should determine two basic facts: (1) the frequency of the power line you are presently using; and (2) the frequency of the power lines in your new location. If you plan to move your appliances, you may find they will work poorly or not at all in your new location, and so it might have been financially more advisable to dispose of them before moving.

Appliances that change electrical energy to heat can be moved without concern. This includes electric blankets, electric ranges, irons, and electric heaters.

Fluorescent fixtures designed to work on 60 Hz may flicker, and if they use a ballast, you will find the ballast (described in the chapter on lighting) will have a much shorter life. Incandescent light bulbs will work equally well at 60 Hz and 50 Hz, but if the power-line frequency is lower than 50 you may notice an annoying flicker.

Many home and workshop appliances use motors. Your electric clock has a motor; so has your vacuum cleaner, washing machine, and hair dryer. Some motors, such as those in electric clocks, are specifically designed to work at a particular frequency. A clock made for 60 Hz will not keep correct time at 50 Hz. A vacuum cleaner made for 60 Hz may not supply as much suction when worked at 50 Hz. Some household devices, such as television receivers that are transformer operated, may not produce as bright a picture or may even have a smaller picture if designed for 60 Hz and forced to work on 50 Hz. On some data plates on appliances you may find a designation: 50 Hz/60 Hz, indicating that such an appliance is made to operate well on either frequency. You may find it helpful to contact the electric-power company in your new location to learn the prevailing frequency, and also what effect, if any, this new frequency will have on your household appliances.

NATIONAL ELECTRICAL CODE

Yes, it is your home or apartment and is your castle, and you can regard it as such, but as far as electrical wiring and installation of appliances are concerned, there are certain things you may do and others you may not. Electrical wiring is hemmed in by all sorts of restrictions specified not only by your municipality but also by home-owners' insurance policies that you bought and paid for. When you sign an application for a policy, the presumption is that you are aware you are affixing your name to a contract and intend abiding by its terms. If a fire occurs in your home due to some contributory negligence on your part, and if that fire is in some way associated with improper use of appliances or wiring installation, you may have difficulty in collecting; or, if you do collect, you may not get the full amount to which you would otherwise be entitled.

Under the aegis of a number of insurance companies, we have a group known as the National Fire Protection Association. Every few years this group publishes a summary of electrical-wiring rules under the general heading of National Electrical Code. The purpose of this code is to provide guidelines for safety in wiring. You can get a copy of the code by writing to the National Fire Protection Association, 470 Atlantic Avenue, Boston, Massachusetts 02210. Your existing local municipality code and your state code, if such a code exists, also affect home wiring. And your home owners' policy may have a clause that all wiring must be done by a master electrician or must be approved by him. This does not mean you cannot do your own wiring. It does mean that you, or a professional electrician for that matter, must follow certain rules. These rules are not capricious or arbitrary. They are based on substantial experience and are for your own protection, as well as the protection of your neighbors, and possibly your neighborhood. Electrical fires can and do happen and when they occur can spread to adjacent homes or apartments. Fortunately, you can make numerous electrical repairs, you can replace worn-out electrical equipment, and you can keep your home or apartment in tiptop electrical shape by making your own repairs, provided you do so in a good way, an approved way. The purpose of this book is to show you how to do so.

UNDERWRITERS' LABORATORIES

Every home electrical repair requires two basic items: labor and materials. Materials are not only good, but they are in plentiful supply and you have a tremendous variety from which to pick and choose. Buying electrical equipment is like shopping in a supermarket. You do best if you know which items are the greatest value for the money. By knowing and understanding just the kind of electrical part you want to buy, by understanding just what that part is supposed to do for you, by understanding the particular jargon of the electrician, you put yourself in the good position of being able to buy the best for the lowest cost.

Many electrical parts carry a label indicating they are approved by the Underwriters Laboratories. You will see the logo or identification symbol of the Underwriters' Laboratories, and possibly the abbreviation UL. Use only those parts that are UL approved. Underwriters' labels come in a variety of sizes, styles, and shapes, but if you read the label carefully you will have no doubt about the intent.

UL approval is not a guarantee of top quality, but simply indicates that certain minimum standards have been met. You can buy two switches, both UL approved, but one costing more than the other and of superior quality and workmanship. Both will be safe to use, will work as you expect, but one may last longer, be quieter than the other, be easier to mount, install, handle, or may have other features over and beyond the normal functions of a switch. But the less expensive switch will also work, and will do so safely.

The Underwriters' Laboratories was set up as a laboratory for making exhaustive tests of electrical products submitted to it by manufacturers. If the item's components meet all tests, it is then eligible for listing in the "List of Inspected Electrical

Various types of labels indicating Underwriter Laboratories inspection.

Appliances," and may then carry a label indicating that such components are UL approved. Manufacturers of electrical products are interested in UL approval since this gives them a competitive edge over products that have not been approved. This does not mean that a product has UL approval in perpetuity. Electrical products that go through materials or design changes must be submitted for re-approval.

The UL stamp or label means the product you buy has met tests imposed by an outside agency and is for your protection. The UL label may actually be that: a label adhering to the surface of the product. Or, it may be stamped or printed on, or be a tiny metallic disc. But whatever its shape, size, color, and no matter how it is printed, look for the words or abbreviation, Underwirters' Laboratories or UL.

FOLLOWING THE RULES

The UL tag of approval does not give you carte blanche to use electrical equipment beyond its specifications. Thus, if you buy a length of wire rated to carry a load of 2 amperes, you may not arbitrarily decide to send 4 amperes through it. UL approval is approval for a product to be used within the specification limits indicated by the manufacturer. These are the specifications submitted to the Underwriters' Laboratories, together with the material to be tested. One of the functions of the Underwriters' Laboratories is to make certain that electrical products do meet the specifications claimed by the manufacturer.

HOW CAN YOU BE SURE?

You can always, somewhere, find a small, marginal merchant, willing to sell electrical equipment at bargain prices. Often the equipment will be sold with the statement that it is as good as UL approved, or there may be an implication that UL-approved manufacturers have gathered together to stifle competition. That's just so much nonsense, of course. Buy only from a reputable electrical-parts merchandiser. If you buy appliances make sure you get a warranty, but before you leave the store make certain you understand just what labor and parts, and for what length of time the warranty is valid.

YOUR LOCAL POWER COMPANY

If you have any doubt about wiring changes in your home, about what you are allowed to do or are not permitted to do, check with your local power utility. It is their function to deliver electrical power to your home and they can supply useful advice, without charge, particularly if you know precisely what you want to do about the electrical wiring in your home and just how you plan to do it.

WHEN SHOULD YOU MAKE REPAIRS?

How do you know if your home needs electrical changes? Right now, before considering anything else, you should know that your home is very probably inadequately wired, particularly if it is more than 20 years old. Two decades ago far fewer electrical appliances were used, and those that were available didn't have the current demands of today's components. As an example, consider the electrical toaster. When first introduced it would handle a single slice of bread, toasting one side at a time. The toaster was then modified, subsequently, to handle two slices, then four, and now you have some that handle six or more. An automatic pop-up feature was then added, and then a control for governing the degree of toast "browning." More elaborate toasters were then made available that would toast simultaneously on both sides, and there are some that act as miniature top-of-the-counter stoves. But every one of these changes meant one thing—more current for the appliance. And so the power consumption of the modern toaster has climbed from about a hundred watts into the kilowatt region.

There are also many appliances today that did not exist 20 or more years ago—color-television receivers, self-cleaning ovens, and central air conditioning. The result is that many homes today have inadequate wiring—that is, wiring incapable of carrying the large currents required by these more recent appliances. Since the trend is toward more, not fewer electrical components, wiring changes must be made not just to meet immediate needs, but with even the heavier current loads of the future in mind.

HOW CAN YOU TELL?

If all appliances in your home work well, and continue to do so even if most or all of them are turned on at one time, if your lighting remains steady and brilliant, if your television pictures fill the entire screen and have adequate brightness, if you do not need to replace fuses, then you can be fairly sure your home wiring is adequate. This does not mean it has not reached the limit of its capacity. It may have. It does indicate that with your existing appliance setup your electrical system is working well. However, it does not mean you can continually and arbitrarily keep adding one appliance after the other, without expectation of trouble.

Here are some trouble symptoms that supply clues about your wiring:

- You install a new air conditioner and its performance is disappointing. Further, you have fuse troubles, something that has never happened before.

- Your master fuse box in the basement of your home has circuit breakers and you find it necessary to reset these breakers fairly often. Or, since the box contains a number of circuit breakers, you find that more of these need regular resetting. If your box uses replaceable fuses, you find that you must put in new fuses more often. Also, you may now be using fuses having higher current ratings than the originals.

- Lights in various rooms seem dimmer, particularly when you turn on an air conditioner, television set, or electric range. At times the lights seem to flicker. Conversely, the lights in one or more rooms may seem much brighter when appliances are turned off.

- You need to "jiggle" one or more of your switches to get lights to go on. Or, you may have noticed that some switches ordinarily making a clicking sound when turned on or off no longer do so.

- You have started to use cube taps at your outlets and now you find yourself connecting a cube tap right on top of a cube tap.

- Upon removing a plug from an outlet, you touch the prongs of the plug and you find they are quite warm. Or, you touch the insulated wire leading to an appliance and find it surprisingly hot.

- Your television picture no longer seems as bright. Your local TV repairman talks about a new picture tube, even though the one you have is just a few months old, and your television set doesn't get much usage.

- The automatic feature on some of your appliances functions erratically. Your toaster doesn't pop up when it should; your washing machine is now in the habit of skipping a cycle or two.

These are just some of the possible symptoms. If you have such troubles, then your home is due for an electrical update.

Chapter 2

TOOLS FOR ELECTRICAL WORK

The number of tools you will need for electrical repairs will depend on whether you have an apartment or your own home, on the extent to which you are motivated by the desire to save money on electrical repairs, and on the amount of work, other than electrical, you may want to do in your home. There is no question that a complete set of tools will not only enable you to do a better job, but a quicker, neater, and more professional one as well. Many of the tools needed for electrical work can also be used in home carpentry or for any of the dozens or other jobs that home maintenance demands.

Tools are inexpensive. Even a professional set doesn't cost that much in relationship to the overall cost of an apartment or house. Further, the money you save by doing electrical jobs yourself will soon more than pay for your original investment in tools. And, fortunately, most tools will have a useful life span equivalent to that of your home, or possibly better.

SCREWDRIVERS

These are available in a variety of sizes, shapes, lengths, and with various types of handles. There are just two basic types, though: The first is the regular kind with a straight edge. The other is known as a Phillips head. The advantage of the Phillips-head type is that the head of the tool gets a better grip on the head or the screw being turned.

Tool steel is generally used for making bet-ter-grade screwdrivers. The screwdrivers have a long shank embedded in a handle, preferably made of plastic, but you will also find handles made of wood. Plastic handles are preferable. When buying such a screwdriver, make sure the round metal portion extends well into the handle, that it is secure, and that the handle is grooved, engraved, or shaped so that you can get a good grip on it. The handle should be long enough to fit in the palm of your hand. If you cannot get a good grip on the handle of the screwdriver, you will have trouble using it.

Every screwdriver has three parts: a handle, a round metal shank, and a blade shaped to fit the slotted head of a screw. The blade is actually part of the shank. Most screwdrivers have round shanks, but the larger ones have square shanks. The purpose here is to let you use a wrench as an aid in turning screws that present turning problems.

The function of the blade is to fit into the slotted head of a screw. The word "fit" means precisely that. The entire edge of the blade must fit in and be parallel to the slot of the screw. If the screwdriver blade is too small, you will find that the edges of the blade are shorter than the slot, and you will also see that the screwdriver will turn a short distance before engaging or touching the edges of the screw. You may be able to turn the screw with such a screwdriver, but you will be making unnecessary work for yourself. There is also the possibility of damaging the screwhead, making a replacement necessary.

It is both advisable and helpful to have a variety of screwdrivers of different sizes. Using a single screwdriver for electrical repairs is not only difficult, but sometimes impossible. Get the regular screwdrivers, and also several having a Phillips head.

Screwdrivers are available with detachable heads so that the same head can be used for a variety of screwdrivers. These are often available in kit form so that you can have a number of screwdrivers of different sizes, in both regular and Phillips-head arrangements. If you do opt to buy the detachable-head type—and it may be more economical than purchasing individual screwdrivers—make sure that the blade fits easily, smoothly, and tightly into the handle. With cheaper types the fit of the handle is very poor, with the handle having a tendency to drop off when least expected. As a start you should have at least three regular screwdrivers: a small one for removing screws from outlet base plates; a medium-sized one for turning screws such as nos. 6, 8, or 10; and a large one for handling fairly big machine and wood screws.

While these are the basic screwdrivers you should have, you can also get an offset screwdriver for turning screws that cannot be reached with an ordinary screwdriver. There is also a ratchet screwdriver that drives screws in or removes them by means of a handle you can push down or rotate.

THE DO'S AND DON'TS OF SCREW-DRIVERS

The purpose of a screwdriver is simple: to turn a screw in or to take it out. That's all. Don't use it for opening cans of paint or other household chores. To keep the screwdriver from rusting, put a bit of machine oil on scrap cloth and rub the metal portion with it.

Don't use the screwdriver for poking into outlets that may be "live." And, when working on any electrical wiring or appliances with screwdrivers, keep your hand on only the plastic handle.

When you use a screwdriver, make sure that the screwdriver is straight, and not tilted—that is, the screwdriver must be at right angles to the screw it is turning.

Always keep the screwdriver in the same place, preferably a toolbox or a tool carrier. A carrier, unlike a toolbox, is open and has a handle so you can carry all or most of your tools at the same time.

Don't select the first screwdriver that comes to hand. Instead, try to match the screwdriver to the screw.

Do not use a screwdriver whose head is very worn or which has become rounded. If you have the equipment and you know how to grind a screwdriver head, do so. If not, replace the screwdriver, and now that the old screwdriver has lost its original function, keep it for opening cans of paint.

PLIERS

Pliers do more than give you the equivalent of an extra hand. Because of the length of their handles, you can exert considerable pressure, much more so than if you used your hands alone.

Like screwdrivers, pliers come in just about every size and some of them have rather odd shapes. Pliers are available with handles that are either insulated or uninsulated. If you have a choice, use insulated handles. This will give you an added measure of protection against possible shock.

As a minimum requirement you should have a gas pliers and a diagonal cutting pliers. The gas pliers have a slip feature giving the jaws of the pliers a considerable opening distance. Further, such pliers have considerable holding force. Diagonal cutting pliers aren't actually pliers, and should more correctly be called cutters. Use them for cutting wire. Another member of the pliers family that would be helpful is the long-nose. These are useful for reaching into areas where your fingers cannot or should not go. Consider them an extension of your fingers, for that is what they are intended to be. You can also use them for retrieving small bits of hardware that inevitably roll or fall into hard-to-reach places. Their true function is to work in bending wire into different shapes, and also for holding wire or hardware.

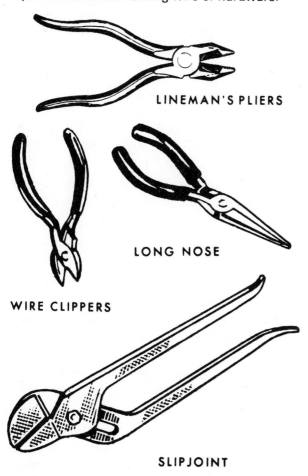

LINEMAN'S PLIERS

LONG NOSE

WIRE CLIPPERS

SLIPJOINT

Various types of pliers: The long-nose is useful for holding wires. The lineman's is for crushing insulation to help in its removal; its cutting jaws are for snipping wires. Wire clippers are intended only for cutting and stripping. The slipjoint pliers are used for tightening locknuts or small nuts. The slipjoint feature permits its use on nuts of various sizes.

The safest procedure when buying tools is to purchase brand names. In this way you pay more but can depend on the manufacturer's wish to be remembered for quality. When buying pliers, make sure that the two moving sections of the pliers, joined by some kind of central pivot, move smoothly and easily without excessive play. The jaws of the pliers should meet and rest on top of each other so that one jaw does not extend over the other. When buying cutting pliers, hold the pliers closed with the cutting edges up to a light. There should be no cracks or damage visible in the cutting edges. The cutting edges should rest in a straight line on top of each other, with no light shining through.

Diagonal cutters are designed for cutting wire made of a metal that is soft compared to other metals. Cutters are not intended for slicing screws, or cutting bits of steel. Doing so will nick the edges and reduce the usefulness of the tool. Some cutters come equipped with a tiny cylindrical slot in the cutting edges, intended as an aid in stripping insulation from wires. This is a useful feature.

There is one type of pliers that combines the features of the diagonal cutters and gas pliers. Known as electrician's pliers, or as side cutters, you can buy them in various sizes. You can use these for cutting, stripping, and slicing wires. Check the cutting edges of electrician's pliers just as you would diagonal cutters. Make sure the cutting edges are straight, smooth, and undamaged, and that they allow no light through when closed.

Pliers are often used for holding and function as a sort of portable vise. For holding small and thin objects you'll need a pair of long-nose pliers. The electrician's pliers will do for larger, thicker materials.

Some pliers, particularly electrician's pliers, are equipped with rubber-grip handles. This allows a more secure hold on the pliers when working with them, and at the same time insulates the hands from contact with voltage.

FUSE PULLERS

There are various sizes and types of fuses (to be described later), among them the cartridge type. The cartridge fuse looks like a small cylinder and is mounted and held at its ends by a rather strong, spring-action metal clip. Removing a cartridge fuse does present the possibility of electrical shock since it is wired directly in the power line. The ends of the cartridge fuse are metal and so you should not touch these ends if you need to remove the fuse. Still better is a fuse puller, which eliminates the shock risk of replacing cartridge fuses by hand. It is also useful for bending fuse clips, adjusting loose cutout clips, and for handling "live" electrical parts—"live" in the sense that an electrical current flows through them.

Whether you need a fuse puller, or not, depends on the kind of fusing you have. If you use circuit breakers only, for example, you do not need the fuse puller. But if your power line is protected by cartridge fuses, the small expense is very worthwhile. Mount the fuse puller near the fuse box, or put it on top of the fuse box, so that in the event of power failure due to an open cartridge fuse, you need not suddenly wonder about the location of the tool.

Fuse pullers are made of some insulating material such as plastic so you can use them safely. One type, made of see-through plastic, contains a small neon glow tube. The fuse puller has a pair of test probes coming out of each handle, and so this tool can be used for both removing cartridge fuses and for testing to determine if line voltage is present. An open fuse is a common cause of failure of an appliance, but the fault can be elsewhere. The neon glow-tube fuse puller can be used right at the fuse box to determine im-

mediately whether or not the cartridge fuse is at fault.

WRENCHES

Pliers are often used for fastening machine nuts, but they are actually holding tools. When pliers are used for fastening a nut, you must do three things simultaneously: Maintain firm pressure on the handles of the pliers, make sure the jaws of the pliers have a firm grip on the nut being turned, and apply a turning force. This doesn't make the task impossible, just difficult. A more logical tool for machine nuts is the wrench, designed specifically for this purpose. The handle of the wrench does not need to be squeezed, and its jaws can either be adjusted to fit the nut, or may fit the nut without adjustment.

There are many different types of wrenches, and some used by other crafts, such as plumbers, are either the same or similar to those used by electricians. One of the more common wrenches for electricians is the adjustable open-end wrench, also called a crescent wrench. One of the jaws of the crescent wrench is fixed; the other is adjustable by a helical-type screw near the head of the wrench. Crescent wrenches are available in different sizes. Very large wrenches are used where substantial turning effort is needed but for home use a medium-sized wrench is satisfactory.

The pipe wrench is another type of open-end wrench, but as its name implies, is intended for pipe and conduit. It can be used for tightening nuts on machine screws, but it will not do this job as well as a crescent wrench. The pipe wrench, though, is well suited for tightening threaded fastenings on pipe.

An open-end wrench consists of a tool made of a straight length of metal in the form of a bar. Each end of the wrench is designed to fit a single-size nut. Since nuts come in different sizes, a complete set of open-end wrenches would be needed to handle all fastening problems. However, the majority of nuts used in electrical work fall into a few size categories, and so wrenches capable of handling nuts from ¼″ to ½″ would be satisfactory. Some open-end wrenches are open at one end and box at the other. A box wrench is one made in the form of an enclosed serrated circle. The ridges inside the circle fit on the four edges of the nut.

Screwdrivers, pliers, and wrenches are the most widely needed tools for do-it-yourself electrical home-repair jobs. The tools are easy to use, and you can save enough on just one or two electrical jobs to pay for complete sets of all of them. This doesn't mean that these are the only tools. There are others we use around the home for various purposes but that can also be used for electrical repairs.

HAMMER

The best kind is one in which the handle and the head form a continuous piece. Use a hammer made of steel with a rubber-insulated handle. This will give a better grip and electrical protection as well. You'll need the hammer for driving staples, nails, or fastening hangers. The hammer is also useful for tapping electrical parts, such as switch boxes, into position.

JACKKNIFE

The jackknife is at best a dubious aid for the home electrician. It can be a dangerous tool since the knife blades can fold back into the knife unexpectedly. The jackknife may contain a screwdriver, awl, scriber, but it is much better to have individual tools. The jackknife can be used for removing insulation from wires, but it is much better, easier, and faster to use a wire-stripping tool.

TEST LIGHT

A test light is simply a neon lamp designed to operate at 115 volts AC. The light is connected to a pair of insulated test leads that terminate in metal tips. You can use the test light to check for the presence of voltage. If all you ever want to do is to test outlets, then an ordinary house lamp will do as well. With a test light, though, you can run checks on wiring not readily accessible for testing with a house lamp. A test light is an inexpensive and extremely useful tool and you won't find an electrician without one.

WIRE STRIPPER

There are many ways of stripping insulation from wire, something you must do if you want to join two or more wires or to fasten the wire to a terminal. You can use a jackknife, but diagonal cutters are better. The trouble with both of these tools is that if you cut through the insulation too deeply you will nick the wire, weakening it at that point and starting the way for a possible break. This does not mean electricians do not use a jackknife or cutters for this purpose. It just takes a lot of experience. For home use it is better to buy a wire stripper. There are various types, but an inexpensive wire cutter and stripper combination should do. It doesn't take much practice to learn to remove insulation with this tool, so handy and so necessary that it is a must for your home-electrician's tool kit.

LEVER JAW WRENCH

This is a combination tool that can be used as pliers, a lock wrench, or a pipe wrench. If you plan to do a substantial amount of electrical work, you'll find it helpful. However, if all you need is maintenance in your house or apartment and you do have pliers and a pipe wrench, you won't have enough work to justify buying this tool.

HACKSAW

This is a very useful tool to have, not only for electrical work but for other household chores. While the hacksaw is designed for cutting metal cable, you can also use it for cutting other metal parts. You can replace the blades when they become worn since the blades are removable and you can buy blades for making fine or coarse cuts. Insert the hacksaw blade so its teeth point away from you as you hold the handle of the saw. This is an inexpensive tool and packages of replacement blades are also low-cost.

DRILL

Both hand drills and electric drills are needed for electrical work. When using a drill of either type, make sure the drill is straight before tightening the chuck. Tighten the chuck only with a chuck key (if using an electrical drill) or by hand with a hand drill. If you plan to drill through metal, make sure the metal is securely fastened. Use a center punch to provide a correct starting point before drilling.

An electric drill comes under the classification of portable power tools. Before using such a tool, make sure you know what you plan to do. Since the tool will have a part that turns or moves in some way, make sure that it is impossible to have your clothing caught. Neckties and power tools do not go together. Neither do long, loose sleeves. If you have long hair, cover it with a cap that will hold it securely in place and also keep your hands away from any moving parts. The safest power tools to use are those that require both hands on the tool, with an automatic stop switch when your hand is removed.

Power tools can produce sparking so do not use them in any place where there may be flammable vapors. Make sure the line cord delivering power to the tool does not come in contact with any moving power blade while you work with it. Don't let the power-line cord come in contact with oil, grease, hot surfaces, or chemicals. If the cord becomes damaged, replace the entire cord instead of patching it with tape. When unplugging power tools from receptacles, grasp the plug, not the cord.

EXTENSION LIGHT

An extension light consists of a length of line cord with a light at one end. The light is generally put in a wire cage at the end of the cord to protect against accidental burns when using the lamp, and also to protect the lamp from breaking when coming in contact with hard surfaces. The cage has a hook at its end so that you can hang the lamp in a convenient position. The purpose of the extension light is to supply a strong light at the spot where you work. In addition, there will be one or more convenience outlets right below the lamp cage, giving you a power outlet to which you can connect power tools.

CONDUCTORS AND INSULATORS

A conductor is any substance, usually metal, that permits the easy flow of current. Copper and aluminum are good conductors, but so is salt water. An acid is also a conductor. The liquid in your storage battery is a water solution of sulfuric acid and permits the flow of current, inside the battery, from the positive to the negative plates.

An insulator is a substance that does not usually permit the flow of current through it. Glass is an insulator, as are rubber and plastic materials. Dry wood is an insulator, but can become a conductor when wet.

This division of substances into insulators and conductors is a rough one. Theoretically, there is no substance that is a perfect insulator, for if the electrical pressure is high enough, a current will flow. Thus, under certain circumstances, an electric current can find its way through dust or oil. For home electric wiring and repair purposes, you can consider rubber, glass, and plastic suitable insulators; and copper, aluminum, and other metals as good conductors.

METAL WORKING TOOLS

In your home you may need to drill through

wood, metal, brick, or cement to make an electrical installation or repair. Cold chisels can be used for working on steel panels. You can use a knockout punch for making or enlarging a hole in a steel cabinet or outlet box. If you need to work through masonry, you may find it useful to have several masonry bits. These are normally carbide-tipped and are used to drill holes in brick or concrete walls, either for anchoring equipment with expansion screws or for the passage of conduit or cable.

FISH WIRE AND DROP CHAINS

It may sometimes be necessary to pull wires through conduits and for this purpose you can use fish wire. Getting wire through conduit sometimes requires quite a bit of force and so a fish-wire grip is needed to get enough force on the wire. Fish wire is made of tempered spring steel about ¼" wide and you can get it in various lengths. While fish wire is fairly stiff, you can still push or pull it around bends or elbows of conduit. When pulling wires and cables in existing buildings, electricians will use a fish wire or sometimes a drop chain. A drop chain consists of small chain links attached to a lead or iron weight. It is used only to feed through wall openings when a vertical drop is to be made.

ELECTRICAL TAPE

The purpose of an electrical conductor is to carry a current to its destination. This means a trip from the source, such as a generator or battery, to and through the load, and then back to the source again. But given the opportunity, the current will seek a shorter path, generally referred to as a short circuit. The trouble with a short circuit is that it reduces the resistance in the path between source voltage and load; consequently the current flow can increase dramatically. The resultant excessive current can "blow" a fuse, opening it and interrupting the flow of current. But the tremendous current surge can heat the wire conductors, caus-

ing a fire. Ordinarily, this does not happen because wire is covered with an insulating material such as cotton, rubber, or plastic, or some combination of these. However, it is often necessary to strip away the insulating substances to make a connection of one wire to another. These exposed connections must be covered and protected in some way. Electrical tape is one of the methods used to supply insulating protection.

There are various kinds of electrical tape. One is friction tape, a cotton tape impregnated with an insulating compound that has adhesive qualities. One of the problems with this tape is that it tends to become very dry with time, which causes it to lose its adhesive qualities and unravel. Never re-use tape. And if you buy friction tape, buy rolls that come sealed or packaged in some way, rather than less expensive rolls that aren't covered. Unfortunately, electrical tape isn't dated, but if you touch a roll that is fresh you will be able to feel its softness and moisture content. An older roll will not be as tacky and will feel dried out. When the older roll is used, it will tend to unravel almost as quickly as you wind it around a connection. With a fresh roll you will be able to wind the tape around a connection, pull it tight, and count on it to hold securely.

You can "cut" friction tape by pulling smartly across the width of the tape. It requires a little practice but is easy to do once you get the knack. If not, cut it with scissors.

Another type of electrical tape, but a little more costly, is rubber or varnished cambric tape. However, plastic electrical tape, made of a plastic material with adhesive on one face, has just about replaced friction and rubber tape. It has a longer life span than the other tapes, and is elastic enough to be pulled tightly around a connection.

Whenever you join a pair of wires, be sure to cover the joint with tape. The purpose of using the tape is to replace the insulating material that has been removed from the wires to permit connecting them. Start the tape at some point before the exposed wire—that is, the tape should begin on the insulated portion and not on the bare, exposed wires. Apply the tape on the bias so that each succeeding wrap of tape will bring you to the other wire. As you proceed you will see that each wrap of tape partially covers the preceding wrap. Continue with the tape until you cover the entire exposed wire and reach the next insulated portion of wire.

The objective of a tape wrap is to make a very tight covering, not a mountainous bundle. The purpose of tightness is to improve the effectiveness of the adhesive substance.

For added protection, you might want to use a second layer over the first. The best type of tape to use is plastic electrical. It does not yield loose threads, makes a very tight joint with good adhesion, and has excellent insulating properties.

SPLIT-BOLT CONNECTORS AND WIRE NUTS

The larger the amount of current that is to flow through a wire, the thicker it will be and the more difficult it will be to handle. It is fairly easy to join thin wires. They are quite flexible and you can easily twist a pair of wires, preferably by using gas pliers. But thick wires are stiff and it becomes difficult to twist such wires together so that they are in good, intimate contact throughout their entire exposed surface.

For this sort of situation you can take advantage of various types of solderless connectors. One of these is the split-bolt connector into which the exposed ends of the heavy conductors are pushed. The split-bolt connector can then be taped to provide insulation protection.

When wires are joined they should be wrapped around each other. A common mistake is to take one wire and wrap it around the other. Instead, place the two exposed wires side by side and with your fingers or gas pliers apply a twisting action to both wires simultaneously. Each wire will then be soldered, but in modern electrical practice, soldering is generally omitted. Electricians like to save working time, but if you are wiring around your own home or apartment, the few extra minutes required by soldering will be worthwhile.

Wire nuts are used by electricians to join wires without soldering and without using electrical tape. There are various kinds. In one type the two bare wires are twisted together and then the wire nut, a sort of plastic shell, is screwed down over the exposed wires. The inside of the wire nut is threaded and so the turning action cuts a small groove in the wires. The result is that the wire nut makes a firm, tight, insulating fit over the exposed wires.

The advantage of the wire nut over tape is that it is fast and supplies excellent protection, but can also be removed easily in the event the joint must be unspliced. With a soldered, taped connection this can be a messy job. Another advantage of the wire nut is that it has a longer life than tape.

USING SOLDERLESS CONNECTORS

The purpose in joining two or more wires is to permit current to flow easily from one wire to the next. If the bare wire ends are dirty, covered with oil, or if there are loose strands of insulation over them, the wire-to-wire contact will be imperfect. The effect is an increase of resistance at the joint, causing a voltage loss at that spot. If the current through the wires is substantial, the joint may become warm or even hot. Further, there will be a loss of voltage at the joint—that is, a voltage drop. The net effect is that the appliance being operated will have less operating voltage than it should have. To avoid these unnecessary consequences, make sure that the wires being joined are sparkling clean. Scrape the wires gently and lightly with a knife or rub them with fairly fine-grade sandpaper, using a rotary motion to make sure the entire copper surface is covered. When twisting them together prior to the use of the solderless connector, make sure that the twist is a tight one. The solderless connector should cover the entire length of the twist with no part of the copper joint exposed. If some of the copper can still be seen after the solderless connector has been put on, it is obvious that the twisted wires are too long. Cut a small section of the exposed ends and replace the solderless connector.

HOW TO TAKE CARE OF TOOLS

The best arrangement for making tools available when you want them is one in which the tools are individually held in a vertical position by spring clips or some type of metal support. A large section of pegboard is excellent for this purpose. The advantage is that the tools can readily be seen and that a vacant spot immediately indicates a missing tool. Arrange tools on the pegboard by family—that is, all screwdrivers together, all pliers together. The difficulty with this setup, though, is that it does require wall space, not always available.

A somewhat more expensive method is to use a drawer-type tool chest. Again, similar tools are kept together, and if the drawers are identified in some way, finding tools when needed becomes easy. However, when fully loaded with tools, the tool chest becomes quite heavy and so a useful adjunct is a tool caddy. The tool caddy is an open, metallic tool carrier with a handle. When you have a wiring job or electrical repair work to do, load the caddy with the tools and parts you will need. Tool caddies are extremely convenient, so much so that the tendency is to leave the tools in the caddy when the work is finished. Inevitably, this results in a frantic search for the right tool at a later date.

If you have absolutely no space, find a drawer somewhere and use it to store your tools. Keep miscellaneous electrical hardware away from tools. For electrical hardware, such as washers, nuts, screws and bolts, use screw-type glass jars. You can buy such jars, or, more economically, use empty food jars. Separate hardware just as you would tools—that is, all washers together, machine screws separated from wood screws—or every electrical-repair job will mean a stop while you search for a particular bit of hardware.

Tools, particularly power tools, are not for children. Some tools have fairly sharp edges and should be considered dangerous. If you have small children on the premises, a lock on the toolbox is better than threats not to touch.

Replace tools when worn out. A screwdriver with a rounded edge, or a tool with a loose handle that cannot be fixed, a hacksaw blade whose teeth are dull, a drill that will not produce a smooth hole and will not "bite" into wood or metal—these and others like them are time wasters and will hinder your work, not help it.

ELECTRICAL METERS

For almost all homes, the line voltage—the voltage delivered to the home by an electrical-power company—has a nominal value of about 115 volts and is AC. The precise amount of voltage isn't a matter of great interest, for it is controlled at the source by the power utility. In the home the question is usually one of whether line voltage is available or not. Any household lamp in working order can be used to determine if voltage is present at all the outlets. Or, you can get a simple tester consisting of a neon lamp and a pair of test leads, for use anywhere in the home, not just at outlets. The household lamp is used for testing and the neon-lamp tester are go-no go devices. They will indicate whether voltage is present or not, but will give no direct indication of the amount of voltage. However, when using either household lamp or neon-lamp testers, you can assume full line voltage is present if the lamps glow with full brightness. If they do not glow at all, there is no voltage. If they glow feebly or possibly flicker, then you are not getting full voltage.

THE AMMETER

An ammeter is an electrical measuring instrument that supplies two important bits of information. It indicates whether or not current is flowing, and if current does flow, tells you how much current is moving. Yet, despite these apparent advantages, the ammeter isn't suitable for home wiring and repairs. It is discussed here since it is used in some branches of electrical work, and since it is available as a test instrument.

While the ammeter is helpful, you can get all the information you need without its use. To determine if current is flowing (one of the jobs of an ammeter), simply connect the appliance and turn it on. If the appliance functions, then your first question—how much current—has also been answered. The appliance is taking the required amount of current. The only thing you don't know is the amount of current. But you can calculate that. Divide the power rating of the appliance, in watts, by the line voltage.

$$I = W / E$$

Thus, if the data plate on the appliance is marked 2 kilowatts (2000 watts), the current bill will be:

$$I - \frac{2,000}{115} = 17 \text{ amperes, approximately}$$

Aside from its cost, using an ammeter is a nuisance since you must disconnect one of the wires and insert the ammeter in series with it. If there is no convenient disconnecting point, then you must cut one of the wires, first making certain that the power has been turned off. Then, after completing the measurement, you must join the wires. Since a current of 17 amperes requires a fairly heavy wire, simply using the ammeter and

then reconnecting the wires can be a chore. The elementary arithmetic involved in calculating the current is easier.

WHY SHOULD YOU KNOW THE AMOUNT OF CURRENT?

Knowing the current demands of an appliance is essential since the connecting wires must be able to carry the current. Ideally, it is best to position current-hungry appliances as close to the voltage source as possible, and so a knowledge of current requirements may have some influence on the ultimate location of such appliances. Finally, since more than one appliance may be connected to the same wires going back to the source, you may want to know whether more appliances may be connected to the same line at some future date. Various wiring networks are used in your home and so it is helpful to know which are underloaded and which are working to near-capacity. The objective is to distribute the load as evenly as possible. Proper current distribution may help you avoid installing additional but unnecessary wiring.

THE VOLTMETER

Like the ammeter, an AC voltmeter will supply two bits of information: whether voltage is present, and if so, how much. Unlike the ammeter, the voltmeter does not require disconnection of circuits. Instead, use it just like a test lamp or neon tester. Either the test lamp or neon tester can let you know whether voltage is present or not, and so the only advantage of the AC voltmeter is that it supplies information on how much voltage is present, information which isn't that essential. This does not mean that AC voltmeters aren't used by electricians. For home use, however, the neon tester is adequate, costs much less, and is easier to carry.

With very few exceptions, all the appliances in your house use the same operating voltage. Your toaster, mixer, electric fans, electric shaver, electric toothbrush, blender, all the lights in the house, the electric clocks—all of these and similar appliances use line voltage: 115 volts, AC. To determine if voltage is reaching an appliance, turn it on. If it works, it is getting voltage. If not, use your test lamp to determine if the outlet to which the appliance is connected is getting voltage.

THE OHMMETER

An ohmmeter is an instrument for measuring resistance. The instrument has wide use in certain types of electrical work, such as radio and television repair, but its value for home electrical-wiring installation and repair is practically zero. You can use Ohm's law for calculating resistance:

$$R = \frac{E}{I}$$

E is the line voltage and I is the amount of current being used by the appliance. If an appliance takes a current of 1 ampere, then its resistance is 115 ohms.

$$R = \frac{E}{I} = \frac{115}{1} = 115 \ ohms$$

But now that you know the resistance, what can you do with it? As a general rule of thumb, appliances with very low resistance take large amounts of current; those with higher resistance values take correspondingly smaller amounts of current. Devices that turn electrical energy into heat energy, such as toasters, broilers, electric ranges, and baseboard electrical heaters, all take substantial amounts of current, and so you know, without measuring, that these are low-resistance components. A radio receiver rated at 35 watts takes much less current and so, as far as the power line is concerned, this component has a much higher resistance.

This doesn't mean resistance isn't important. It is. It is especially important when wiring a new home or when making wiring changes in an older house. This topic, though, is covered fully in Chapter 4.

THE MULTITESTER

The multitester, sometimes called a volt-ohm-milliammeter (abbreviated as VOM), is a single instrument that can be used for measuring voltage, current, and resistance. Instead of requiring three separate meters—the ammeter, voltmeter, and ohmmeter—it uses a single meter that can do all functions. Some multitesters are fairly low-cost units, are conveniently small, and would make a nice addition to your collection of electrician's tools. Whether you would ever use it is another matter. You can learn just about everything you want to know with nothing more than Ohm's law and a neon-lamp tester. The disadvantage of the multitester is that the meter scale is crowded, the readings obtained on the meter are approximate, and the unit can be damaged if you do not follow the operating instructions properly. The VOM is more useful for radio and television repair than for home electrical work.

There is an exception. If you plan to repair home appliances, including motors, then you will find the VOM very useful. Whether you get the VOM or not, then, depends on the extent to which you want to do electrical work. You can, for example, test the filament of a light bulb with the ohmmeter section of a VOM to determine if the filament is in good condition. An easier and equally rapid check is to insert the bulb in a light socket. If the light turns on, you have your answer. But, in the later section on repairs, you will see that the VOM can be very useful.

MISCELLANEOUS TOOLS

Buying tools is a personal decision. The total number of tools you get and their variety depend entirely on how much you are willing to pay for the convenience of having tools, even if you use them infrequently. There is nothing more exasperating than needing a tool and not having it. This is almost as exasperating as having an electrician's tool and never using it. For an apartment, a limited tool supply should do. For a house, an extensive collection is better, since many of the tools can be used for jobs other than electrical.

CRIMPER

Quite commonly a wire will be connected to some device by stripping one end of the wire and wrapping it around the terminal of a machine screw. When making this sort of connection, expose only enough wire to go around the screw. If not, you will have bare wire exposed beyond the screw head, which can lead to the possibility of a short. Wrap the wire around the screw in the direction in which the screw will turn. Thus, when tightening the screw, you will be closing the loop the wire makes around the screw. If, by error, you wrap the wire in the opposite direction, tightening the screw will tend to undo the loop of wire and will make poor contact.

When screws are tightened, they are turned in a clockwise direction. This means, then, that the wire should also be wrapped around the screw body in a clockwise manner.

If the wire is thin enough and sufficiently flexible, you can attach a metal terminal to it. This makes connecting the wire to the screw much neater and also supplies a better connection. For fastening the metal terminals to the wire, you will need a crimping tool. All that this does is fasten the terminal to the wire. The terminal can then be slipped over the screw and the screw can then be tightened.

If you use stranded wire, make sure that every one of the strands is present before wrapping around the screw or before attaching a terminal. To give the strands a "solid" effect, twirl them with your fingers.

POP RIVETER

Some small appliances are held together with rivets. You can poke these rivets out of place with the help of gas pliers and a screwdriver, but this method is slow because the pliers and screwdriver aren't designed for such an application. A pop riveter is an excellent tool for removing small rivets.

NUT RUNNER

A nut can be the head portion of a machine screw or a separate part. They are usually hexagonal in shape, but the larger sizes may have only four sides. The smaller sizes are often slotted so that they can be removed with a screwdriver. A nut runner is a better tool for this purpose since it can be made to slip right over each of the six sides of the hexagonal nut. You can then apply much more turning power than with a screwdriver. The disadvantage is that machine nuts come in different sizes and so you will need a complete set of runners. To minimize the expense of buying individual nut runners, you can get a set of runners that have a click-in feature permitting them to use a single handle.

CONDUIT BENDER

Conduit is pipe available in various straight lengths. However, when you put conduit into a wall, you may find it necessary to bend the conduit to avoid existing obstructions. Or, you might need to have the conduit travel around the 90° angle made by a pair of walls. To bend the conduit it is helpful to have an electrician's tool called a conduit bender. The conduit bender fits the conduit, but you will need to supply a handle. A scrap length of 3/4″ pipe will do, but make sure the pipe is long enough. About 4′ or 5′ should be about right.

SOLDERING TOOLS

Although the modern trend in home wiring is to get away from soldering, you will find a soldering iron or gun useful to have. The whole purpose of soldering is to help you make a good electrical connection. For home use, soldering is important enough to warrant a separate chapter, and so you will find a full description of this tool and its use in Chapter 5.

SYMBOLS

Before making wiring changes, it may be helpful to draw up some sort of plan, depending on the complexity of the wiring you intend doing. You might want to install a wiring arrangement involving nothing more than a set of switches for opening and closing downstairs lights from upstairs, or upstairs lights from downstairs. It sounds simple, and it is, if you know in advance just how the wiring is to be handled.

Your wiring plan can consist of pictorial draw-ings—actually pictures—of the wiring and ot parts such as bulbs, switches, fuses, outlets, and fixtures. An easier method, and one that will be more accurate, is to use electrical symbols. An electrical symbol is a sort of shorthand. Thus, if you plan to install a fluorescent fixture, you could draw a picture of the fixture itself, which is quite difficult to do; or use its electrical-symbol equivalent, nothing more than a small rectangle with a circle in the center.

Electrical symbols will be supplied, where applicable, throughout the pages that follow. The illustrations show some of the more commonly used electrical parts and their symbols.

ITEM	SYMBOL
WIRING CONCEALED IN CEILING OR WALL	
WIRING CONCEALED IN FLOOR	
EXPOSED BRANCH CIRCUIT	
BRANCH CIRCUIT HOME RUN TO PANEL BOARD (NO. OF ARROWS EQUALS NO. OF CIRCUITS, DESIGNATION IDENTIFIES DESIGNATION AT PANEL)	A1 A3
THREE OR MORE WIRES (NO. OF CROSS LINES EQUALS NO. OF CONDUCTORS TWO CONDUCTORS INDICATED IF NOT OTHERWISE NOTED)	
INCOMING SERVICE LINES	
CROSSED CONDUCTORS, NOT CONNECTED	
SPLICE OR SOLDERED CONNECTION	
CABLED CONNECTOR (SOLDERLESS)	
WIRE TURNED UP	
WIRE TURNED DOWN	

Electrical parts and their symbols.

31

ITEM	SYMBOL	ILLUSTRATION
LIGHTING OUTLETS*– CEILING		
WALL		
FLUORESCENT FIXTURE		
CONTINUOUS ROW FLUORESCENT FIXTURE		
BARE LAMP FLUORESCENT STRIP		

*LETTERS ADDED TO SYMBOLS INDICATE SPECIAL TYPE OR USAGE

J-	JUNCTION BOX	R-	RECESSED
L-	LOW VOLTAGE	X-	EXIT LIGHT

ITEM	SYMBOL	ILLUSTRATION
RECEPTACLE OUTLETS**– SINGLE OUTLET		
DUPLEX OUTLET		
QUADRUPLEX OUTLET		
SPECIAL PURPOSE OUTLET		
20-AMP, 250-VOLT OUTLET		
SINGLE FLOOR OUTLET (BOX AROUND ANY OF ABOVE INDICATES FLOOR OUTLET OF SAME TYPE)		

**LETTER G NEXT TO SYMBOL INDICATES GROUNDING TYPE

Electrical parts and their symbols (continued).

ITEM	SYMBOL	ILLUSTRATION
SWITCHES – SINGLE POLE SWITCH	S	
DOUBLE POLE SWITCH	S_2	
THREE WAY SWITCH	S_3	
SWITCH AND PILOT LAMP	S_P	
CEILING PULL SWITCH	Ⓢ	
PANEL BOARDS AND RELATED EQUIPMENT PANEL BOARD AND CABINET		
SWITCHBOARD, CONTROL STATION OR SUBSTATION		
SERVICE SWITCH OR CIRCUIT BREAKER	■ OR ■ OR ⊗	
EXTERNALLY OPERATED DISCONNECT SWITCH		
MOTOR CONTROLLER	◁▷ OR MC	
MISCELLANEOUS – TELEPHONE	◄	
THERMOSTAT	Ⓣ	
MOTOR	Ⓜ	

Electrical parts and their symbols (continued).

Chapter 3

BATTERIES

At one time batteries were widely used in the home, not for electrical work, but for radio receivers. When these receivers became electrified, batteries made a hasty exit. Electrical power—power obtained from an outlet—was so convenient, and the batteries so large and messy that it was no contest.

However, line-powered equipment does have one problem and that is the electrical cord or pair of wires that connect the equipment to the nearest available outlet. This cord is a restraining influence. It generally means that the appliance must be fairly fixed in one spot. You can carry a lamp from one spot to another in your home, but it is a nuisance to do so, for the lamp must be unplugged from one outlet and connected to another. A flashlight is more convenient. It is more convenient not because it is a flashlight, but because it carries its own power source along with it, and so there is no need to connect to an outlet. Battery-operated components are becoming more popular in home use. The big difference is that battery-operated devices are noted for portability.

THE INSIGNIFICANCE OF VOLTAGE

The battery in your automobile is probably rated at 12 volts. It is also possible to buy a hand-held portable transistor radio whose battery is also 12 volts. Car batteries and transistor radio batteries have identical voltages, yet one cannot be substituted for the other. The difference isn't a matter of voltage, but one of current. It takes hundreds of amperes to start your car; the transistor radio is satisfied with less than half an ampere. And so, while voltage is one of the criteria when discussing batteries, current availability is just as important, if not more so. The current-delivering ability of a battery is called its capacity.

CURRENT CAPACITY

Every battery is a miniature chemical factory, engaged in changing chemical energy to electrical energy. But no battery can deliver current indefinitely, nor does the quantity of available current remain constant. The current capacity of a battery is the amount of current it can supply multiplied by time. A battery that can supply 6 amperes for 1 hour has a capacity of 6 ampere hours. A car battery rated at 120 ampere hours can, theoretically, supply 120 amperes for 1 hour, or 60 amperes for 2 hours, or 30 amperes for 4 hours: 120 x 1 equals 120; 60 x 2 equals 120; 30 x 4 equals 120. Similarly, the same battery should be able to supply 240 amperes for 1/2 hour since 240 x 0.5 equals 120. The starting current of your car may be as much as 300 amperes. But since you keep your starter key turned for just 1 or 2 seconds, a battery having a 120-ampere hour capacity can supply the current needed.

Your transistor radio battery could have a capacity of 6 ampere hours. It can furnish 6 amperes for 1 hour, or 3 amperes for 2 hours, or 1 ampere for 6 hours. Since an ampere is equivalent to a thousand milliamperes, it can furnish 500 milliamperes for 12 hours. This battery, however, while rated at 12 volts, the same as a car battery, could not possibly supply 300 amperes, the amount of starting current needed.

As a general rule, batteries that are capable of yielding large amounts of current are substantial in size and quite heavy. Those from which you require just small amounts of current will often fit into the palm of your hand.

POLARITY

All batteries, regardless of size, voltage, or current capacity, have a plus terminal (sometimes called the positive terminal) and a minus terminal (also called the negative terminal). Sometimes the terminals are identified by plus (+) and minus (-) symbols, but equally often just a plus symbol is used. Sometimes the plus terminal is marked in red, with the understanding that the other terminal is minus. And, of course, there are batteries that aren't marked at all. The consumer is supposed to know which terminal is which. Polarity is a reference to the plus and minus terminals. Plus polarity simply means the plus or positive terminal; and negative polarity, the minus or negative terminal.

BATTERY SYMBOLS

Experienced electricians are often so familiar with the wiring arrangement of a house that they can easily visualize it. But when a new home is to be constructed, a wiring plan must be made. This wiring plan uses lines to represent the various connecting wires and symbols to represent various parts such as switches, lights, fuses, fuse boxes, and outlets.

A combination of various symbols plus connecting lines is called an electrical diagram. For the home owner as well as the practicing electrician, an electrical diagram is a simple, easy way to plan circuit arrangements.

The electrical symbol for a battery is shown in the illustration. Technically, this is more correctly

called a cell since a battery consists of a combination of cells. The battery in your car, presumably a 12-volt type, consists of 6 cells connected together.

BASIC-CIRCUIT DIAGRAM

A circuit consists of various electrical parts, generally designed to be connected by a conductor such as wire and intended to work together. A simple diagram could consist of a voltage source, such as a battery, a pair of connecting wires, a switch, and a bulb. This is the setup for the wiring of a flashlight. When the switch is closed, current will flow from the negative terminal of the battery (assuming that as the starting point), through the connecting wire to the closed switch, through the switch to the next connecting wire and then to the bulb. The current will flow through the bulb. The bulb contains a tiny bit of wire called a filament, designed to glow when the correct amount of current passes through it, the same procedure that takes place when a current flows through a house electric light. The current then continues through the return connecting wire to the positive terminal of the battery. Here it moves inside the battery from the positive electrode inside the battery to the negative. This is the starting point, and so the entire process repeats. Actually, the current in this circuit starts and stops at the same time in any part of the circuit, but it is a convenient bit of fiction to assume a starting point.

This circuit diagram is simple, deliberately so, but it is essential to know something about the path of current flow to be able to modify home wiring. As an example, consider a single electric light bulb in your home. The power for this bulb is supplied by a huge generator at your local utility. Since the generator is an AC type, its terminals will become alternately negative and positive. If we start from the terminal that is momentarily negative, current will flow through a wire connecting your fuse box to the generator. From the

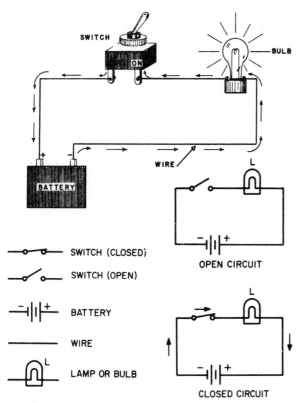

SWITCH —o o— SWITCH (CLOSED)

—o o— SWITCH (OPEN)

—|‖|+ BATTERY

——— WIRE

LAMP OR BULB

OPEN CIRCUIT

CLOSED CIRCUIT

Current flows in a closed circuit, but does not flow in an open circuit. Voltage is available whether the circuit is open or closed. Upper drawing is a pictorial, difficult to draw, but easy to understand. Equivalent electrical circuits are shown below, at right. Symbols used here are at lower left.

fuse box the current will pass through the appropriate fuse to the outlet to which you have connected the light bulb. The current will then move out of the outlet, through the wire to the lamp, through the lamp, and then back to the other wire. That's not the end of the line, though, for the current will now retrace its path all the way back to the utility company and through the generator. The only thing that will happen when the polarity of the generator reverses is that the direction of current flow will also reverse. Naturally, this explanation is one that is highly stripped, for the current must also pass through various meters, both in your home and at the utility, and it may also be used in connection with a transformer (to be described later).

THE BASIC DRY CELL

A cell consists of two dissimilar conductors placed in a conducting solution. You could make a

cell by putting a bar of iron and one of tin in a liquid such as salt water. The voltage of such a cell would probably be very small and the amount of current you could get out of it would be insignificant. Making a cell is easy; making one that is useful and practical is quite another matter.

Like metals, many liquids are good conductors of electricity. Acids are good conductors, and so are salt solutions. Pure water is an insulator—that is, current won't flow through it readily. You can change that situation just by adding a pinch of salt. For the most part, you won't have to do that since most water does contain dissolved minerals and salts.

In the cell the action is a chemical one. The acidic solution attacks one of the metals, stripping electrons from it. The electrons migrate through the liquid to the other plate. This gives us a situation in which one of the plates has an excess of electrons, and since all electrons have a negative charge, we now have one plate that has been made highly negative. The other plate, having lost electrons or negative charges, is called positive. Positive and negative are just relative terms. All substances, including yourself, are literally smeared with electrons. If you have an average amount, you can regard yourself as neutral, whatever that word might mean. If you gather more electrons on your body surface, you become negative, just another way of saying that you have more of them on you than before. If you can manage to get rid of your electrons, then you are positive, also another way of saying that you have less of them on you than before. The same thinking applies to a cell, except that in the case of a cell we can, through electrical design, emphasize this behavior of electrons and then put it to work for our own purposes.

A flow of current consists of a movement of electrons. Made to move through the body in huge quantities, simultaneously, they produce the effect known as electrocution. On your body surface, they have limited movement and it is random.

ELECTRODES

The two dissimilar conductors in a cell are termed electrodes, with the one having a surplus of electrons called negative; and the other, positive. It is this difference in electron quantity that produces the effect known as voltage. Voltage, then, is simply the pressure caused by an electron difference. Gather more electrons in one area than in a nearby area, and you will have developed or generated a voltage. It is so easy to produce a voltage that it is almost impossible not to do so. You generate a voltage every time you walk. When you go across a rug, a voltage develops because the act of walking attracts free electrons to your body surface. But a nearby doorknob hasn't moved and so has far fewer electrons than you have. When you approach the knob with your fingers, there is an electrical discharge because you represent one electrode and the doorknob the other, with the air between working as a conductor. It may not seem that way, but this action is quite similar to what happens in a cell.

A pair of metal plates with the same number of electrons are electrically neutral. There is no voltage and no electrical pressure between the plates.

In the cell we separate the two electrodes to make sure that electrons do not jump from the electron-rich electrode to the one that has been deprived of them. Instead, we connect a wire to the negative electrode, and allow the electrons to move through the wire from the negative to the positive electrode. But we make the electrons pay a price, by forcing them to go through an electrical part such as a lamp, or a toaster, or a clock, en route.

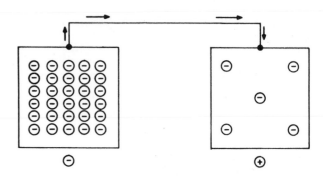

Both plates have electrons. The one with the greater number of electrons is negative with respect to the other plate. The plate at the right, with fewer electrons, is positive with respect to the plate at the left. The words positive and negative are relative. Because of the difference in electron quantity, a voltage or electrical pressure exists between the two plates. If connected by a wire, electrons (an electrical current) will flow from the negative to the positive plate and will continue to do so until approximately equal quantities of electrons are on both plates.

SHORT CIRCUIT VS. WORK CIRCUIT

Connecting a wire from the negative to the positive terminal of the battery is called a short circuit. It is known as short because it provides the most direct and the easiest path for the passage of electrons. If there are enough electrons on the negative electrode, and on a cell of the type used in an automobile there would be, the movement of a tremendous quantity or electrons would produce enough heat to cause the wire to glow and possibly to melt. Large quantities of electrons in uniform motion can be a blessing or a disaster.

Instead of allowing a short circuit, we break open the connecting wire and insert a load, possibly an electric-light bulb. Because the bulb has resistance, it limits the current to a reasonable amount. We get two benefits from this. The first is that we keep the current flow within tolerable limits. The second is that we get some use from this action, in this case a bulb that lights.

Returning electrons to the positive terminal of a cell through a work circuit, consisting of an electric light in this case, does not mean the end of the action. Simultaneously, the liquid, gas, or conducting paste in the cell, known as electrolyte, is attacking the positive electrode, removing more electrons from it, and these promptly migrate to the negative electrode.

The process is thus a continuous one, but this does not mean it will last indefinitely. Ultimately, the positive electrode will be eaten away and so the cell will have reached the end of its useful life.

RECHARGING CELLS

All cells can be recharged to a greater or lesser extent. As a general rule of thumb, cells that have a liquid electrolyte can be recharged rather easily; others are more of a problem. Whether a cell should be recharged or not is a matter of economics. It is certainly worthwhile to recharge an automobile battery, but whether it is monetarily feasible to recharge your transistor radio cells is another matter.

Recharging is just a technique in which the normal direction of flow of the discharge current is reversed. The cell is connected to a DC-voltage source, with that DC-voltage source driving a current into the cell. When making a connection to a charger, attach the minus terminal of the cell to the minus terminal of the charger; and the positive terminal of the cell to the positive terminal of the charger. The EMF of the charger is generally just a few volts higher than that of the cell being charged. Better-grade chargers, such as those used for automobile batteries, have a built-in ammeter to indicate the amount of current flow. When a battery is first being charged, flow of current from the source into the battery will be maximum. As the battery builds up a charge, the voltage across its terminals will increase, and will oppose the charging voltage. The net effect of this will be that the amount of charging current will reduce, producing an effect known as a tapered charge. This is perfectly normal and is to be expected.

There are also chargers for the cells used around the house. Such cells, when recharged, do not have the life expectancy of a new cell, and since you pay for the charging current, it becomes a moot point as to whether the time, effort, and expense are worth it.

CELLS VS. BATTERIES

A cell is a single unit consisting of a pair of electrodes immersed in a conducting electrolyte. A combination of cells wired together is a battery. Your 12-volt auto battery consists of 6 cells. The word "cell," however, is gradually falling out of the electrician's vocabulary, with the word "battery" being applied whether a unit is a single cell or a combination known as a battery.

TYPES OF BATTERIES

The great advantage of a battery is its portability. Its significance is that you can carry electrical power with you wherever you go. We now have battery-operated toothbrushes, battery clocks, battery-operated toys, battery-operated radio receivers, battery scissors, battery grass cutters, and so on. The result is that in the average home you will find appliances being worked from battery power as well as from line power. Batteries supply a DC voltage; your line supplies AC.

There are still other differences between line voltage and battery voltage. Line voltage remains constant. It is always about 115 volts, and remains that way except in emergency conditions. Battery voltage can be anything you want it to be, and is always dictated by the requirements of a particular appliance. Your transistor radio may require 9 volts; your electric clock 3 volts; your flashlight 1½ volts. Your 115-volt AC line can supply a tremendous amount of current. There is no appliance you can install in your home that will remotely exhaust the current-delivering capabilities of the generators in your local power utility. But when you buy a battery you buy a component whose current capacity is quite limited.

TYPES OF BATTERIES

Because batteries for home use have become so popular and because they are so convenient, a number of different types have been developed. This accounts, in part, for the large variation in cost. Batteries designed for long life cost more than those having a shorter expectancy. Both may have the same amount of voltage—that's not important. One 3-volt battery may cost twice as much as another, but will have 4 times the current capability. It is obviously a better buy, economically, but some people do prefer to pay less, in effect spreading their payments over a period of time.

We now have silver-zinc, nickel-zinc, nickel-cadmium, silver-cadmium, magnesium-magnesium perchlorate, mercury, thermal, nickel-nickel oxide and sponge lead, lead peroxide combinations.

THE DRY CELL

Because there are so many different types of cells, they are arranged into two basic types, to bring some clarity out of chaos. Thus, there are two basic types of cells: a dry cell in which the electrolyte is a moist paste, and a wet cell in which the electrolyte is a liquid. Your car battery is made up of wet cells; your battery shaver uses a dry cell.

Technically, there is no such thing as a dry cell. An electrolyte can be a paste, but the paste is moist. When the paste becomes dry, the cell becomes worthless. Generally, wet cells are easier to recharge than dry cells, and in this context easier means that a wet cell will retain its charge for a much longer time.

LOAD VS. NO-LOAD VOLTAGE

A battery always has voltage whether it is being used or not. When a battery is not in use, the voltage measured across its two terminals is called the no-load voltage. No-load voltage is the voltage of a battery when it is not delivering current to some device, such as a bulb. The load voltage of a battery is the voltage measured across its terminals when it is under load—that is, when it is supplying current.

The no-load voltage of a battery is meaningless. To say that a dry cell has 1-½ volts isn't significant, since even a worn-out cell ready for the junk heap could register almost 1-½ volts. The important measurement for a battery is the full-load voltage. The word "full" as used here means the normal load of the battery. If you habitually use a particular battery to operate 6 lamps, turning on 1 lamp is just 1/6th of normal load. A battery that is fresh and in good condition will measure almost identical no-load and full-load voltages. A battery that is worn-out can have a drop of as much as 50 percent of its no-load voltage when a load is applied. When the no-load voltage of a battery drops by 20 percent of its usual full-load voltage, it is time to discard or recharge it. Your car battery normally measures a bit above 12 volts, but if the battery is weak and run-down, you can be sure that voltage will drop considerably the moment you turn the ignition key. And because the battery cannot deliver current since the electrical pressure is much too low, your car will simply grunt instead of starting.

To test a battery, then, connect it to its usual load, and measure the voltage across the terminals of the battery with a DC voltmeter or with the DC voltmeter section of a multitester. If you do not have a voltmeter, an easier technique is to substitute a new battery for the old one. If the appliance works after you make the change, you can be certain that the old battery is defective.

MAXIMUM CURRENT VS. LOAD CURRENT

The maximum-current output of a battery is the short-circuit current, the current that would be obtained by shorting the terminals—that is, connecting a heavy conductor, such as thick copper wire, from one battery terminal to the other. This shouldn't be done, of course, but a manufacturer may do so to learn the maximum-current output of which the battery is capable.

The load current is always less than the maximum current and is the amount of current taken by the load. When using a battery, then, you have two electrical concerns: The first is whether the battery has the right amount of voltage; and the second is whether the battery will be able to meet the continuing current demands of the load.

There is still another problem. You must also be concerned with the physical size of the battery. Since a battery is a portable source of power, it must fit into some kind of container. If the battery is too small, it will not make contact with the terminals of the load; if the battery is too large it simply will not fit in the space provided for it.

SHELF LIFE

There is no economy to be had in buying a dry cell and never using it. With time, a cell consumes itself and so all batteries must ultimately be discarded. One of the problems in buying dry batteries is that you never know how long they have been on the shelf in a store. It is always better to buy in a store with substantial traffic on the supposition that some of these must be battery buyers and that the turnover will be large enough to ensure fresh stock. You cannot determine if a battery is fresh by looking at it. It is the interior that decomposes, not the label. The only checks are a possible date on the battery, to measure its voltage under load, or to use it. Even then, a partially self-consumed battery will still perform. It will just not work as long as it should. But that is what you pay for and to that extent you will have been cheated.

The function of a battery manufacturer is to sell as many batteries as possible and so you will sometimes see batteries being sold in groups of two, four, and six in a plastic-sealed blister pack. The price per individual battery will be lower than usual since you will be buying in quantity instead of one at a time, and so you will be tempted to take advantage of what may appear to be a bargain. However, it is not a bargain if you will simply be moving some of the batteries off the dealer's shelf onto your own. They will deteriorate just as fast, and so, when you come to use them you may find they do not work or their actual working life is shorter than you expected. If you buy batteries, buy them for use. If not, do not.

BATTERY POLARITY

Every battery has a plus and a minus terminal. The polarity symbols, plus and minus, may or may not be marked on the terminals. Quite often they will not be, but you may find some information on the battery label or on the package. If not, ask the salesman from whom you purchased the batteries.

When you replace a battery in an appliance, common sense dictates that you should take a look at the used battery before you remove it. How is the battery connected? How is it held in position? Is there more than one battery, and if so, what are their respective positions? To make sure you get an exact replacement, copy whatever information you can from the battery label and take it with you when you make your purchase, or take the battery along.

One of the most common faults of battery-operated appliances is the battery and so if such an appliance stops working, or does not work as well as it should, replace the batteries. Quite often the appliance will have a printed date sheet pasted on the back or somewhere near where the batteries are locked in position. If present, it will give you some information about the type of batteries to use for replacement and possibly how to remove them. It is always an excellent precaution to learn about the batteries at the time you buy a battery-operated appliance. Get the salesman to show you where the batteries are located and how to replace them. In some instances, appliances are sold without batteries and so getting this information at the time of purchase becomes even more essential. Also, ask for information about the expected life of the batteries. For your own satisfaction, keep a record of the date on which the batteries started working for you on a label pasted inside the appliance. This will give you a check on the replacement batteries you buy, so that ultimately you will be able to get substitute batteries supplying the greatest working life for the lowest cost.

BATTERY HOLDERS

A battery holder may consist of spring clips that hold the battery in position and at the same time make contact with the battery terminals. Unless the batteries are inserted in the correct way, the appliance will not work, and you may possibly damage the batteries. Some battery connectors are snap-on types, others depend on a tight-fit arrangement. Whatever the kind of connection, be sure the battery connectors are clean. Battery terminals tend to corrode—after all, the battery is a chemical factory—and so if the appliance is to work well, or if it is to work at all, the connectors must be free of any corrosion materials. If not, wipe them clean with a cloth. You may need to sandpaper them a bit or scrape them with a knife if the deterioration has continued for a long time.

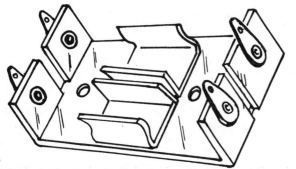

Device for holding two cells: The central portion is made of spring-clip metal. The terminals at the end are for making connections to the cells. Holder are usually made so that the cells are automatically connected when correctly inserted in the cell holder.

When replacing batteries, use those that are not only physically identical but those that are electrical equivalents having the same voltage and current ratings. In use, batteries do not become consumed at the same rate, so if a particular appliance uses two cells, you'll get better results if you replace both cells at the same time. In electrical apparatus, a weakened cell always acts as a drag on the stronger one. The stronger cell tries to do a double job: to operate the appliance while at the same time doing its best to recharge the weaker cell. The result is that this extraordinary effort rapidly discharges the stronger cell, and so, instead of having a strong cell, the net result is a pair of weak ones.

Some appliances come equipped with fasteners for attaching batteries. While these are for making connections, they do not hold the batteries in position. The fasteners are usually the snap-on type.

Batteries should fit snugly into their holders. They should not rattle about, particularly if the appliance is a portable one instead of being well mounted. If the batteries are loose, shim them—that is, tighten them into position by pulling on the spring clips to give them more holding tension, or fit a bit of paper or cardboard in with the cells to hold them more firmly. With small-voltage, small-current cells, there is no danger of fire.

Battery holders usually come with a cover plate. The plate has a twofold purpose: to keep the cells from falling out; and to exert a small amount of pressure on the cells to keep them tightly in position. Always replace the cover plate after checking on or putting in new cells. If, for any reason, you have trouble removing the cover plate or don't know how to do so, take the appliance back to the store in which it was purchased, or to any store selling that particular appliance, and get firsthand instructions from a salesman. Get him to demonstrate the procedure and then you try it while he watches.

It is best not to store cells at home, not from any possible danger of shock or fire, but simply because they will become weaker with time. If you must do so, keep them in a cool, dry place. Put each cell in an individual, thin-type, see-through plastic bag. This will not only keep the cell clean, but will protect it against becoming excessively dry. Another practical reason is that you do not want the cell accidentally shorting against a stray length of metal, nor would you want one cell shorting against another. Most supermarkets supply plastic bags in abundance without charge.

NO. 6 DRY CELL

This is a workhorse among dry cells, for not only is it large in an age when batteries are being made smaller and smaller, but it can deliver current in the order of ampere seconds. Known either as the No. 6 dry cell or the standard size cell, it is about 2½″ in diameter and approximately 6″ long. The voltage measured between its positive and negative terminals is 1½ volts, but this is when the cell is fresh. When the cell voltage drops to about 1 volt, it is about time for the dump. Do not incinerate cells as strong heat can produce some unexpected chemical reactions. Some types of cells explode. There is no danger in putting your fingers across the terminals of a cell. The low voltage isn't capable of producing a shock.

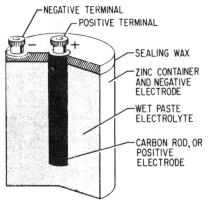

Cross section of a dry cell. The terminals may be screws, as shown, or spring clips.

The no. 6 cell has a rated current capability of ⅛ ampere for several hours, but it can supply much larger currents for shorter periods of time. A cell, any cell, will have a longer life in intermittent rather than continuous service. If you can give a cell a brief rest between periods of use, it will last longer. Cells have a small amount of recuperative ability and can regain their strength in some measure if permitted to do so.

The short-circuit current of the no. 6 dry cell is about 25 amperes, possibly a bit more. As the cell works over a period of time, its terminal voltage decreases and its current capacity—its ability to deliver current—also drops.

The positive electrode of this cell (and there are smaller cells that use this type of construction) consists of a cylindrical length of carbon rod down the center. A knurled screw or spring clip is attached to the top of the rod so that a wire can be easily connected to it. The negative electrode is a zinc can that also serves as a holder for the contents of the cell. The zinc, of course, is covered with some sort of wrapper. A knurled screw or spring clip is mounted at the top of the zinc can and is the connection for the negative electrode. The electrolyte is a moist paste containing a mixture of ammonium chloride, powdered coke, ground carbon, manganese dioxide, zinc chloride, graphite, and water.

While only one of the electrodes is metal, the carbon electrode is a conductor and so can be used for this purpose. The terminals of this cell may not be marked, but it should be easy to remember that the center clip is positive; the case negative. In some cells of this type, such as those used in flashlights, there is no knurled screw or spring clip on the ends of the electrodes. Instead, the center positive terminal has a small mound of metal at the top of the cell, while the bottom part of the cell is exposed metal. The flat bottom portion is the negative terminal, while the small mound at the top is positive. Connection is through direct physical contact. In a flashlight, the positive part of the cell touches one end of a bulb. The negative part of the cell makes contact with a spring clip that is part of the flashlight circuit.

For a long time no. 6 dry cells were popularly used in homes for operating doorbells. They have now been replaced by transformers, but you may still find them in some older residences. They do have excellent current capacity, but their large size has decreased their popularity and you will now find them only in specialized applications.

SIZE D CELL

The size D cell has the same construction as a no. 6 cell but is much smaller in size. It is sometimes called a flashlight cell, somewhat misleading since flashlight cells are available in various sizes. The size D cell has a short circuit current of about 6 amperes and a terminal EMF of about 1.5 volts. Ordinarily, a pair of these cells are used in flashlights, but some extra-large flashlights use 4 of them.

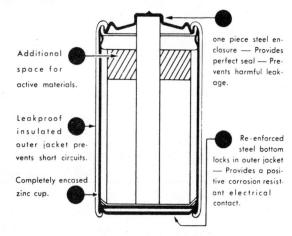

Additional space for active materials.

one piece steel enclosure — Provides perfect seal — Prevents harmful leakage.

Leakproof insulated outer jacket prevents short circuits.

Completely encased zinc cup.

Re-enforced steel bottom locks in outer jacket — Provides a positive corrosion resistant electrical contact.

Cross-sectional view of size D cell, commonly used for flashlights and electrically operated toys. The center rod is carbon and is the plus electrode. Connection is to a metal button at the top. The exposed bottom of the cell is the negative terminal.

The no. 6 cell and the size D, both dry-cell types, tend to corrode after being in use for sometime. Corrosion consists of a chemical ac-

cumulation around the terminals, plus a swelling of the case. This may make it difficult, and in some cases impossible, to remove the dead cells without damaging the appliance. If you have battery-operated appliances that you do not plan to use for a long time, possibly a period of 6 months or more, remove the cells and store them. Put a note inside the appliance, in the battery compartment, as to when the cells were purchased and where you have stored them. This will prevent buying duplicate batteries unnecessarily and a frantic search for batteries you may want quickly. Or, if you prefer, you can buy steel-encased D cells. The steel casing means the cell is better mechanically only, not electrically. Swelling of the cell will be contained within the steel jacket and so there will be no appliance damage. A cell that swells, whether steel-encased or not, is worthless. The steel-jacketed type is more costly than ordinary D cells.

SILVER-OXIDE BUTTON-TYPE CELLS

Very small cells are required for hearing aids and electric watches. When buying appliances of this kind, be sure to get personal instructions at the time of purchase on how and when to replace batteries. These cells have an output of 1.5 volts, and supply very small currents. The size is approximately 0.455'' x 0.165'' although, as in the case of other cells, other dimensions are available.

MERCURY CELLS

The mercury cell was one of the earliest efforts to decrease cell size while supplying required current without an excessive loss of battery voltage. Like other type of cells, mercury cells are available in different sizes and shapes for various applications. The voltage is just a bit higher than that of dry cells and is about 1.34 volts.

The basic mercury cell is contained in a small steel case and uses an electrolyte of potassium hydroxide. The positive plate is amalgamated zinc while the negative electrode is mercuric oxide. The three basic types of mercury cell are the wound anode flat, flat pellet structure, and cylindrical.

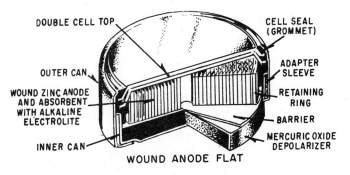

WOUND ANODE FLAT

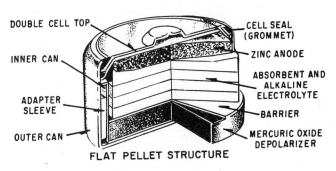

FLAT PELLET STRUCTURE

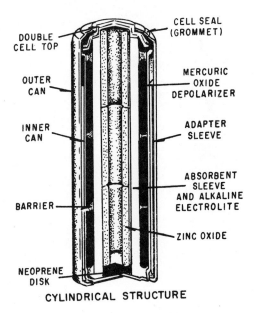

CYLINDRICAL STRUCTURE

Mercury cells are available in different sizes and shapes, some of which are shown here.

Short circuiting a battery, sometimes done accidentally, can be dangerous. Even a small cell can supply an astonishing amount of current. A short across a storage battery can make the shorting wire glow hot and result in a serious burn. This could be accompanied by a shattering of the battery case, or ripping of the vent caps, and a discharge of acid. The mercury cell, in its steel jacket, has no way of venting, and so can explode. An incinerator is no place for worn-out mercury cells.

PRIMARY AND SECONDARY CELLS

All dry cells come under the heading of primary cells. As such, they are not designed to be recharged, although you will find dry-cell rechargers available in some electrical-parts stores. While you can get some additional life from a primary cell after recharging, it isn't too effective, and whether the time, effort, and expense are worthwhile is debatable.

A wet cell is one in which the electrolyte is a liquid. Such cells are designed to be recharged. Recharging is not only easy, but in some instances, such as your automobile, is automatic. If you have a house and a garage, or have garage space available, a wet-cell battery charger is convenient. Battery-operated power tools are available with individual chargers. With such appliances frequent recharging is required, since the current capacity of the built-in batteries isn't too large. Most such chargers are sealed units, with a pair of male prongs exiting from one side, and a line cord going to the battery operated appliance out of the other. To know if the charger is working, connect it to an outlet and let it remain there for an hour or so. If, at the end of that time, the charger is warm to the touch, you can be sure it is delivering current. This does not automatically mean the battery in your appliance is in good condition. Current can be sent by a charger into a defective battery. If, after charging for a number of hours, an appliance does not work, a defective battery could be one of the causes. In some instances, chargers must be connected overnight to supply an adequate charge.

THE LEAD-ACID CELL

While the lead-acid cell has its greatest use in automobiles, you will find variations of it in home-operated power tools, including tools used for gardening. It could also be used as an independent power source for a home theft-and-fire-alarm system.

The electrolyte in the lead-acid cell is a water solution of sulfuric acid. During operation the temperature of the acid increases and there is some evaporation of liquid. However, this evaporation is of water only, not acid. Never add acid; use water only. Always make sure that the water level is such that it covers the plates inside the battery.

The positive plate (actually a large group of connected similar plates) is made of lead peroxide, while the negative is of pure sponge lead. Chemically, these are dissimilar metals, even though they are variations of the same element, lead. The terminals of a lead-acid battery may be marked with plus for the positive terminal and minus for the negative. Sometimes just the plus terminal is so identified, or it may have a touch of red near or on it. In some lead-acid cells, the positive terminal is slightly larger than the negative. When connecting a charger, make sure that the plus or positive lead of the charger (marked plus or coded in red) connects to the positive terminal of the battery. The negative lead of the charger (marked minus or color-coded black) should connect to the negative terminal of the battery. If the battery is the type that has removable vent caps, take them off during charging. Hydrogen gas is given off

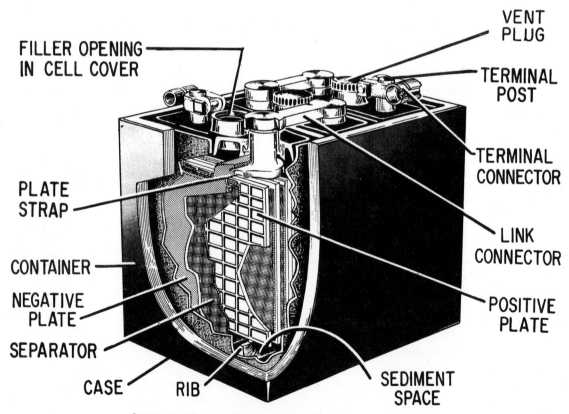

FILLER OPENING IN CELL COVER

VENT PLUG

TERMINAL POST

TERMINAL CONNECTOR

PLATE STRAP

LINK CONNECTOR

CONTAINER

NEGATIVE PLATE

POSITIVE PLATE

SEPARATOR

CASE   RIB

SEDIMENT SPACE

Construction of a lead-acid battery: Vent plugs permit escape of hydrogen when battery is being recharged. Typical lead-acid batteries have ratings between 60 ampere hours and 120 ampere hours.

during the charging process and you may see this as the formation of tiny bubbles on the top surface of the electrolyte. Hydrogen is explosive, and so if you are simultaneously charging a large number of batteries, supply a venting hood. Keep sparks or lighted matches or lighted cigarettes away from charging batteries.

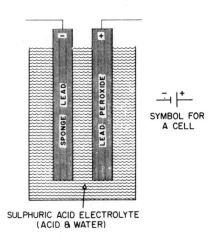

SYMBOL FOR A CELL

SULPHURIC ACID ELECTROLYTE
(ACID & WATER)

Basic lead-acid cell: The electrolyte is a liquid mixture of sulphuric acid and water. The negative electrode is pure sponge lead; the positive electrode is lead peroxide. Evaporation from the cell is water only, not acid. Replace evaporation losses with water only.

CHECKING LEAD-ACID CELLS

The easiest way to check a wet cell that has vent caps is with a hydrometer, or equivalent tool. A hydrometer measures the specific gravity or the electrolyte, about 1270 when fully charged and about 1150 when discharged. To use the hydrometer, open one of the battery vents and insert the rubber tip of the hydrometer. Squeeze the hydrometer bulb and draw some electrolyte into the hydrometer. Hold the hydrometer so you can take a reading of the top level of the liquid. Repeat this process for each of the cells making up the battery.

Hydrometers are now available that contain several colored balls. Each of these balls will respond to a different specific gravity, and so you can get a rough estimate of the state of charge of a battery, depending on which one rises and floats

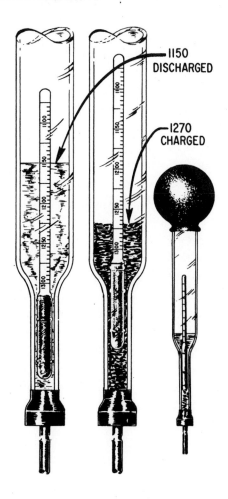

1150 DISCHARGED

1270 CHARGED

A hydrometer with a graduated float is one of the best ways of checking the charge of a lead-acid cell.

near the surface of the electrolyte. After using a hydrometer, flush it with clean water to make sure no acid remains. If you get some acid on your skin, even in small quantities, the result can be an annoying or even a serious burn. Wash the area with large amounts of water as soon as possible, then apply boric-acid ointment or zinc ointment. Clean lubricating oil will do in an emergency. If you spill electrolyte on your clothing, neutralize as soon as possible with dilute ammonia or a solution of baking soda and water.

NICKEL-CADMIUM CELLS

While wet cells such as the lead-acid type are rather large and heavy, there are other types of small-size wet cells such as nickel-cadmium designed for a number of in-house electrical applications. You'll find them in electric toothbrushes, portable vacuum cleaners, electric combs, etc. Nickel-cadmium cells are storage types and can be recharged often. They are given the same type numbers as equivalent dry cells and are interchangeable with them. Like dry cells, nickel-cadmium are available in AA, C, D, and other sizes, and also in the so-called "button" size, only 29/64" x 7/32". The output voltage of a single cell is 1.25 volts.

Nickel-cadmium batteries are better than lead-acid types, and in some instances are interchangeable with them. Some nickel-cadmium batteries are sealed units so there is never a problem of level of electrolyte. Both nickel-cadmium and lead-acid cells can be made to have the same current capacity, but the nickel-cadmium can stay idle in any state of charge for an indefinite time and keep a full charge when stored for a long time.

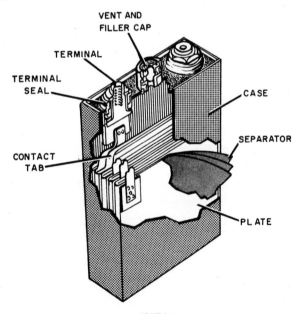

VENT AND FILLER CAP

TERMINAL

TERMINAL SEAL

CONTACT TAB

CASE

SEPARATOR

PLATE

Construction of a nickel-cadmium cell.

The positive plate is made of nickel hydroxide while the negative is cadmium hydroxide. The electrolyte is a 30 percent by weight solution of potassium hydroxide in distilled water. The spe-

cific gravity does not change during use and so there is no way of using a hydrometer to check the state of charge. Another characteristic of the nickel-cadmium cell is that the voltage remains much more constant than that of the lead-acid type. Thus, a voltage test under load isn't very helpful. If you have an appliance that uses such a cell, the best check is to substitute a new battery for the one you suspect may be defective. If the appliance works with the new battery, but not with the old, your suspicions are verified.

There are many other types of wet cells, including the silver-zinc and the silver-cadmium. These are made especially for particular characteristics, such as fast charge, fast discharge, larger current capacity, and so on.

GETTING MORE VOLTAGE

The voltage of a single cell is about 2 volts or less. A dry cell may have a median voltage of 1.5 volts; and a fully charged lead-acid cell, about 2.1 volts. To get more voltage than that supplied by a single cell, they can be electrically connected in series. In a series circuit, the plus terminal of one cell is wired to the minus terminal of another. Thus, if two 1.5 volt cells are used, the total voltage available then becomes the sum of the voltages of the individual cells. For two 1.5-volt cells in series, the total would be 1.5 plus 1.5 equals 3 volts.

In a flashlight using a 3-volt bulb, the two cells inside the flashlight are automatically connected in series when they are inserted in the flashlight. If you buy a 9-volt battery for a transistor radio, the battery you get will have a single case but inside that case will be six 1.5 volt cells wired in series. Since the wiring is done for you by the manufacturer, you need not concern yourself with doing it. If cells come equipped with knurled nuts and machine screw terminals, connecting cells in series is no problem. If you have a transistor radio and its operating potential is 6 volts, you will probably buy four small cells, each rated at 1.5 volts. When you insert them individually into the battery holder in the radio, you will at the same time be connecting them in series, automatically, to supply a total of 6 volts.

THE SERIES CURRENT CAPABILITY

When cells are connected in series, the total current capability is that of a single cell. If you have four cells in series, and each has a maximum current output of 1 ampere, then the total current output can be no more than 1 ampere. Actually, the current output is limited to that of the weakest cell. If one of the cells of this group, through some defect, or because it is worn, has an output of only ¾ ampere, that will be the maximum current, even though the other cells can supply 1 ampere. That is why, in replacing cells in an appliance, it is important to replace them all at the same time with fresh cells. If, for correct operation, an appliance needs four cells, and one of the cells is worn out, then the appliance cannot work the way it should, even though three of the four cells are fresh.

It is possible, when replacing cells in an appliance, to insert them incorrectly. If this happens, the appliance will not get its correct operating voltage and will either not work at all (most likely) or will work poorly. For dry cells, the center tip is plus and should make contact with the base of the adjoining battery (minus). Be sure to follow the battery-insertion diagram often pasted inside the appliance or supplied with it.

Your automobile battery consists of six lead-acid cells. If these are fully charged, each has an output of 2.1 volts. They are internally connected and since there are six of them, the total battery voltage is 6 times 2.1 equals 12.6 volts. However, if one of the cells becomes defective, the battery will have to be replaced. This also applies to wet cells used in connection with in-home or garden appliances.

GETTING MORE CURRENT

To get more current from two or more cells, wire them in parallel, also known as a shunt connection. In this circuit arrangement, the plus terminal of one cell is wired to the plus terminal of another. The two negative terminals are then joined by a wire. With this arrangement, the total current capacity is that of both cells. As in the case of a series circuit, both cells must be identical. Further, both should have the same amount of charge. If one is weaker than the other, the stronger will charge the weaker, diminishing the total available current by that amount. To get large amounts of current, you can wire more than two cells in parallel.

When cells are connected in parallel, all the plus terminals are joined, and all the minus terminals are connected. The output voltage, that of a singel cell, can be taken from the exposed ends of the two wires.

SERIES-PARALLEL CIRCUIT

Cells can be wired in series-parallel to get a higher voltage and also a higher current. The difficulty with parallel, or series circuits, or a series-parallel, is the limitation imposed by the weakest cell. However, such circuit arrangements are used for household appliances and they work well.

Various symbols are used to show cells connected in series.

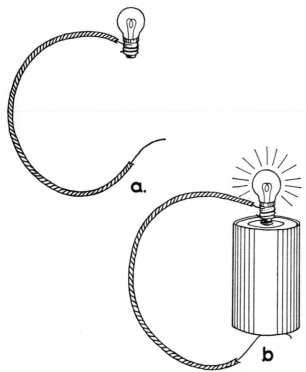

Basic idea of a flashlight: To light, the bulb must have the same voltage rating as the dry cell. The open wire represents a switch. Circuit a is called open; no current flows. Circuit b is called closed; current flows and the bulb lights.

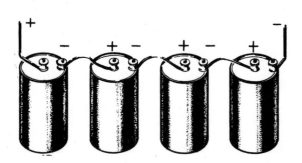

Method of connecting cells in series: The center terminals are plus; the terminals on the edge of the case are minus. The total voltage is the sum of the voltages or the individual cells. Use only identical cells when connecting this way.

CIRCUIT DIAGRAMS

It is a good idea to get into the habit of drawing diagrams of electrical-wiring arrangements, since a simple sketch will often help you decide the way in which the wiring should be done. This is particularly true with switching circuits. A jagged line can be used to represent a load, whether that load is a lamp, a heater, or an iron. The electrical

symbol for a cell is a short line and a longer line, parallel to each other. If more than one cell is used to form a battery, then use a succession of such lines. Marking the diagram with current and voltage values helps clarify the work done by the circuit.

PICTORIAL VS. CIRCUIT DIAGRAMS

A pictorial diagram, as the name indicates, shows actual electrical parts. It is much more difficult to do a drawing of this kind than a circuit diagram, since it does require some drawing ability. However, pictorials are valuable in instructions issued by electrical manufacturers, since they make methods of connections quite obvious.

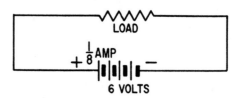

The jagged line represents the load, while the light and dark parallel lines are cells in series. The straight lines are connecting wires. In this schematic diagram, the battery is rated at 6 volts, and the amount of current flow is ⅛ ampere.

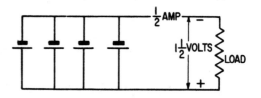

Four cells in a parallel or shunt arrangement. The voltage of each of the cells is 1½ volts and is also the voltage that appears across the load. The current in this circuit is marked as ½ ampere. There is no standardization in drawing electrical symbols, and in this diagram the plus and minus symbols associated with the cells have been omitted.

OPEN CIRCUIT

An open circuit is one through which current does not flow. But be careful. An open circuit can have voltage present. The outlets in your home all have voltage. A turned-off lamp plugged into such an outlet has voltage across its interior wiring, but since no current flows to a bulb, is regarded as being open or open-circuited. Open the switch to a lamp or remove the bulb and you create an open-circuit condition. This does not mean you can make repairs to the wiring of the lamp with impunity with the male plug of the lamp inserted into a wall outlet. When fixing a lamp, or any other appliance, the best procedure—the safest procedure—is to remove the plug attached to the end of the line cord from the power outlet.

CLOSED CIRCUIT

A closed circuit is exactly opposite that of an open circuit. A closed circuit is one in which current flows to a load. This does not mean that the load, possibly an appliance, is receiving the correct amount of current, nor does it mean the appliance is working properly. All it signifies is that the appliance is connected to a voltage source, that the circuit is complete—that is, all switches are closed—and that current is flowing from the source to and through the load. If an appliance works correctly, it is obviously receiving the correct amount of current. If it does not work well, or doesn't work at all, it may be receiving less current than it should.

A short circuit is a type of closed circuit. With a short circuit an appliance can receive much less current than it should or possibly no current at all. And yet the current taken from the source will be maximum.

CURRENT CONTROL

For home appliances, the amount of line voltage is very rarely changed. If any voltage change is required, it is handled inside the appliance. Thus, a radio receiver or a television set connected to an outlet will take the voltage available from an outlet and modify it or change it in some way. But that is done completely automatically. However, you can modify the amount of current flow to some home equipment. Thus, if you have a light dimmer, you can increase or decrease the amount of current flowing to electric light bulbs, producing an effect from complete darkness to maximum light, with intermediate lighting conditions. Modern electric irons have various settings, depending on the fabrics to be ironed. This is handled by a current control.

THE CONDUCTIVE LINK

The electrical setup in every home consists of three basic parts: (1) one or more appliances to be operated from an AC or a DC voltage; the DC voltage is supplied by batteries and the AC voltage from an outlet; (2) a voltage source; and (3) a conductive link between the appliance and the voltage. This conductive link is wire, and because it is used for delivering current, is as important as either of the other factors.

Chapter 4
WIRING

An oil company delivers fuel to your home by truck; your electric utility delivers electrical energy by wires. Thus, there is a physical connection between the generators of your local power company and every appliance of every shape and description in your home.

Your home wiring is your responsibility or that of your landlord. Generally, most home wiring is inadequate and is so because of the growth and development of appliances. It isn't easy to add more wiring to an existing installation, since so much of it is buried behind walls. Some people have the idea that an unlimited source of electrical power is available through their baseboard outlets. There is no question that your local power company can usually supply the average home. The problem is whether your wiring can accommodate increased electrical demands. It is possible to overload wiring just as it is possible to overwork or overload an appliance.

MEANING OF CONDUCTORS

A conductor is any substance—gas, liquid, or solid—that permits the relatively easy passage of an electric current. For home wiring the most common conductors are copper and aluminum. Copper wiring is preferable, since volume for volume, it has better conductivity than aluminum. Further, copper is easily soldered; aluminum can be soldered but it is much more of a job. However, the present trend in commercial installations of home electrical wiring is to eliminate soldering as much as possible.

Substance	Relative conductance (Silver = 100%)
Silver	100
Copper...........	98
Gold	78
Aluminum........	61
Tungsten	32
Zinc	30
Platinum	17
Iron.............	16
Lead	15
Tin	9
Nickel	7
Mercury..........	1
Carbon...........	0.05

Relative conductivity of various metals on a scale of 0 to 100. Copper has almost as good conductivity as silver. Aluminum is not quite as good as copper in this respect.

WIRE TYPES

The simplest kind of wire is single conductor covered with some sort of insulation such as plastic or synthetic rubber. The conductor can be either solid or stranded copper wires. If stranded, the total number of strands is equivalent in conductivity to a particular size of solid conductor.

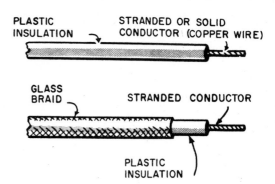

53

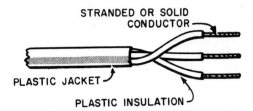

Wire conductors can be single or stranded and can also be covered by various kinds of insulation.

The insulation around a conducting wire can be paper, cotton, silk, plastic, asbestos, neoprene (a synthetic rubber), varnished cambric, or any other commercially made substance such as polyvinyl chloride (PVC). Depending on wiring requirements, the insulating substance may consist of one or more layers. Thus, SCC wire is single-cotton covered, DCC is double-cotton covered. The purpose of the insulation is to prevent the accidental transfer of electric currents from one wire to another or from the wire to the metal conduit or cable that covers it. Wires may be single, solid, or stranded, or may come in pairs, or larger groups, depending on the final use.

WIRE SIZE

The size of a wire is not its length, but is determined by its cross-sectional area. This is the area you see when looking at a wire end-on. The area of a wire is measured in a unit called the circular mil, and abbreviated as CM. A circular mil is the area of a wire whose diameter is equal to 1 mil, or 1/1,000", or 0.001". Wire size is specified by gauge number usually extending from 0000 wire to no. 40. The thickest is 0000 wire; and the thinnest, no. 40. You can verify this by examining the table of wire sizes.

The first column in the table is the gauge number of the wire. The second column is the diameter of the wire in mils. Note that no. 40 wire is 3.1 mils while 0000 wire is 460 mils or ½" in diameter. The third column is the cross-sectional area in CM. Note how rapidly the area increases as the gauge number becomes smaller. The area in CM of no. 40 wire is only 9.9 mils (little less than 10 1/1,000") while that of 0000 wire is 212,000 circular mils. By examining the last column, you can get some idea of the weight of the wire. A thousand feet of no. 40 wire weighs 0.0299 pound and 1,000 feet of 0000 wire weighs 641 pounds. However, neither no. 40 wire nor 0000 is used in the home. For home wiring, no. 14 gauge is quite common, while you will find nos. 16 and 18 used in cords connected to various appliances. Service wires coming into the home are about no. 6 or no. 8. And while the table shows wires only up to no. 40, wire sizes all the way up to no. 60 are available. Such very fine wires, possibly thinner than a human hair, are used in the wiring of some electronic instruments.

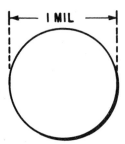

The diameter of wire is measured in mils. A mil is 0.000" or 1/1,000". To get the area in circular mils, multiply the diameter by itself. A wire having a diameter of 5 mils, has a cross-sectional area of 5 x 5 equals 25 circular mils.

The greater the cross-sectional area of a wire in circular mils, the more current it can carry. At the same time, it is more expensive than thinner wires and is more difficult to handle in making connections. However, cross-sectional area isn't the only factor in governing current-carrying capacity. This is also affected by the length of the wire, the temperature, and the insulation surrounding the wire.

(American wire gauge — B & S)

| Gauge Number | Diameter (mils) | Cross section | | Ohms per 1,000 ft. | | Ohms per mile 25° C. (=77° F.) | Pounds per 1,000 ft. |
		Circular mils	Square inches	25° C. (=77° F.)	65° C. (=149° F.)		
0000	460.0	212,000.0	0.166	0.0500	0.0577	·0.264	641.0
000	410.0	168,000.0	.132	.0630	.0727	.333	508.0
00	365.0	133,000.0	.105	.0795	.0917	.420	403.0
0	325.0	106,000.0	.0829	.100	.116	.528	319.0
1	289.0	83,700.0	.0657	.126	.146	.665	253.0
2	258.0	66,400.0	.0521	.159	.184	.839	201.0
3	229.0	52,600.0	.0413	.201	.232	1.061	159.0
4	204.0	41,700.0	.0328	.253	.292	1.335	126.0
5	182.0	33,100.0	.0260	.319	.369	1.685	100.0
6	162.0	26,300.0	.0206	.403	.465	2.13	79.5
7	144.0	20,800.0	.0164	.508	.586	2.68	63.0
8	128.0	16,500.0	.0130	.641	.739	3.38	50.0
9	114.0	13,100.0	.0103	.808	.932	4.27	39.6
10	102.0	10,400.0	.00815	1.02	1.18	5.38	31.4
11	91.0	8,230.0	.00647	1.28	1.48	6.75	24.9
12	81.0	6,530.0	.00513	1.62	1.87	8.55	19.8
13	72.0	5,180.0	.00407	2.04	2.36	10.77	15.7
14	64.0	4,110.0	.00323	2.58	2.97	13.62	12.4
15	57.0	3,260.0	.00256	3.25	3.75	17.16	9.86
16	51.0	2,580.0	.00203	4.09	4.73	21.6	7.82
17	45.0	2,050.0	.00161	5.16	5.96	27.2	6.20
18	40.0	1,620.0	.00128	6.51	7.51	34.4	4.92
19	36.0	1,290.0	.00101	8.21	9.48	·43.3	3.90
20	32.0	1,020.0	.000802	10.4	11.9	54.9	3.09
21	28.5	810.0	.000636	13.1	15.1	69.1	2.45
22	25.3	642.0	.000505	16.5	19.0	87.1	1.94
23	22.6	509.0	.000400	20.8	24.0	109.8	1.54
24	20.1	404.0	.000317	26.2	30.2	138.3	1.22
25	17.9	320.0	.000252	33.0	38.1	174.1	0.970
26	15.9	254.0	.000200	41.6	48.0	220.0	0.769
27	14.2	202.0	.000158	52.5	60.6	277.0	0.610
28	12.6	160.0	.000126	66.2	76.4	350.0	0.484
29	11.3	127.0	.0000995	83.4	96.3	440.0	0.384
30	10.0	101.0	.0000789	105.0	121.0	554.0	0.304
31	8.9	79.7	.0000626	133.0	153.0	702.0	0.241
32	8.0	63.2	.0000496	167.0	193.0	882.0	0.191
33	7.1	50.1	.0000394	211.0	243.0	1,114.0	0.152
34	6.3	39.8	.0000312	266.0	307.0	1,404.0	0.120
35	5.6	31.5	.0000248	335.0	387.0	1,769.0	0.0954
36	5.0	25.0	.0000196	423.0	488.0	2,230.0	0.0757
37	4.5	19.8	.0000156	533.0	616.0	2,810.0	0.0600
38	4.0	15.7	.0000123	673.0	776.0	3,550.0	0.0476
39	3.5	12.5	.0000098	848.0	979.0	4,480.0	0.0377
40	3.1	9.9	.0000078	1,070.0	1,230.0	5,650.0	0.0299

Standard annealed solid copper-wire table, using American Wire Gauge (AWG). Another gauge, Browne & Sharp (B & S), is identical to AWG.

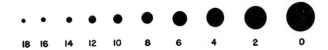

Cross-sectional areas of some copper wires from gauge 18 to gauge 0.

RESISTANCE OF WIRE

The smaller the cross-section of a wire, the greater is its resistance per unit length. A foot of no. 12 wire, for example, has more resistance than a foot of no. 8 wire. Whether resistance is important in home-wiring calculations depends on wire length and on how much current is to flow through the wire.

There are two possibilities when using the wrong gauge of wire for current-demanding appliances. Because of the resistance, there will be a voltage loss in the wire. Further, the wire may become exceptionally hot. Assume, for instance, that 10 amperes of current is to flow through the wire, and that the length of the wire between the source and the appliance has a total resistance of 1 ohm. To find the voltage loss in the wire, multiply the current flow by the resistance of the wire. The current is 10 amperes, the resistance 1 ohm: 10 times 1 equals 10. This means the appliance will receive 10 volts less than it should. If the line voltage is 115 volts, then 115 less 10 equals 105 volts. Whether or not the appliance will work well with 105 volts is a guess. It may or may not. Or, it may not function at all.

When selecting a wire size for installation, take two factors into consideration: (1) how much current the wire is required to handle; and (2) how many additional appliances will be used to load this line in the future. The safest procedure to follow, is always to use a heavier gauge of wire, but this, of course, will also increase the installation expense. The smaller the gauge number of a wire, the more it costs.

STRANDED WIRE

The cross-sectional area of a wire becomes larger with smaller gauge numbers. The cross-sectional area of no. 8 wire, for example, is about 10 times as great as that of no. 18 wire. But as a wire is made thicker, it becomes increasingly difficult to handle. It is quite easy to wrap a no. 16 wire around the screw terminal of a switch. Doing it with a no. 8 wire is quite an accomplishment. For this reason, wires having about a no. 8 or no. 6 gauge are usually stranded types. Stranded wire consists of thinner wires twisted together.

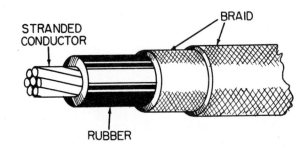

Stranded conductor: The strands are generally twisted, and if made of copper, are shielded from the rubber with cotton. The rubber is protected by more and more outer sheaths of cotton braid. When connecting stranded conductor to another wire or to a screw terminal, be careful not to break any of the strands. Twist them to ensure good electrical contact.

If, when buying wire, a single number is indicated, then the wire is a solid type. Thus, the label on a spool of wire will state: "No. 18" or "No. 16". Stranded wire is always referred to by a pair of numbers such as: "18/30". This means that the wire consists of 18 strands of no. 30 wire.

Like solid wires, stranded types have current limitations. Sixty-five strands of no. 34 wire will carry the same amount of current as a solid no. 16 wire, and so for wiring purposes you can use either 65 strands of no. 34 (supplied as a cable) or no. 16 wire. Some manufacturers, instead of referring to the wire as "65/34", will identify it as no. 16 stranded. Of course, there are any combination of wires that could be made into an equivalent of no. 16. The thicker the wire, the fewer the number of strands. And so a designation such as no. 16 stranded does not tell you anything about the number of strands nor the gauge of the individual wires.

HOW TO CALCULATE THE SOLID CONDUCTOR EQUIVALENT OF STRANDED WIRE

Assume you have stranded wire consisting of 37 strands, each of which is 0.002" thick. Since 0.002 is the same as 2 mils, to calculate the area in circular mils, multiply the diameter by itself: 2 times 2 equals 4, and so each individual strand has an area of 4 circular mils. However, there are 37 strands and so the total cross-sectional area is 37 times 4 equals 148 circular mils.

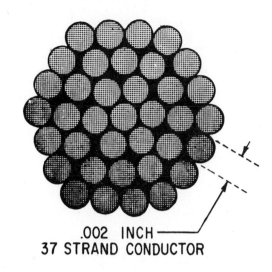

.002 INCH
37 STRAND CONDUCTOR

Cross-sectional view of wire consisting of 37 strands of 2-mil wire.

Look in the wire table, and under the heading "Cross Section" in the third column, you will find areas in circular mils. Move down this column and you will see that there is no single solid conductor that has an area of 148 circular mils. No. 29 wire is 127 circular mils and no. 28 wire is 160 circular mils. And so 37 strands of 2-mil wire could be considered somewhere between no. 28 and no. 29 gauge.

COPPER VS. ALUMINUM WIRE

Aluminum wire has a greater resistance per unit volume than copper. The chart shows wires ranging from no. 14 to no. 0. Examine the two columns at the right and you will see that aluminum wire has about 50 percent more resistance than copper. Wire gauge alone doesn't tell the whole story. If you are planning to rewire, or are planning to have an electrical contractor do the job, be sure to specify whether copper or aluminum wire is to be used. No. 14-gauge copper wire has a greater current-carrying capacity than no. 14 gauge aluminum. If the substance of the wire isn't specified, your wiring may have much less current-carrying capacity than you realize.

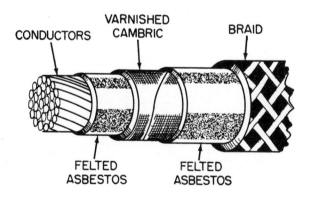

CONDUCTORS — VARNISHED CAMBRIC — BRAID

FELTED ASBESTOS — FELTED ASBESTOS

While solid conductors can be used for heavy currents, stranded conductors of smaller gauge are easier to handle. Two layers of asbestos are sometimes used, as shown here, separated by varnished cambric. The outer sheath can be metal braid.

57

Trade Name	Type Letter	Size AWG	No. of Conductors	Insulation	Braid on Each Conductor	Outer Covering	Use		
Heater Cord	HC	18–12	2, 3 or 4	Rubber & Asbestos	Cotton	None	Portable	Dry Places	Portable Heaters
	HPD	18–12	2, 3 or 4	Rubber with Asbestos or All Neoprene	None	Cotton or Rayon	Portable	Damp Places	Portable Heaters
Rubber Jacketed Heater Cord	HSJ	18–16	2, 3 or 4	Rubber with Asbestos or All Neoprene	None	Cotton and Rubber	Portable	Damp Places	Portable Heaters
Jacketed Heater Cord	HSJO	18–16	2, 3 or 4	Rubber with Asbestos or All Neoprene	None	Cotton and Oil Resistant Compound	Portable	Damp Places	Portable Heaters
	HS	14–12				Cotton and Rubber or Neoprene			
	HSO	14–12				Cotton and Oil Resistant Compound			
Parallel Heater Cord	HPN	18–16	2	Thermosetting	None	Thermosetting	Portable	Damp Places	Portable Heaters
Heat & Moisture-Resistant Cord	AVPO	18–10	2	Asbestos & Var. Cam.	None	Asbestos, Flame-Ret. Moisture Resistant	Pendant or Portable	Damp Places	Not Hard Usage
	AVPD		2 or 3						
Range, Dryer Cable	SRD	10–4	3 or 4	Rubber	None	Rubber or Neoprene	Portable	Damp Places	Ranges, Dryers
	SRDT	10–4	3 or 4	Thermoplastic	None	Thermoplastic	Portable	Damp Places	Ranges, Dryers

Chart of flexible-cord types.

Trade Name	Type Letter	Size AWG	No. of Conductors	Insulation	Braid on Each Conductor	Outer Covering	Use		
Parallel Tinsel Cord	TP	27	2	Rubber	None	Rubber	Attached to an Appliance	Damp Places	Not Hard Usage
	TPT	27	2	Thermoplastic	None	Thermoplastic	Attached to an Appliance	Damp Places	Not Hard Usage
Jacketed Tinsel Cord	TS	27	2 or 3	Rubber	None	Rubber	Attached to an Appliance	Damp Places	Not Hard Usage
	TST	27	2 or 3	Thermoplastic	None	Thermoplastic	Attached to an Appliance	Damp Places	Not Hard Usage
Asbestos-Covered Heat-Resistant Cord	AFC	18–10	2 or 3	Impregnated Asbestos	Cotton or Rayon	None	Pendant	Dry Places	Not Hard Usage
	AFPO		2	Impregnated Asbestos	None	Cotton, Rayon or Saturated Asbestos	Pendant	Dry Places	Not Hard Usage
	AFPD	18–10	2 or 3	Impregnated Asbestos	None	Cotton, Rayon or Saturated Asbestos	Pendant	Dry Places	Not Hard Usage
Cotton-Covered Heat-Resistant Cord	CFC	18–10	2 or 3	Impregnated Cotton	Cotton or Rayon	None	Pendant	Dry Places	Not Hard Usage
	CFPO		2	Impregnated Cotton	Cotton or Rayon	Cotton or Rayon	Pendant	Dry Places	Not Hard Usage
	CFPD		2 or 3	Impregnated Cotton	None	Cotton or Rayon	Pendant	Dry Places	Not Hard Usage
Parallel Cord	PO-1	18					Pendant or Portable	Dry Places	Not Hard Usage
	PO-2	18–16	2	Rubber	Cotton	Cotton or Rayon	Pendant or Portable	Dry Places	Not Hard Usage
	PO	18–10					Pendant or Portable	Dry Places	Not Hard Usage
All Rubber Parallel Cord	SP-1	18					Pendant or Portable	Damp Places	Not Hard Usage
	SP-2	18–16	2	Rubber	None	Rubber	Pendant or Portable	Damp Places	Not Hard Usage
	SP-3	18–12		Rubber	None	Rubber	Refrigerators or Room Air Conditioners	Damp Places	Not Hard Usage

Chart of flexible-cord types (continued).

59

Cord	Type	Size	No. of Conductors	Insulation	Braid	Covering	Use	Location	Usage
All Plastic Parallel Cord	SPT-1	18	2	Thermoplastic	None	Thermoplastic	Pendant or Portable	Damp Places	Not Hard Usage
	SPT-2	18-16							
All Plastic Parallel Cord	SPT-3	18-10	2	Thermoplastic	None	Thermoplastic	Refrigerators or Room Air Conditioners	Damp Places	Not Hard Usage
Lamp Cord	C	18-10	2 or more	Rubber	Cotton	None	Pendant or Port.	Dry Places	Not Hard Usage
Twisted Portable Cord	PD	18-10	2 or more	Rubber	Cotton	Cotton or Rayon	Pendant or Port.	Dry Places	Not Hard Usage
Reinforced Cord	P-1	18	2 or more	Rubber	Cotton	Cotton over Rubber Filler	Pendant or Portable	Dry Places	Not Hard Usage
	P-2	18-16							Hard Usage
	P	18-10							
Braided Heavy Duty Cord	K	18-10	2 or more	Rubber	Cotton	Two Cotton, Moisture-Resistant Finish	Pendant or Portable	Damp Places	Hard Usage
Vacuum Cleaner Cord	SV, SVO		2	Rubber	None	Rubber	Pendant or Portable	Damp Places	Not Hard Usage
	SVT, SVTO	18		Thermopl'		Thermoplastic			
Junior Hard Service Cord	SJ	18-16	2, 3, or 4	Rubber	None	Rubber	Pendant or Portable	Damp Places	Hard Usage
	SJO					Oil Resistant Compound			
	SJT, SJTO			Thermopl' or Rubber		Thermoplastic			
Hard Service Cord	S		2 or more	Rubber	None	Rubber	Pendant or Portable	Damp Places	Extra Hard Usage
	SO	18-2				Oil Resist. Compound			
	ST			Thermopl' or Rubber		Thermoplastic			
	STO					Oil Resistant Thermoplastic			
Rubber-Jacketed Heat-Resistant Cord	AFSJ	18-16	2 or 3	Impregnated Asbestos	None	Rubber	Portable	Damp Places	Portable Heaters
	AFS	18-16-14							

Resistance characteristics of copper and aluminum wire.

The largest gauge size is no. 0000, but there are wires larger than this, not for home, but for commercial installations. Wires that are larger than no. 0000 are classified in size by their cross-sectional area in circular mils. Sizes normally used have even numbers, such as nos. 12, 10, and 8. For interior home wiring, the most commonly used wires are nos. 14, 12, and 10.

Single conductors may be thinned—that is, the copper conductor is coated with an outer layer of tin, making such wires very easy to solder. The wire is then covered with one or more layers of insulating material, with an outer insulating layer of braided cotton covered by rubber. Such wire is called rubber-covered.

WIRE IDENTIFICATION

Since there is a tremendous variety of wires of all kinds, they are often designated by letters, rather than the more elaborate process of describing them in detail. Rubber-covered wire is called type R; and the better grade is known as type RH, because of its greater heat resistance. Thermoplastic materials, with the letter T as the designation, are now used more widely than rubber. The letters NM and NMC are used for non-metallic sheathed cable. The charts show some of the different kinds of wires, their type letter, gauge size, number of conductors, type of insulation, and use. However, a list of this kind is sometimes modified. Thus, the insulation material may change, but the chart is still useful in allowing a comparison of various kinds of wire.

AMERICAN WIRE GAUGE

The standard for wire sizes is American Wire Gauge, abbreviated as AWG. American Wire Gauge refers to wire sizes, such as no. 16, no. 18, etc. Wire sizes in the home may range from no. 18, possibly used for a bell-ringing circuit, to no. 3/0, (3 strands or no. 0 wire) for bringing current into your home. For wiring various outlets, either no. 14 or no. 12 AWG wire is commonly used.

WIRE GAUGE

Without considerable wire experience, it is difficult to estimate the gauge of a wire simply by inspection. If the wire you buy is on a spool, the gauge will be indicated somewhere on one of the side supports.

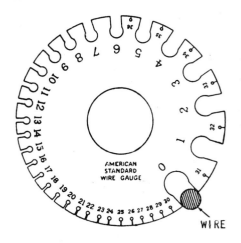

Wire gauge is an inexpensive, useful tool for determining wire thickness and gauge number.

The wire gauge, shown in the illustration, is a very useful and handy tool for measuring wire sizes. You can determine wire gauge by measuring wire thickness with a micrometer, but the wire gauge is easier and faster. To use the wire gauge, remove insulation from the end of the wire. If the wire is stranded, twirl the individual strands until the wire is as uniform as possible. Select a hole in the wire gauge that looks as though it will allow the wire to pass through it. If it does so very easily, try the next smaller hole. Continue until you find the one hole that will permit the wire to pass through snugly.

The wire gauge has each hole marked with wire-size data. On one side you will find the diameter of the wire in decimal fractions—that is, in thousandths of an inch. On the opposite side of the gauge, using the same hole, you will find the AWG gauge number. If, as an example, you pass a wire through a hole and it seems to make a good fit, you will possibly find the dimension .064 on one side. On the other side of the same hole, you will find the wire gauge number—in this case, 14.

CURRENT-CARRYING CAPACITY

The chart shows the current-carrying capacity of copper wires commonly used in the home. The first column is the gauge number of the wire, while the second column is the allowable amount of current in amperes. According to this table, no. 14 copper wire has a capability of handling 15 amperes, while no. 8 wire can tolerate 40 amperes.

Size AWG	
14	15·
12	20
10	30
8	40
6	55
4	70
3	80
2	95
1	110
0	125
00	145
000	165
0000	195

Current-carrying capacity of copper wires.

Size AWG	
12	15
10	25
8	30
6	40
4	55
3	65
*2	75
*1	85
*0	100
*00	115
*000	130
*0000	155

Current-carrying capacity of aluminum wires.

Size AWG	No. wires	Diameter in.	Diameter mm	Resistance Ohms per 1,000 feet Copper	Resistance Ohms per 1,000 feet Aluminum
14	solid	.0641	1.63	2.57	4.22
12	solid	.0808	2.05	1.62	2.66
10	solid	.102	2.59	1.02	1.67
8	solid	.129	3.27	.640	1.05
6	7	.184	4.67	.410	.674
4	7	.232	5.89	.260	.424
3	7	.260	6.60	.205	.336
2	7	.292	7.41	.162	.266
1	19	.332	8.42	.129	.211
0	19	.373	9.46	.102	.168

Chart of flexible-cord types (continued).

The next chart shows the current-carrying capacity of aluminum wires. In this table, no. 12 wire can handle 15 amperes and no. 10 can carry 25 amperes. As a general rule of thumb, to get the same current handling ability in aluminum wire as in copper, you must go to one size larger. No. 14 copper wire can carry 15 amperes, but to get the same current capacity in aluminum, you must use no. 12 wire.

IMPORTANCE OF WIRE LENGTH

It isn't enough to go to these two charts and select a wire based on current capacity alone. The distance from the main fuse box to the appliance is also important, particularly if the distance is rather long and the current demands are heavy. Generally, the allowable voltage loss in a wire from fuse box to appliance is 3 percent. Thus, if your line voltage is 110 volts, the loss should not be more than 3.3 volts. The voltage at the appliance will then be 110 minus 3.3 equals 106.7 volts. This voltage is measured at the appliance with the appliance working and drawing its full amount of current.

LOAD IN AMPS.	FOR 110V CIRCUIT DISTANCE TO LOAD IN FEET									
	50	75	100	125	150	200	250	300	400	500
15	10/12	8/10	8/10	6/8	6/8	4/6	4/6	3/4	2/4	1/3
20	10/12	8/10	6/8	6/8	4/6	4/6	3/4	2/4	1/3	0/2
25	8/10	6/8	6/8	4/6	4/6	3/4	2/4	1/3	0/2	(2/0)/1
30	6/10	6/8	4/6	4/6	3/4	2/4	1/3	0/2	(2/0)/1	(3/0)/0
40	6/8	4/6	4/6	3/4	2/4	1/3	0/2	(2/0)/1	(3/0)/0	(4/0)/(2/0)
50	4/8	4/6	3/4	2/4	1/3	0/2	(2/0)/1	(3/0)/0	(4/0)/(2/0)	
60	4/6	2/4	2/4	1/3	0/2	(2/0)/1	(3/0)/0	(4/0)/(2/0)		
70	4/6	2/4	1/3	0/2	(2/0)/2	(3/0)/0				
80	4/6	2/4	1/3	0/2	(2/0)/1	(3/0)/0				
90	2/4	1/3	0/2	(2/0)/1	(3/0)/1	(4/0)/(2/0)				
100	2/4	1/8	0/2	(2/0)/1	(3/0)/0	(4/0)/(2/0)				

Chart for calculating wire size between appliance and fuse box.

A voltage loss in a line connecting an appliance to your main fuse box takes place only when current is flowing between the two. If the appliance is turned off, the voltage measured at its control switch will be the same as the line voltage. If the line voltage is 110, then that will be the voltage at the appliance. The drop in voltage or the voltage loss takes place only when current flows.

The chart shows the wire size to use in accordance with the distance between source (the fuse box) and the load (any one of your appliances). The upper number refers to copper wire; the lower to aluminum. To use the chart, first decide what the load current will be, in amperes. Next, measure the distance, in feet, between the fuse box and the appliance. Finally, determine whether you will use copper or aluminum wire. As an example, assume that the load will draw 20 amperes and that it will be 75' from the fuse box. Locate 20 in the left column. Move across to the column headed by the number 75. The number given is 8/10. The upper number is for copper wire; the lower for aluminum. For this application, then, you can use either no. 8 copper wire, or no. 10 aluminum wire.

TYPES OF METALLIC ARMOR

Metallic armor has a number of advantages. It supplies a tough, protective covering for cables and it is fireproof. It can be easily grounded and it should be, but do not use it as the ground or "cold" line of a two-wire system.

There are six types of metallic armor. If you need a metallic armor that is light and very flexible, use wire covered with wire braid. The individual wires used for the outer braid are woven together and can be made of steel, copper, bronze, or aluminum.

Another type of armor is made of steel tape, which is then wrapped around the cable and covered with a serving of jute.

BX is a more common type of armor used around the home, but where there are conditions of moisture, there is a type of BX in which the armor is put over lead sheath.

Finally, there are two types of conduit: thin-walled and heavy. The thin-walled conduit is much easier to bend and is lighter and easier to handle, but the heavy-walled is much more substantial, and supplies greater protection.

LEAD-SHEATHED CABLE

Wires that may be immersed in water or that must be placed in terrain subject to water flow must have a cover that is completely watertight. You can put a rubber sheath around the cable, but the problem with rubber is that as it ages it cracks. Lead is a more useful, but more expensive, outer sheath.

Lead-sheathed cables are often used in power work. Lines that come into a home may be of this type. As shown in the drawing, there are three conductors, each one of which is made of stranded wire. The stranded conductors are covered with some kind of insulation, and then wrapped in a layer of rubberized tape. Fillers are added to give the wire-insulation combination a rounded form. Another layer of tape known as "serving" is used both for insulation and to keep the wire-filler assembly together. Finally, a lead covering or lead sheath is molded around the cable.

You will have two basic types of wire in your home. One is exposed—that is, you can see it. This is the wire that you use to plug a lamp, or a radio receiver, or a mixer, or blender, into an outlet. The other type of wire is that hidden by your walls and is known as cable or a run. Cable can consist of one or more wires and may be enclosed in flexible armor, and is then known as armored cable. Metallic cable is sometimes called BX. BX is designed only for indoor use. It is flexible and can be cut with a hacksaw or a cutting tool designed specifically for this purpose.

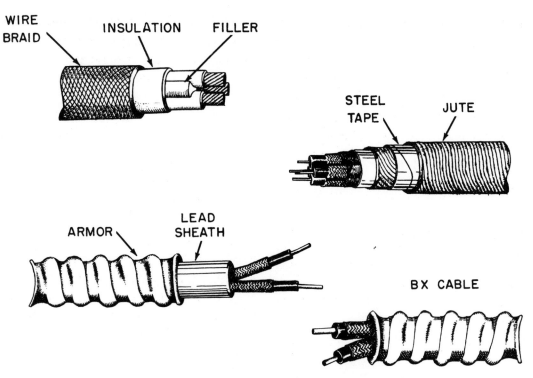

Some types of armored cable: Conduit, not shown in this drawing, is now preferred for re-wiring and for new home installations.

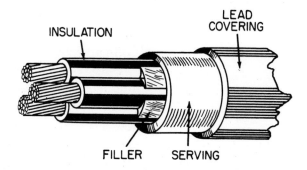

For wiring installations where there is a possibility of water seepage, cable with a lead covering offers good protection.

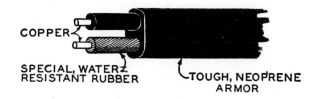

NMC cable is imbedded in Neoprene, a synthetic rubber substitute, and the wires are covered with special water-resistant rubber. There is no space between the wires and the Neoprene armor and so no filler material is needed. As a result it is impossible for moisture to seep in to rot the wire insulation. Neoprene is impervious to moisture, mildew, or rot.

BX

BX is one type of armored cable—that is, it consists of two or more conductors surrounded by metal. In the case of BX, the metal armor around the wire is flexible. The wires in BX are twisted together and are then wrapped in a paper coat. Until recently, BX was the most widely used form for interior wiring. It supplied fireproofing, something exposed wires do not do. Further, the armor also supplied automatic grounding.

Ordinary BX isn't suitable for outdoor wiring. For wet locations, or for use through masonry or concrete building partitions or through cinder block, the cable is supplied with a lead sheath.

CUTTING BX

You can cut BX by using a hacksaw with a fine-tooth blade. Insert the blade in the hacksaw so that the cutting teeth are away from you. Select one end of the BX and notch the cable lightly or mark it in some way so that you will recognize the starting point. Allow enough room from the end of the cable so that the wires you will expose from the armor will be long enough to reach the connecting points you plan to use. It is much easier to cut off excess wires with diagonal cutters than to go through the process of cutting the armor again.

Mount the BX in a vise and clamp it so that the section you wish to cut is close to the edges of the vise. Cut carefully so that you make a definite groove in the armor, and then rotate the cable after loosening the vise. In this way make a succession of notches all the way around. Then go back and join each notch by using the hacksaw. When finished you will have a groove all the way around the BX. And now, using the hacksaw slowly and carefully, deepen each notch until you can see it is practically cut through.

Remove the cable from the vise and bend it back and forth and you will find the cut section coming apart. Use the hacksaw to cut through any portion that still remains together. Remove the cut portion of the outer BX armor, and the wires and their paper wrapper will be exposed.

If the cut edges of the BX are rough, smooth them with a file. Cut away the excess paper insulation with a razor blade or scissors. If you want to protect the wires against possible cutting by the edges of the armored cable, you can buy an insulating sleeve to fit over the wires at the point where they exit from the armor. The insulating sleeve is a fiber bushing.

CONDUIT

Metallic cable, or BX, is gradually being replaced by conduit. Conduit is a hollow pipe that does not have the flexibility of BX. BX can be bent by hand; conduit requires a special bending tool. Conduit is now being used in new home construction and is often required by local electrical codes.

For home use, conduit is most often 1/2" or 3/4" in diameter. After the conduit is installed, the required wires are snaked through or "fished" through. BX comes complete with its wires and so "wire fishing" isn't needed. However, this isn't as much of an advantage as it might seem. In cutting away the outer metallic sheath of BX to get at the wires, it is quite possible to cut through the insulation of the wires. Further, the rough edges of the BX that has been cut can also cut into the insulation, unless protected by a bushing.

Conduit is available in two basic types: rigid and thin wall. You can buy rigid conduit cut to length and threaded, or, if you plan to do a substantial amount of wiring installation, you can get a tool for cutting threads. For the amateur home electrician, thin wall conduit is preferable. It costs less, and instead of having threaded fittings, uses a force-fit type. Because of its structure, you will also find it easier to bend.

Before replacing any wiring, check your local electrical code to determine whether you may use BX or not. Your fire insurance policy may be affected by the type of wire housing you select. Rigid and thin wall conduit can be used either indoors or outside, but rigid conduit is preferable for underground work. Again, there may be local restrictions on how you may use rigid conduit underground. While both types of conduit, rigid and thin wall, are galvanized, some soils and building materials may be too corrosive.

NON-METALLIC CABLE

The problems with conduit, whether thin-walled or rigid, are the difficulty in handling, the need for fishing wires through, and bending. For indoor wiring, such as exposed basement wiring, you could use wires covered by a non-metallic sheath. This does not mean rubber-encased wire of the type used for lamps, but a tough, plastic-impregnated outer sheath. There are various kinds of non-metallic cable. Romex, one of the better known, is easier to use and costs less than armored cable. In some areas, non-metallic cable is permitted for inside wall use; in others, it is prohibited. Once again, it is always best to learn something about your local electrical code.

Both BX and various types of non-metallic cable have the disadvantage that improper handling can damage the wires. Stapling or nailing non-metallic cable to wood beams, for example, can result in penetration of the wires by the nails or staples. The insulation of non-metallic cable can also be damaged by hammer blows.

NM AND NMC CABLE

NM (non-metallic) and NMC (non-metallic cable) are two more of the family of non-metallic cables. NM is for indoor use only and since it costs less than NMC, which is intended for either indoor or outdoor work, is preferable if you do not plan outdoor wiring. The sheath or protective covering of NMC is tough, much more so than NM, although it isn't possible to determine this by making a side-by-side comparison with NM. NMC is available in various grades, so which you use depends on what you intend doing with it. You can get NMC for outdoor work, for outside underground use, or for stringing through the inside holes of concrete blocks. You should be able to get catalog sheets of manufacturers' literature at your local electrical supply. These are highly informative and you should be able to use such literature as a guide in making a selection.

UF AND USE CABLE

Other types of non-metallic cable are UF and USE types. Some underground cables must be fused; others need not be. Again, before you make a selection, decide what you want to do, read the mechanical and electrical characteristics of the various cables, and then make price comparisons. In this way you will be able to avoid unnecessary costs.

RIGID CONDUIT INSTALLATION

The finish on rigid conduit is either black enamel or galvanized. Galvanized conduit is generally approved for indoor or outdoor installation, while the black-enamel type is restricted to in-house use. Conduit costs more than other types, such as NM cable, but it can carry more conductors in a single run. With BX the wire is an integral part of the cable, and so you do not have the option of adding more wires.

Foot for foot, conduit does cost more than BX. But consider that at some future date you may wish to increase the current-carrying capacity of a run. If you have BX you have two choices: You can either replace the existing BX with sheathed wire having a larger current capacity, or you can parallel the existing run with another set of wires. However, if you have conduit whose diameter is sufficiently large, you can fish through new wires at less cost. If you plan for the future, your long-term cost may be lowered by using conduit. Of course, in some cases you may have no choice where a local electrical code requires the use of conduit.

Rigid conduit has the same size designations as water pipe. The size of the conduit is specified by its inside diameter. While ½" is a commonly used size, some 5/16" conduit is permitted where extensions are to be made under plaster. Incidentally, ½" conduit has an actual inside diameter of 0.622". Standard conduit sizes used in interior wiring are ½, ¾, 1¼, 2, and 2½", but sizes up to 6" are available for commercial installations.

While the dimensions of conduit are the same as those of water pipe, one isn't a substitute for the other. Conduit is softer than water pipe, so you can bend it more easily. The inside finish of conduit is smoother so that the insulation of wires will not be abraded as the wire is fished through. Some conduit is available in aluminum, copper alloy, or is plastic-jacketed for installation where the atmosphere is corrosive.

WIRES FOR RIGID CONDUIT

There are some wires whose outer insulation is especially prepared to facilitate fishing through rigid conduit. This treatment consists in giving the insulation a wax coating so that wires can be made to slide more easily against each other or against the inner walls of the conduit. Rubber-covered wire, known as R or RH, is used with conduit in most interior wiring installations, although thermoplastic insulation types, known as T or TW, are now preferred because of their superior insulating characteristics. Underground or wet installations require the insertion of lead-covered cables in rigid galvanized conduit for permanent protection.

INSULATION

All house wiring, whether behind the wall or exposed, or used outdoors, must be insulated. Insulation may be minimum and may consist of nothing more than a covering of rubber over copper wires, or may include several layers of different kinds of insulating materials. The greater the amount of insulation, the more rigid the wire, and the more expensive it becomes. Lamp cord, a pair of wires for connecting a lamp to an outlet, is extremely flexible, but carries the minimum amount of insulation.

RUBBER INSULATION

Rubber for insulating wires may be either natural rubber or one of the various synthetics. The amount of insulation obtained depends on the thickness of the rubber. When natural rubber is used, the copper conductor may have a thin coating of tin. This separates the copper wire from the rubber and has a double purpose. The first is that it is easier to solder to tin-coated copper. The other is that a chemical action takes place between copper and natural rubber, and if the two make contact, the rubber becomes soft and gummy. Instead of tin, a layer of cotton threads is sometimes used.

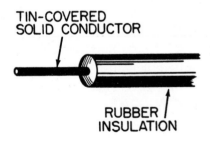

TIN-COVERED
SOLID CONDUCTOR

RUBBER
INSULATION

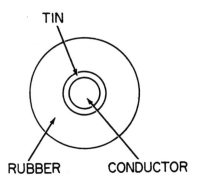

Single conductor with rubber insulation: The tin coating prevents chemical interaction between the copper wire and rubber.

PLASTIC INSULATION

A large variety of different plastics are used as insulating materials for wires. Natural rubber is a vegetable product and so ultimately decays. In time, rubber becomes hard and then cracks. Wire covered with aged rubber is a fire hazard. Plastic insulation has excellent flexibility, is moisture resistant, and, depending on the type of plastic, may have a longer useful life than rubber.

VARNISHED CAMBRIC

Whenever a current flows through a wire, heat is produced. The cambric has little insulation value when used alone. When impregnated with high-grade mineral oil, it works well as an insulating material for high-voltage cables. Paper insulation is sometimes used for underground service conductors.

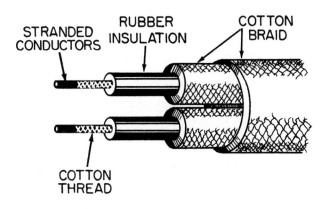

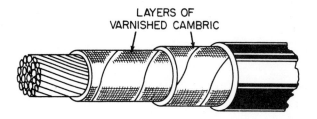

Multi-strand cable with varnished-cambric covering. For service-entrance work, stranded wire is used instead of a single heavy-gauge wire. The varnished cambric may be covered with a lead sheath. This wire arrangement is used for carrying the total current sued by a home.

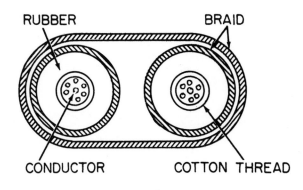

Two-wire conductor: The wire is stranded, although single conductors are also used. The wire is covered with cotton thread to separate the rubber insulation from the copper. Each of the rubber-insulated wires is covered with cotton braid. The two insulated conductors are then held together with an outer wrapping, also cotton braid.

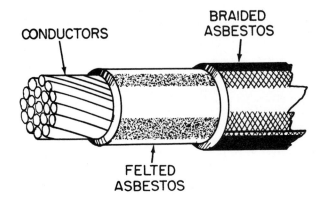

One type of conductor used for carrying heavy currents to an appliance, such as an electric iron: Two layers of asbestos may be used, felted covered by braided. The outer braided asbestos will be covered by some water-impervious material, such as impregnated cotton.

SILK AND COTTON

Cotton is more commonly used in connection with home wiring than silk. Either of these may consist of a single wrap or double. SCC wire is single cotton-covered. DCC is double cotton-covered. SSC is single silk-covered and DSC is double silk-covered. Cotton-covered heat resistant wire is often used for fixture wiring.

ENAMEL

Enamel is an insulating material and when used for this purpose is a synthetic compound of cellulose acetate, made of wood pulp and magnesium. The thickness of the enamel depends on the number of times the wire is coated during its manufacture. One of the advantages of enamel is that it is the thinnest insulation that can be put on wires. However, the enamel has a tendency to crack when the wire is flexed. You may find it as a primary insulating material in some types of home wires, never used alone, but covered by some other insulating substance. You cannot solder directly to enamel-covered wire. The enamel must be removed from the soldering area first. Similarly, if you plan to connect enameled wire to a screw, such as the screw of a light switch, it is important to remove the enamel before wrapping the wire around the screw. Failure to do so means either no contact or an extremely poor one.

FORMVAR

There are various synthetic enamels that look like enamel but do not have its shortcomings. One of these is Formvar. Enamel is easy to remove with a knife; Formvar and other enamel-like compounds having various trade names, are not. Formvar does not crack when flexed. It is a much better insulator than enamel, but is more difficult to work with when making connections.

PROTECTING WIRES

Despite the fact that wires are generally fixed in position, they are subject to outside effects that

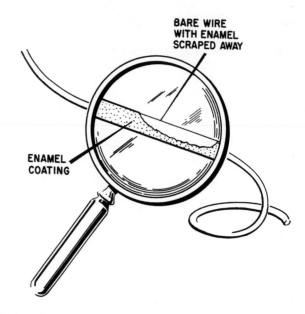

BARE WIRE WITH ENAMEL SCRAPED AWAY

ENAMEL COATING

Beofre soldering to enamel-coated wire or before connecting such a wire to other wires or to a screw terminal, scrape the enamel coating away with a knife. Scrape the entire surface area of the wire and not just one side. Enamel is an insulator and will prevent good electrical contact.

lower their useful life. Moisture, high temperatures, polluted air, or contact with other materials, all contribute some form of corrosion. Cables buried in the ground used for outdoor lighting are affected by moisure, chemical action, and abrasion.

For these reasons, wires are protected by some form of covering, possibly some type of insulating material such as plastic or rubber. Over this may be an outer covering of fibrous braid, which, in turn, may also be covered.

FIBROUS BRAID

Cotton, silk, rayon, linen, and jute are members of the fibrous-braid family. They are used as an outer covering when the wires or cable aren't exposed to possible mechanical injury. Interior wiring for lights or power is usually done with impregnated cotton, braid-covered, rubber-insulated wire. Generally, the wire is further protected by a flame-resistant outer covering, or by thin-walled conduit or by rigid conduit, or by a flexible metallic covering as in BX cable.

LAMP AND POWER CORD

Although referred to as lamp cord, this type is used for fans, lamps, radios, TV sets, and stereo speakers. The wires are covered with a plastic insulating material. There are two solid conductors of no. 18 wire, or stranded wire can be used that consists of 41/34 wire—that is, 41 strands of no. 34 wire. The cord has a current rating of 7 amperes. The cord is supplied with a polarity ridge over one conductor. This is helpful in applications in which it becomes necessary to identify one of the two conductors. The cord is rip-type construction, meaning you can separate the conductors just by holding the two conductors and pulling apart. The cord will then split down the center of the insulating material, facilitating connections with the individual wires. The identification letters for this type of lamp and power cord are SPT.

Type SPT lamp and power cord: A plastic-covered cord, it is available in brown, white, gray, or black.

There are many types of lamp and power cords, a few of which are shown in the illustration. The most common types are the single-paired, rubber-insulated, and twisted-paired cords. The twisted-paired cords consist of two cotton-covered conductors, which are then covered with rubber with a final covering of cotton braid. Heater cords also belong to the flexible power-cord family, except that the first coating around the copper conductors may be asbestos. Heavy-duty or hard-service cords are usually supplied with two or more conductors surrounded by cotton and rubber insulation. When manufactured, the conducting wires are twisted, and then the assembly is covered with some material to shield it from an outer rubber coating.

The extensive chart shown earlier starting on page OO is a listing of some of the more commonly used flexible cords, their type letter, wire size, type of insulation, and expected use.

EXTENSION CORDS

These are used for making temporary connections between a power outlet and some appliance. In effect, they extend the fixed outlet to a point some distance away, and are available in lengths from 6' to 100'. The extension cord, in its basic form, consists of a male plug at one end and a female plug at the other. The male plug is connected to the power outlet at the baseboard in a room, while the appliance is connected to the female plug at the other end.

Like other types of wire, each extension cord can be identified by letter. In the chart, the top row shows that a 6' extension cord can consist of two no. 18 conductors, or a pair of conductors made of 41 strands of no. 34 wire, and that this cord will have a 7-ampere rating. Instead of quoting these specifications, just ask for SV-type extension cord. SV is also available in 9' lengths, so you will need to indicate the length. This chart is for two-wire extension cords only.

COND. SIZE	COND. STRANDING	RATING (AMPS.)	U.L. STYLE	NOM. O.D.	CORD LENGTH FT.
18/2	41/34	7	SV	.245	6
18/2	41/34	7	*SV	.245	9
18/2	16/30	7	SJ	.300	10
18/2	16/30	7	SJ	.300	25
16/2	26/30	10	SJ	.325	10
16/2	26/30	10	SJ	.325	25
16/2	26/30	10	SJ	.325	50
16/2	26/30	10	SJ	.325	100

Specifications for two-wire extension cords.

You can also get extension cords containing three wires, in lengths from 10 to 50′, although longer cords are available. The chart shows that any length of three-conductor extension cord has the code name SJ. A 10′ length contains three no. 18 conductors, or is made up of three 16/30 conductors (16 strands of no. 30 wire) and is capable of carrying 7 amperes.

18/3	16/30	7	SJ	.330	10
18/3	16/30	7	SJ	.330	25
18/3	16/30	7	SJ	.330	50
16/3	26/30	10	SJ	.365	15
16/3	26/30	10	SJ	.365	10
16/3	26/30	10	SJ	.365	25
16/3	26/30	10	SJ	.365	50

Specifications for three-wire extension cords.

Using the correct extension cord is simply a matter of knowing the current requirement of the appliance to which you will connect the cord. If, for example, you are using an electric-type lawn mower that requires 10 amperes, and you need a three-wire extension, you would order a 50′ length of SJ. This would meet the current requirements.

Some extension cords come equipped with a lamp mounted at one end, placed in a shielded cage for protection. The lamp may be seated on a housing containing one or more female outlets to which various appliances can be connected. The light, which can be switched on or off, is convenient to have for areas needing more illumination. The switch at that end of the extension cord controls current to the lamp only and does not control the current flowing to the appliance. However, when a lamp-type extension cord is used, you must remember that the extension cord supplies current to the lamp as well as to the remotely fed appliance. For that reason it is best to switch off the lamp if it isn't needed, or to use the lowest wattage-rating lamp that will supply a satisfactory amount of light.

For lamps or small appliances you can use a no. 16 or no. 18 extension cord. The extension might be made of ordinary lamp-cord-type wire, such as type POSJ or SPT. But for heavy-duty use, such as motors, or lawn mowers, for example, you would need a wire with a gauge number of either 10, 12, 14, or 16.

Extension cord is often sold by gauge number. You can select the right extension with the help of this table:

Distance	Gauge No.	Current Load in Amperes
25′	18	7
25′	16	7 to 10
25′	14	10 to 15
50′	16	7
50′	14	7 to 10
50′	12	10 to 15
100′	14	7
100′	12	7 to 10
100′	10	10 to 15

If your extension cord has outlets into which you can connect more than one appliance, use the total current demand of all the appliances, even if you do not plan to use more than one appliance at a time. When extension cords are too long and must carry substantial current, using an extension having too small a gauge will result in a voltage loss in the cord, with the result that the appliance that is connected will simply not get enough current and will either not function, or may do so poorly. This type of use may also result in overheating the cord.

When you use an extension cord, make sure that the male plug end fits firmly and securely into the outlet. If the prongs of the male plug are loose or if they do not fit tightly, you will get a voltage loss right at the outlet. After using an extension cord for some time, remove the male plug from the outlet and touch the prongs of the plug. They may be mildly warm, but if they are not, then you have poor contact between the plug and the outlet. The fault may be in the plug, the outlet, or both. Try twisting the prongs of the male plug slightly to see if this will give a better fit in the outlet. If the plug wobbles back and forth easily when in the outlet, quite probably the outlet needs replacement.

BELL WIRE

The appliances in your home get power from outlets, or else are battery operated. Your front and rear doorbells may also be battery operated, but more likely use a step-down transformer. A step-down transformer is one that changes the 115 volts AC of the power line to a much lower voltage, possibly less than 30 volts, AC. It is this low voltage that is used for operating your door chimes or bell.

Annunciator or bell wire is designed for low-voltage circuits only. Insulation is easily pushed back for making connections.

Since the bell or chimes work with low voltage and with low current, a fairly inexpensive wire known as bell wire or annunciator wire can be used for wiring. The wire is generally no. 18 gauge, has no rubber, but instead has two layers of cotton, wound in opposite directions, and then is

impregnated with paraffin. The copper conductor is easily exposed by pushing back on the insulation. Do not use bell wire for 115-volt AC connections and do not use it as a substitute for lamp cord. You can use it for any battery-operated device, or where low voltage is supplied by a transformer.

GROUND

One part of your electrical system is known as ground for the simple reason that one of the wires is actually connected to the earth through a pipe. The ground connection is established at the service entrance, and may consist of a heavy metal strap attached to an in-ground metal pipe.

Ground is also known as neutral, and to make sure the correct wire is selected for grounding, its outer insulation is color-coded. The white wire is always the ground wire, or neutral. It is sometimes called the "cold" lead or wire.

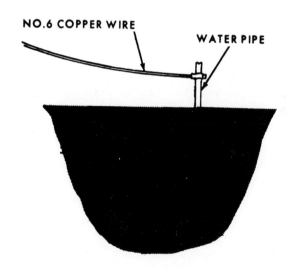

One of the wires, the white wire, is grounded at the service entrance to the home.

In a cable, there may be one or more wires other than the white ground or neutral wire. These will be color-coded black. They are sometimes referred to as "hot" leads or "live" wires. For home use, an electrical pressure of 115 volts AC exists between the hot and cold wires. If you have three wires, two black and one white, the voltage between any one of the black wires and the white neutral will be about 115 volts AC, but the voltage between the two black or hot wires will be double this, or 230 volts AC.

Ground is a reference point for voltage, just as the left side of a ruler is a reference point for any measurement you might want to make. Since we stand on the ground, and since the white wire of a home-wiring system is also grounded, there is no potential or voltage between you and the white wire. You are both at the same voltage level. That is why you can safely touch the metal plates of your outlets or the metal box containing your fuses. You are both at the same potential—ground potential. This means, also, that one of the wires going to all your appliances is neutral or grounded, while the other wire is 115 volts above ground. Both wires carry current, however. The wire that is color-coded white referring to voltage, not current, is as much a current carrier as a black-coded wire.

Another advantage of grounding one side of the electrical system is that it helps protect you against shock. If both wires going to one of your appliances were above ground—that is if both wires measured 115 volts with respect to ground—you could easily get a shock if one of them accidentally touched the metal housing of the appliance at the same time you did. That is why it is very important that all appliances be grounded. You still have one "hot" wire coming into the appliance. In the event this wire should touch the metal frame of the appliance, it will simply create a short circuit, blowing the fuse or tripping a protective circuit breaker.

To supply added protection, flexible cords connected to powered equipment such as electrical drills, washing machines, dryers, etc., have a third wire known as a grounding wire. It ensures grounding of the metal frame of the appliance. The appliance will work without it, but you will then not have as much protection.

CONNECTING WIRES

When connecting wires in the home, never connect a black wire to a white one. Always connect black to black.

PARALLEL LOADING

All of the electrically operated devices in your home are connected in parallel. A parallel connection means the components are shunted across or are connected directly to the two wires that supply current. The advantage of a parallel or shunt connection is that each appliance in your home is completely independent of any other appliance. Thus, if you have an electric clock it will have two leads or wires. One of these will be connected to the black or hot lead of your two power wires, while the other will be connected to the white or cold lead. The clock is now connected in parallel or shunt with the two wires supplying power. If you now want to connect a toaster, you can do so without interfering with the operation of the clock. The two leads of the toaster are also connected, one to the hot power wire (black) and the other to the cold power wire (white).

The electric clock requires or "draws" current to operate properly. The amount of current taken by the clock is automatic. It is determined by the clock, and not by you. Thus, the clock may take 0.1 ampere from the power-line wires. When you connect the toaster, you increase the current drain drastically, for the toaster may require 6 amperes. The total current drain is now 6 amperes plus 0.1 ampere or 6.1 amperes. The more appliances you connect, the more current you use, and the greater your electric bill.

Homes are wired for a 115-230-volt three-wire system. This consists of a neutral or ground, coded white, and a pair of black wires. The voltage from black to black wire is 230 and that from white to either of the black wires is 115 volts. What you have, then, are a pair of black wires and a single neutral. Any appliance connected across the black wires receives 230 volts. Your outlets, however, have 115 volts only.

TWO- AND THREE-WIRE SYSTEMS

All of the outlets in your home supply 115 volts AC. The appliances in your home, though, are of two types. One is the plug-in kind, including toasters, broilers, electric shavers, fans, and lamps. The other type of appliance may not be the plug-in type and includes heavy current devices such as an electric range.

The power used by an appliance is the product of voltage and current. If one of the appliances takes 2 amperes of current, the power it uses will be 2 times 115 equals 230 watts. However, we could redesign the appliance to work with a lower voltage, such as 57.5 volts. This is one-half the original value. But since the appliance is a 230-watt type, the current it needs will increase: 4 times 57.5 equals 230 watts. But this presents an immediate disadvantage. Increasing the current flow means a heavier gauge of wire to carry the current. Not only is this more expensive, but the wire is more difficult to handle. Note, though, that the cost of operating the appliance remains the same. It is 230 watts in both instances.

If we were to move in the other direction and increase the voltage to 230 volts (this is twice the original value of 115 volts) then the current requirement of the appliance could be reduced to 1 ampere: 1 times 230 equals 230 watts. Again, the appliance uses the same amount of power, but since it now requires only 1 ampere of current, a thinner gauge of connecting wire can be used. This reduces the cost of the wire and makes labor easier as well. That is why a number of appliances

in your home are 230-volt types. However, to keep you from plugging 115-volt appliances accidentally into 230 volts, the 230 volts are often wired directly to the appliance needing it.

WIRE SPLICES

When you join two or more wires, you must do two things: You must make the joint or tape mechanically and electrically secure. These are two different functions. If you twist a pair of bare copper wires securely around each other, you make a good mechanical connection. When you solder the joint or use a solderless connector, you make a good electrical connection. For every connection, both conditions must be met. Simply wrapping a pair of wires together isn't enough. They must either be soldered or joined with a solderless connector, for the wrapping process is mechanical, not electrical.

When copper wires are thin enough they are quite malleable, and so it may seem possible to twist them together using fingers only. But fingers are not electrical tools. Using a pair of gas pliers, hold the two wires firmly together and then use the pliers to twist the ends. A better approach is to mount the wires in a vise and then to use the pliers. Hold the wires taut and make as many twists per inch as you can without breaking or damaging the wires.

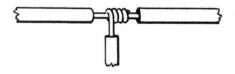

How to form a tap: The exposed wires are at right angles to each other.

The purpose of making a good mechanical connection is to keep the wires from separating; a good electrical connection makes sure the current can flow from one wire to the other. A poor connection can result in all sorts of faulty operating conditions and is sometimes very difficult to trace.

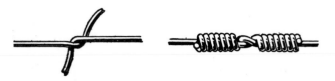

How to make a splice: Make sure the exposed ends of wires are clean. Twist one wire around the other as shown at the left. Continue the wrapping process until the two wires form a tight mechanical joint as shown at the right. The best tools to use are a vise and a pair of pliers. Mount the two wires in the vise and twist with the pliers. This will complete one-half of the splice. Remove and repeat with the other half.

The best thing to do about wire splices is to try to avoid them. If you must splice a wire, then the splice must be so good that the two joined wires behave electrically and mechanically like a continuous wire. When making a wire run from a fuse box to an outlet, it is much better to use a continuous wire rather than one made up of splices, even though it may seem more economical to you to use scrap lengths of wire. If, however, you must splice, then protect the splice by putting it in an electrical box. Do not pull a splice through conduit, nor permit a splice to remain inside conduit.

TYPES OF SPLICES

There are various types of splices, a few of which are shown in the illustration. However, there is a difference between a splice and a tap, although they may seem alike. If you join the exposed ends of a pair of wires, you form a splice. If, however, you strip insulation from somewhere along the length of a wire and join another to it at right angles, you have formed a tap. Always make sure, whether making a splice or tap, that the wires to be joined are bright and clean and that they are free of any scraps of insulation. Some insulation, when cut, may leave long threads. Trim these threads away with scissors or sharp blade.

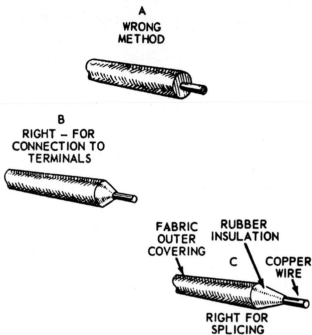

When removing insulation from wire, taper the insulation slightly.

HOW TO SPLICE WIRE

Start about three inches in from the end of the wire and remove the insulation. It will be much easier to make a splice if you work with solid conductor, but whether you use solid or stranded, try to avoid damaging the wire or wires when removing the insulation. This is more difficult to do with stranded wire, since the individual strands may be quite thin. After you have removed the insulation, scrape the wires very gently with a single-edge blade or fine-toothed file to remove any wax and to give the conductors a shiny finish. With stranded wire, twirl the exposed wires between your fingers so that no individual strand is loose and so that the wires form the appearance of a solid conductor. It is also a good idea to count the nunder of strands before doing this to make sure that no single strand has been cut through and has en off. If you find you are missing one or more strands, completely cut off the exposed strands and start over again, this time more carefully.

A split-bolt connector is convenient for joining heavy wires.

SOLDERLESS CONNECTORS

Split-bolt connectors are commonly used for joining wires that are too thick to splice. There are various types of split-bolt connectors; some use screws for tightening the wires and holding them firmly in place, while others use a snap-in metal for locking the wires into position. The screw type is better, provided the screw does not work its way loose. It may do this if the wire vibrates or if a lockwasher isn't used with the screw.

Two types of wire nuts: At left, plastic shell is slipped over twisted wires. Wire nut at right has removable shell to permit wires to be screwed together. Shell is then put back over joined wires.

Wire nuts are another type of solderless connector, and these also are available in various shapes and styles. The wire nut at the left in the illustration contains a threaded insert. To use this wire nut, join the exposed ends of the wire and then screw the wire nut in over the wires. The wire connector is soft enough to let the wire nut cut small threads into the conductor, forming a sort of screw-and-nut combination. Twist the plastic housing firmly over the joined wires until the plastic reaches over and beyond the insulation of the wires.

The wire nut at the right in the illustration has a removable insert. This insert has a setscrew for clamping and holding the two wires in position. After the wires are joined and the screw is tightened, screw the plastic shell onto the insert to cover the joint.

WESTERN UNION SPLICE

If you want to splice wires, but do not intend soldering them, then the splice must serve a double purpose. It must be mechanically strong and must at the same time make a good electrical connection.

Here is how you can make a test to determine if the connection is satisfactory. After finishing the splice, hold each wire separately about 4″ from the splice. Move the wires back and forth while watching the splice. Neither of the wires forming the splice should move—that is, they should not rub against each other—nor should you be able to move them out of position. You should also not be able to detect any open spaces between the wires forming the splice.

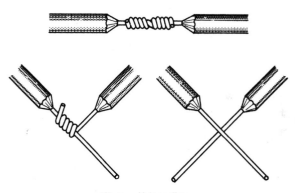

Western Union splice.

The Western Union splice is excellent since it is easy to do and, properly handled, forms a good splice. The first step, of course, is to prepare the wires for splicing by removing the insulation and cleaning the conductors. Bring the wires to a crossed position as shown in the upper-left illustration. Take one of the wires and wrap it tightly around the straight portion of the other wire. You may be tempted to use your fingers to do this, particularly if the wire is thin and flexible, but you will get a tighter wrap with a pair of pliers.

At this stage, you have the left wire wrapped around the one at the right, as shown in the drawing at the upper right. Now take the wire at the right and wrap it around the wire at the left. When you finish, straighten the splice as shown in the bottom drawing. Tug on both wires, holding the insulated portion about 4" from the splice. You should not be able to see any movement in the splice. Rotate the two wires, with each in a different direction. The splice should remain firm.

STAGGERED SPLICE

After making a splice, you must cover it with insulation, such as rubber tape followed by friction tape, or by a vinyl tape. If the joint is poorly made and if the tape is handled sloppily, the result will be a joint that is large and bumpy. If the joint is for external wiring, such as for a lamp, it will look unsightly. If it is to be "in wall" you may have trouble getting it into a metal box.

Staggered splice: The individual splices must be taped.

It is much easier to splice just a single wire, but sometimes you may want to add a section of wire to an existing two-wire line. When this is the case, do not make one splice above the other, but stagger them instead. There are two reasons for this: The first is that if the two splices are offset, there is less chance of a short if the insulating tape unravels. The other is that the total splice becomes less bulky.

After completing the staggered splice, tape each splice individually, and then put tape over both. Vinyl tape is best for this. Tape tightly—that is, don't let the tape become slack when using it—or the final tape wrap will make the job look bulky.

If, when making a staggered splice, you plan to solder the joints, do one splice at a time. You will find it easier to solder if you complete one splice, solder it, and then move on to the other splice. Separate the two wires when soldering to avoid burning the insulation with the soldering iron. Also avoid having hot solder dropping on the insulation.

THE RATTAIL JOINT

Use the Western Union splice to join a pair of wires that must form a single, continuous wire. Do not make a Western Union splice and then bend the wires back on each other. Instead, use a rattail joint as shown in the drawing. Cross the wires as shown at the left in the drawing, and then twist them together with a pair of pliers, producing the result shown in the drawing at the right. You can now solder the joint, or simply cover it with vinyl tape.

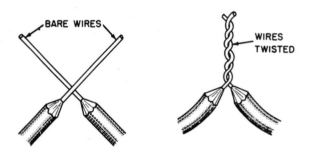

Steps in making a rattail joint: Twist wires as tightly together as possible. Make sure wires are clean and free of an insulation. Rubbing wires with a fine grade of sandpaper before joining is helpful.

When making a rattail joint, or any other kind of splice, make the turns of wire as tightly as you can, especially if you are not planning to do any soldering.

FIXTURE JOINT

A fixture joint is so-called, since it is commonly used for connecting light fixtures to the branch circuit of an electrical system. Generally, in such installations, you will find that the wire supplied with the fixture is smaller in diameter—that is, it has a smaller gauge than the branch wire—the wire that will supply electrical current to the fixture.

Neither the rattail joint nor the fixture joint will withstand much mechanical strain. When using the fixture joint, remember it is not the function of the wires to support the fixture. There shouldn't be any stress or pull on the fixture joint after it is completed.

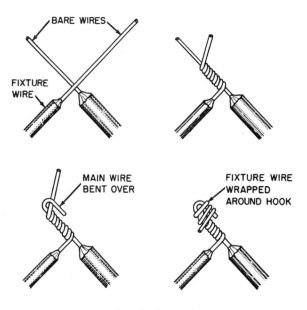

Steps in a fixture joint.

The drawing shows the steps to follow when you make a fixture joint. First, as shown in the drawing at the upper left, cross the wires after you have stripped them clean. The wire at the left is the fixture wire, that at the right is the branch wire. Wrap the fixture wire as tightly as you can around the branch wire. When you finish doing this, the two wires will have the appearance shown in the drawing at the upper right.

At this time take the branch wire, shown as the main wire in the drawing at the lower left, and bend it over the fixture wire. The fixture wire will form a sort of U-shaped hook. Finally, as illustrated in the drawing at the lower right, take the fixture wire and wrap it around the hook. You can now solder the joint or leave it as it is. Cover it with vinyl tape or with a solderless connector. If you do use a solderless connector, make sure it covers every bit of exposed wire and that the solderless connector also reaches over to cover the end portion of insulation.

KNOTTED TAP JOINT

All the splices shown earlier belong to the general family of butt splices. In each instance it is the ends of the wires that are being joined.

To make a knotted tap joint, strip about 1" of insulation from the wire to which a second wire is to be connected. We can call this the main wire, and the second wire the branch. Strip about 3" of insulation from the branch wire. The main wire and the branch, when the knotted tap joint is completed, will look like the capital letter T, with the main wire horizontal and the branch wire vertical, as indicated in the drawing.

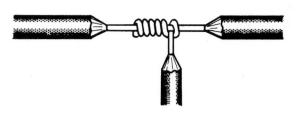

How to make a knotted tap joint: The knot supplies additional mechanical strength.

To make the knotted tap joint, cross the two wires at right angles. Bend the branch wire over the main wire, then under the main wire to form a knot. After making the knot, continue wrapping the branch wire around the main wire, in tight turns.

You can eliminate the knot if you wish. It all depends on whether the wires will be subject to any kind of strain or slip. If there is no mechanical strain, forget about the knot. The knot, however, does make the tap much more mechanically secure.

FUSES

The purpose of a fuse is to prevent current flow from exceeding a predetermined amount. Fuses not only protect appliances, but wiring as well. Properly installed and used, they also reduce the possibility of an electrical fire. A fuse is a type of automatic switch, opening a circuit when current rises beyond a certain amount. It is easy to defeat a fuse simply by shorting it with wire or by using a fuse having a higher rating than it should have. However, these techniques negate the purpose of the fuse and eliminate the protection it supplies. A defeated fuse that results in an electrical fire may also nullify the terms of your fire-insurance policy.

FUSE RATINGS

A "blown" fuse is one whose current rating has been exceeded. Fuses are rated by the safe amount of current they can pass, ranging from about 5 amperes to 30 amperes or more. A common type is the 15-ampere fuse used for protecting no. 14-gauge wire. As long as the current flow through that wire remains at 15 amperes or less, the fuse will remain as a good connecting link.

Fuses have a time lag—that is, they do not blow instantaneously. Thus, a 15-ampere fuse could carry a current of possibly 20 amperes, provided this higher current remained for only a short period of time. An uninterrupted flow of 20 amperes, however, would heat the element inside the fuse and so in a matter of time, possibly a few minutes, the fuse would blow—that is, it would open. Of course, for much higher currents, such as the 50 amperes or 100 amperes produced by a short circuit, the fuse would blow practically at once. A good rule to follow is that the fuse rating should never exceed the current-carrying capacity of the wire it protects. If the wire is designed to carry 20 amperes, the fuse rating should be 20 amperes, or less.

Basically, a fuse contains a short length of wire, designed to melt when a certain amount of current flows through it. Since the melting process can cause the metal to splatter, it is enclosed in some sort of housing, such as metal or fiber.

THE PLUG FUSE

The plug fuse is probably one of the most common types. It is made with a screw-in-type socket and has a window at the top covered with a transparent type of material such as glass

through which you can see the fuse element. These fuses are sometimes available in two different shapes, hexagonal and round. If the fuse is 15 amperes or less the window has a hexagonal shape, while for fuses of more than 15 amperes it is round. However, this isn't standard.

Plug fuse screws into fuse receptacle. Contact is made to receptacle wiring through fuse threads and through small metal area at base of fuse.

Plug fuses are available in current ratings of 3, 6, 10, 12, 15, 20, 25, and 30 amperes. When a plug fuse "blows," it often forms a discoloration, a sort of black smudge against the inside of the window.

There are several ways of checking plug fuses. One of the easiest is to substitute a known good fuse for the suspected defective one. If the appliance begins working again, this is your assurance that the old fuse is blown. In some fuses the fuse element is placed right against the inside of the window so that just by looking at the fuse you can see whether it is good or not. If your installation does use plug fuses, it is a good idea to keep several known good fuses as "test" fuses to check whether an existing fuse is good or not.

One other method of checking a fuse is to use a test lamp. Connect the test lamp into the fuse socket or across the two wires leading into it. If the lamp lights, voltage is present and the fuse can be assumed to be defective.

An old trick is to insert a penny or a five-cent coin in the fuse socket and then to insert the fuse to hold the coin in place, thus bypassing the fuse. This is a dangerous procedure, is probably a violation of your local electrical code and your fire ordinances, and could very well nullify your insurance policy. It is safer and more sensible to replace a blown fuse with one that is in good condition.

The fuse rating of plug fuses is often stamped in the form of a number on the fuse base or may be printed on a card fitted up against the inside of the fuse window. If you do not know the rating of a fuse, it is always better to discard it. When buying replacement fuses, always make sure that the fuse carries some sort of current designation.

Whether or not a plug fuse will blow depends on the amount of excess current, the amount of time the excess current lasts, and the speed with which heat can escape from the fuse. For a short circuit condition, a fuse will open practically immediately. With an overload condition, the fuse may or may not blow, depending on how long the overload lasts. As a rule of thumb, if the overload is 50 percent you can expect the plug fuse to blow in 1 to 15 minutes. Thus, if you have a 10-ampere fuse, a current of 15 amperes will cause it to open, not at once, but within the 15-minute period.

Fuses aren't precision devices, and most of them have a 10 percent overload tolerance: for example, 10 percent of 10 amperes is 1 ampere. Consequently, a 10-ampere fuse will be able to handle a current of 10 amperes plus 1 ampere equals 11 amperes without blowing.

Fuses do not deteriorate in storage and so it is well to have extra fuses on hand so you can replace any fuse at once. If your plug-type fuse box is in a dark location, it is also a good idea to have a battery-operated flashlight placed nearby.

The fact that a fuse blows isn't always an indication of trouble in an appliance. The fuse may be connected into a line that is being overloaded. As more and more appliances are connected to a particular outlet, the current drain increases, depending on the current drain of each appliance. Thus, connecting an electric heater, an electric toaster, a radio, and possibly a broiler to a single outlet could increase current flow through the line beyond the safe current-carrying capacity of the wires.

CARTRIDGE FUSES

Cartridge fuses are in two forms: renewable and non-renewable. The non-renewable type consists of a cylinder made of some hard, fiberlike material containing the fuse element. The fuse element, a metal filament that melts at a predetermined current value, is either soldered to or mechanically fastened to a pair of metal ferrules, one at each end of the fuse housing. The ferrules are actually end caps and are used for clipping the cartridge fuse into a pair of spring metal holders.

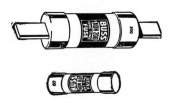

Two types of cartridge fuses: The knife-blade type shown at the top is for heavy currents, usually 60 amperes or more. The lower drawing shows a snap-in type of cartridge fuse. Thirty amperes is a common rating, although these are also available in higher current ratings.

Cartridge fuses are generally designed to handle larger currents than plug fuses, but you can get them in current ratings of 3, 6, 10, 25, 30, 35, 40, 50, and 60 amperes. Up to 30 amperes the fuses are 2″ long, and for currents between 30 and 60 amperes, they measure 3″.

Some cartridge fuses are renewable—that is, the fusible metal strip can be replaced after the fuse has blown. To replace the fusing strip, remove the ferrules, mount the new strip, and then replace the ferrules.

Knife-blade-type cartridge fuses have much higher current ratings than the ferrule type. These can have current ratings of 65 to 600 amperes. Knife-blade cartridge fuses from 60 to 100 amperes are 7⅛″ long, while those having higher current ratings are longer.

TIME-LAG FUSES

In some electric circuits a momentary overload current is a normal condition. A motor, for example, can be practically a short circuit across a power line when the motor is first started. As the motor armature starts to revolve, it develops a counter or opposing voltage, known as a counter electromotive force or counter EMF. This counter EMF opposes the line voltage and in so doing reduces the current taken by the motor to some safe value. A motor might require 30 or more amperes starting current but in operation will take only 5 amperes. If an ordinary fuse is used, it can blow under these working conditions. For circuits using motors, then, you may require a time-lag fuse. This fuse looks just like other fuses, but is capable of tolerating an overload condition for a longer time.

PROBLEM: APPLIANCE DOES NOT WORK

If an appliance stops working, follow these test steps to locate the fault.

1. Make sure the plug of the appliance is in its outlet. Sometimes the plug of an appliance is accidentally removed.

2. Check whether or not you have power at the outlet. You can do this by plugging in an ordinary lamp, such as a portable light, to determine if you have power at the outlet.

3. If the above test shows there is no power at the outlet, go to the fuse box. Your fuse box should indicate which fuse controls the circuit to the inoperative appliance. If the fuses are plug types, examine each for evidence of blowing.

4. If you find a fuse whose window is clear but whose fuse strip is melted, you do have evidence of an overload condition, but the overload is a light one.

5. If you find a plug fuse whose window is badly smudged, the overload is severe. This could also be an indication of a short circuit. A short circuit represents a maximum-overload condition.

6. When you locate the blow fuse, whether by visual examination or through the use of a test lamp, see if you can locate the possible cause of the overload. Remove all appliances connected to the fused line. Replace the fuse. Test the line by inserting a lamp in the socket to which the appliances were connected. The lamp should light. If it does not, check the replacement fuse. If it has blown, there is a short in the line between the fuse box and the outlet.

7. If the test lamp lights, plug in each appliance. Each time you do so, check the fuse. The appliance that causes the fuse to blow once again has some defect.

If none of the appliances causes the replaced fuse to blow, and all the appliances work well, there are two possibilities:

(a) One of the appliances caused a momentary overload.

(b) The load on the line is at maximum or a little above maximum. Accumulation of heat inside the fuse could then cause it to blow. The cure is to reduce the load on the line by connecting one of the appliances to some other line—that is, redistributing the load—or by rewiring so that the line can carry a stronger current.

9. If your tests indicate a possible short in the wiring, trace the wiring to see if there are any splices. A poorly taped splice in an outlet box can result in a short between the splice and the box.

10. If an appliance works intermittently, check to make sure the plug fuse, if one is used, is seated tightly and securely in its socket. If a cartridge fuse is used, make sure that the end ferrules are firmly gripped by the spring metal holders. Check the cartridge fuse by gripping the fiber cylinder portion and try to move it. If it moves easily, take the cartridge fuse out and tighten the spring metal holders. Be sure to turn the power off before doing this.

FUSE PULLERS

Plug fuses can be removed safely by gripping and turning the insulated portion surrounding the window. While the cylindrical portion of cartridge fuses is made of an insulating material, it is easy for your fingers to slip and touch the end ferrules. Since these are made of metal, there is a good possibility of getting a shock. You can avoid this in two ways. You can turn off the power at the main switch but you may not want to do so, since this will cut off all your available light and it will also mean the resetting of all electric clocks. To avoid this, use a fuse puller described earlier in Chapter 2.

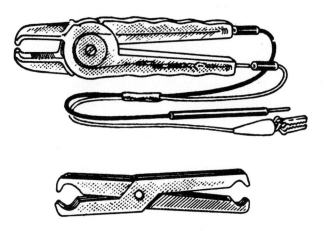

Two types of fuse pullers: These are intended for cartridge-type fuses. The one shown at the top contains a neon glow lamp and a pair of test leads that can be inserted in the ends of the handles of the fuse puller. This fuse puller, then, has a double job: It works as a fuse puller, and also as a test lamp.

MAKE LIFE EASIER FOR YOURSELF

The time to know all about your fusing system is before a fuse blows, not during, or after. Pasted on the inside panel of the fuse box, you should have a description such as the following of which fuse controls what circuit:

Fuse Location	Amperage Controls
#1 top left in box	
20	Upstairs bedroom and hall
#2 left	15
Upstairs bathroom	
#3 left	15
Guest bedroom	
⁰4 left	20
Upstairs bedrooms	

for children
#5 top right in box
20   Kitchen & pantry
etc.

Always keep a supply of fuses on hand, preferably somewhere near the fuse box. Make sure you have a duplicate fuse for each one in the fuse box. Do not keep blown fuses and do not mix them in with good fuses. Dispose of blown fuses immediately.

Before installing a new appliance, decide which circuit it is to be connected to, and then determine if the fuse and the line can carry the added current. If your line has a 15-ampere fuse and the line is already carrying 10 amperes when all appliances are turned on, adding a 7-ampere appliance is sure to blow the fuse. It is a good idea to have a record of the amounts of current demanded by all appliances in your home.

SAFETY SUGGESTIONS

There is always an element of danger when replacing a plug- or cartridge-type fuse, especially when your fuse boxes are located in a dark corner of a damp basement. For cartridges, use a cartridge puller. For plug types, wear an old glove. If your basement floor is damp, put on galoshes or rubbers, or at least separate your feet from the floor by a dry plank. Keep one hand in your pocket or away from possible contact with any metal.

You may never see professional electricians taking such precautions. The first reason is that they are experienced and the second is that they often work on a time basis. But every now and then you will read about an electrical worker, usually a lineman, being electrocuted.

Plug fuses are designed to be screwed into sockets, much as you screw a light bulb into a socket. Never put a fuse into a light socket or into any other socket except a fuse socket.

CIRCUIT BREAKERS

A circuit breaker is a combined fuse and switch. Unlike plug- and cartridge-type fuses, no replacement is needed. When a circuit breaker opens (equivalent to a blown fuse) all that is needed is to correct the fault and to reset the breaker. This is done by depressing the proper breaker switch. Circuit breakers are also available with the time-lag feature described earlier so that they can also be used with motors having a high starting current and much lower operating current.

Circuit-breaker box. The breaker at the top is the main circuit breaker and is the main fuse for all current going into the house. The four other circuit breakers shown in the drawing are for controlling four separate power lines going to various rooms or floors. Most home circuit-breaker boxes are more elaborate than the one shown here, containing many more breakers.

Like fuses, circuit breakers are constructed in various ways. They may be thermal (that is, heat operated), magnetic, or work on a combination of thermal and magnetic properties.

The thermal breaker has a bimetallic element made by bonding two different metals to each other. Each of the metals has a different temperature coefficient of expansion. This means that the two metals are affected somewhat differently by increases in temperature and one will expand more rapidly than the other. But since the two metals are joined, a rise in temperature will make the metals bend. The bimetallic element will then act as a latch, tripping the circuit breaker and causing it to open. The bimetallic element will do this when the current exceeds a predetermined value.

However, once the breaker is open, current stops flowing since the breaker, working as a switch, is now also open. Since current no longer flows through the bimetallic element, it resumes its normal position. The switch, whose external structure is somewhat like an ordinary light switch, can now be reset to its closed position. Current will once again pass through the bimetallic element. If the condition that caused the excessive current flow was removed, the circuit breaker will remain closed. However, if the excessive current condition still remains, the circuit breaker will open once again.

The thermal type of circuit breaker is the one most often used in the home, since it is easily capable of handling typical currents used in the home.

A magnetic circuit breaker, as its name implies, works as a magnet. Whenever a current of electricity flows through a coil, the coil becomes an electromagnet and becomes capable of attracting a bit of ferrous metal. This bit of metal could be part of a switch. As long as current through the magnetic circuit breaker coil remains normal, the magnet isn't strong enough to pull the metal strip away from its closed-switch position. However, in case of an overload or a short circuit, the current through the magnetic circuit-breaker coil increases substantially. The coil becomes a much stronger magnet and attracts the metal strip to itself. But this metal strip is part of a switch and in moving toward the magnet opens a circuit.

Ordinarily, the metal strip would be pulled down immediately, closing the circuit once again, for two reasons. The first is that the metal strip is spring loaded—that is, it is connected to the switch by a spring, and the natural effort of the spring is to keep the switch closed. The second is that once the current is interrupted there is no longer a magnetic field around the coil and so there is no way for the coil to hold the switch strip.

However, the magnetic circuit breaker has a tiny latching mechanism. When an excess current flows through the circuit-breaker coil, it pulls the metal arm of the switch up toward itself. A small mechanical latch then moves into position holding the metal arm against the pull of the spring. When you reset the circuit breaker, this action releases the latch and permits the spring to pull the metal arm toward itself, closing the switch, and allowing the current to flow in the circuit once again. Of course, if the overload condition wasn't removed, the circuit breaker will trip open once again.

Magnetic circuit breakers are used in applications in which fairly heavy currents flow and so are designed specifically for stronger circuit conditions than the thermal type. The thermal type is more sensitive to and more responsive to smaller currents.

The thermal-magnetic breaker is a combination of thermal and magnetic principles. It is used for installations in which there is a wide range of current flow. The thermal element protects against current surges and overloads in the lower range, while the magnetic element protects against higher current shorts.

ADVANTAGES OF CIRCUIT BREAKERS

Circuit breakers have a number of advantages over fuses. There is no possibility of tampering with the thermal or magnetic element, since these are sealed behind a metal panel. Consequently there is no way of changing the current range. Further, it is easy to reset a circuit breaker by depressing a switch. Once the circuit breaker is installed and functioning, there is never a need to buy and replace fuses. There is also no possible danger of shock since the voltage connections are shielded behind a panel. New home installations use a circuit-breaker panel rather than plug- or cartridge-fuse arrangements. When older homes are rewired, it is advisable to replace an existing plug- or cartridge-fuse type with a circuit breaker.

Most home-type circuit breakers have a main breaker used for disconnecting power to the entire home. The main breaker is then followed by a series of breakers, one for each line. Each branch circuit must have a circuit breaker to protect each ungrounded conductor. And so a circuit breaker panel may have 10, 20, or more circuit-breaker switches.

WHAT SHOULD YOU DO WHEN A CIRCUIT BREAKER OPENS?

Follow exactly the same procedure as that outlined earlier in connection with a plug fuse. Remove all appliances from the outlet protected by the breaker. Reset the circuit breaker and then insert a lamp, known to be in good working condition, into the outlet. If the lamp lights, then the entire line from the circuit breaker to the outlet is in good working condition. Connect each appliance, one at a time, to the outlet until you find the one that causes the circuit breaker to open. The fault may be in the appliance—that is, it may have an internal short. Or, you may be overloading that particular line by connecting too many appliances to it. Or, if you are just using a single appliance for that particular outlet, the appliance may be drawing too much current. It is possible to overload a line with just one appliance if the line and its breaker aren't designed to handle the amount of current demanded by that appliance.

If either a fuse blows repeatedly, or if a circuit breaker opens repeatedly, you are getting a warning that something is wrong. Don't ignore it. If it happens often enough it could increase your electric bills, or it could cause the appliance to work poorly. It could also cause a fire. In normal operation fuses and circuit breakers rarely open. When they do, it is time to pay attention.

PLUG-TYPE CIRCUIT BREAKERS

If your fuses are plug types and you would prefer the convenience of a circuit breaker, you can replace the fuse box with a circuit-breaker panel, an expensive job and not one for the amateur home electrician. An easier method is to replace plug fuses with mini-circuit breaker types. These look like plug fuses and fit directly in place of a plug fuse. They have a reset feature consisting of a small pushbutton in the center of the fuse. When the fuse blows, you can reset it by pushing the button in.

Chapter 5
SOLDERING

The purpose of soldering in home wiring is to join electrically two metals, usually copper wires. The solder used for this purpose is an alloy known as soft solder. In soft soldering, one of the metals, the solder, melts with the help of a soldering iron, although other heating devices can be used. The metals to be joined do not melt, for the heat is never high enough to reach the melting point of copper.

There is another soldering process known as brazing or hard soldering in which silver solders or brazing alloys are used. The temperature is much higher than that in soldering, and the metals to be joined actually fuse. For electrical work, soft, rather than hard soldering is used.

SOFT SOLDERS

Soft solders contain mostly tin and lead in some proportion, but may also contain very small amounts of antimony, bismuth, cadmium, and zinc. The quantity could be about 0.1 percent bismuth and 0.1 percent antimony, so electrical solder can be regarded as being primarily a tin-and-lead combination.

EUTECTIC POINT

Lead has a melting point of $620°$ F. while that of tin is $450°$ F. However, when these two metals are combined, the overall melting point is owest melting point obtainable is with an alloy of about 63-percent tin and 37-percent lead. This combination of metals is called eutectic and the melting point is called the eutectic point. The eutectic point is $361°$ F. However, as the percentage of tin in solder is decreased and that of lead is increased, the melting point increases.

HOW THE SOLDERING IRON WORKS

Most soldering irons (not all) work on the same basic principle as a toaster, or heater, or electric iron. A current of electricity passes through a resistive element, a special type of wire that gets very hot, and which is embedded in the body of the unit. The only connection between the tip of the iron and the body is a physical one. As the body of the iron is heated by the resistive element, heat flows into the tip.

The handle of the iron is made of some non-heat conducting substance. A hole is drilled lengthwise through the handle for the power cord. Two leads of the power cord are connected to the resistive element, while at the other end the same two leads are screwed into a plug.

The current flowing into the iron is in the order of one or two amperes, approximately. The cord is generally insulated with asbestos covered with fibrous braid. For some of the smaller irons, such as pencil types, the power cord is rubber-covered wire, similar to lamp cord.

TINNING THE IRON

For soldering you will need some accessories. These include some scrap sections of cloth, a file, medium-grade sandpaper, and some device, such as a vise, for holding the work.

All irons, whether new or old, must be tinned before use. Tinning simply means putting a coat of solder on the tip of the iron. Some new irons are sold with pre-tinned tips. In that case, let the iron get hot, and as it does so, just rub the tip with scrap cloth. If the iron is new and does not come pre-tinned, let the iron get hot and then file the tip lightly. This will remove most of the accumulated oxide and dirt on the surface of the tip. Rub the tip with sandpaper and finish the job by further rubbing with scrap cloth. Apply solder directly to the tip. As you do, a small globule of solder may form on the tip surface. Wipe it away with the cloth and you will note that this action has spread some of the solder along the tip face. Keep repeating until all sides of the tip are coated with solder. Then, and only then, will you be able to solder joints. Tinning a new iron takes time, patience, and some practice.

For some soldering, the tip of the iron must have the correct temperature, neither too hot nor too cold. Some irons come equipped with automatic thermal controls, but these are more expensive. With a non-thermostatic type of iron, if the tip of the iron is too cold, the solder will not melt, or if it does melt will do so slowly and sluggishly, forming a soft, gray blob. If the iron is too hot, the solder won't adhere. The best technique is to plug the iron into an outlet, solder the joint, and then remove the plug. Do not plug in an iron indefinitely while you do other portions of electrical work. Plug the iron in shortly before you expect to solder and remove it directly thereafter.

SOLDERING COPPER

While solderless connectors are useful for making electrical joints with minimum effort and time, there is no question that soldering does produce a better electrical union. A well-prepared joint would be one that is soldered and then reinforced with the help of a solderless connector. The combination of solder and connector then gives the joint optimum mechanical and electrical security.

The purpose of soldering is to make a good electrical connection, not mechanical, and so, before soldering a pair of wires, the joint they make must be mechanically tight.

The watchword in soldering is cleanliness. It is difficult, if not impossible to solder wires that have some traces of wax, enamel, or other insulating materials. Before soldering, scrape wires shiny clean with a penknife, making certain that the entire exposed area is shiny, not just the upper surface.

Follow the correct soldering technique. Put the tip of the iron so that it touches the undersurface of the joint to be soldered. Keep the iron steadily in position and then apply the solder to the top portion of the joint. It is the heated joint that must melt the solder, not the iron. Use just enough solder to barely cover the wire. The soldered joint should then be smooth and shiny, not lumpy and dull gray. An improperly soldered connection is called "cold" soldered.

After the solder has flowed onto the joint, remove the iron and give the solder a chance to cool. Do not move the joined wires before the solder has cooled. If you are holding the wires with one hand while soldering with the other, keep your hand motionless for a few seconds after removing the iron. If, for some reason, the soldered joint looks lumpy, reheat it and allow the excess solder to flow off onto the iron tip. Do not add more solder.

Before soldering, twist wires together to from a good mechanical joint. Wires must be shiny clean over entire exposed surface area. Clean shortly before soldering as copper wire oxidizes. The oxide makes soldering difficult.

It will be necessary to tin the iron repeatedly, but this is easy to do once the first tinning is accomplished. To tin the iron again, simply rub the heated iron tip through some scrap cloth. It is a good idea to wipe the tip with a cloth after each soldering job. The excess solder will help form a tin coating on the tip surface of the soldering iron. The reason for tinning is to help prevent the formation of copper oxide on the tip. When an iron is heated, the hot copper tip joins with the oxygen in the air. The resulting coating of copper oxide is an insulator, preventing the adequate transfer of heat to the joint. Since the function of the iron is to make the joint hot enough to melt solder, make sure that the maximum surface area of the tip is in contact with the joint—that is, don't apply the pointed tip of the iron to the work, but rather its flat surface.

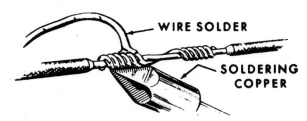

Correct soldering technique: Apply hot iron beneath the joint, solder above it. Use a minimum amount of solder.

Use the minimum amount of solder to produce a good electrical joint. Drawing at left shows use of excess solder; drawing at right indicates correct amount. The solder should fill the spaces between the wires.

SOLDERING ALUMINUM

Aluminum wiring is being used increasingly, but it does present some disadvantages. Its resistance, per unit volume, as mentioned earlier, is larger than that of copper, and so there is a greater power loss when using such wire. Aluminum can be soldered, but it is very difficult to do so. Use aluminum wire for short runs carrying relatively limited amounts of current, and where the connections or joints can be made mechanically through screws or solderless connectors.

INSULATING THE SOLDERED JOINT

Solder is an excellent electrical conductor and so a soldered joint is an exposed joint—that is, it can produce a short circuit if joints touch each other or some grounded surface, such as conduit.

Cover all soldered joints with friction tape. Friction tape is available in rolls 60' or more in length. For home wiring use tape having a ¾" width. Friction tape consists of cloth impregnated with a tacky rubber compound. The problem with friction tape though, is that in time the rubber becomes dry and loses its stickiness and the tape unravels. When buying friction tape, make sure it is fresh. The tape should be boxed and preferably sealed in plastic. If the tape feels dry to the touch and if its edges have started to unravel, the tape is no longer fresh and will be useless.

For best protection of a soldered joint, cover the joint with rubber tape first. Rubber tape is highly flexible and so you can use it to make a very tight wrap around the joint. The rubber tape will supply insulation, and if it is then covered with friction tape, will have added mechanical protection.

Another kind of tape, known as vinyl electrical tape, can be used in place of the rubber-friction combination. Also known as PVC tape, it is available in rolls from about 12' to 100' or more and in ½" and ¾" widths. You can buy vinyl electrical tape in various colors such as black, red, yellow, blue, etc. The color coding is advantageous if, for some reason, you need to identify a particular joint.

Vinyl plastic electrical tapes are available as pressure-sensitive types and supply excellent resistance to abrasion, sunlight, moisture, alkalies, solvents, oil, and some acids.

SOLDER

Like wire, solder is available in rolls, ranging in length from about 7' to 50' or more. It is also sold in the form of bars and tape. Roll solder is sometimes called wire solder. It can be identified by gauge number, with gauge no. 16 as the standard size for home wiring when using an iron in the 100-watt to 150-watt class. For a pencil iron, or any other low-wattage type, it is easier and better to use a thinner gauge of wire solder.

Solder is a mixture of tin and lead in various

proportions. There are three grades used in electrical work: 40-60, 50-50, and 60-40. The first number given is the percentage of tin, the other is the percentage of lead. The greater the tin content, the lower the temperature required for melting, as described earlier. Also, the higher the tin content, the easier the flow of solder and the less time it takes for the solder to harden. Consequently, it is usually easier to work with 60-40 solder than with 40-60.

SOLDER TAPE

You can also buy solder in the form of small tape strips. With these just wrap the solder tape around the joint and then heat the joint. The advantage of using tape is that you do not need to use an iron. A lighted match or candle will do. However, this kind of soldering is just a temporary expedient. It is difficult to avoid burning the wire insulation, and so for better work use a soldering iron and 60-40 rosin-core solder.

SOLDER BARS

Solder bars are used with extremely high-wattage irons or with a torch. Such bars aren't practical for home-type soldering jobs.

FLUX

When soldering copper wire, the intense heat of the iron not only helps form an oxide around the copper soldering tip, but also promotes a similar oxide around the wire joint. These oxides may either make soldering more difficult or may prevent it completely. To avoid the formation of such oxides, soldering requires the use of a flux. For home electrical work the preferred flux is rosin. Fortunately, solder is available as a rosin-cored type—that is, wire solder contains a core of rosin and so the flux is applied automatically together with the solder.

There are also various other types of fluxes, such as muriatic acid, hydrochloric acid, ammonium chloride, or zinc chloride, but these are soldering fluxes for metals other than copper wire, although acid flux can also be used on copper.

Rosin is the preferred flux most often used for electrical work. It is easier to work with acid flux, but joints soldered with acid flux tend to corrode.

While the rosin in rosin-core solder does keep oxides from forming on the wires to be soldered, it will not remove existing dirt or oxides. A wire must be shiny clean if the solder and the rosin flux are to be effective.

SOLDERING IRONS

As you might expect, soldering irons are available in a large variety of sizes, shapes, and wattage ratings. For home use, the most practical iron will have a rating between 100 and 150 watts. A lighter-weight iron, such as a 25- or 35-watt size is also helpful for soldering narrow-gauge wires. Irons are also available as soldering guns—irons having fixed tips, irons having replaceable tips, battery-operated irons, and AC-operated types.

For average work around the home, a fixed-tip iron is quite satisfactory. An iron with replaceable tips will let you do a greater variety of soldering jobs, but unless you expect to become a professional electrician, isn't usually necessary. One advantage of the interchangeable tip feature is not only having a variety of tips, but also a hot knife attachment. The hot knife consists of assorted blades that can be attached to the iron. When the blades become hot, they can be used for cutting through and removing wire insulation quite easily. This insulation, of course, is a fibrous or plastic type only, and does not include enamel or similar coatings.

BATTERY-OPERATED IRON

The battery-operated soldering iron uses a single Ni-Cad (nickel cadmium) battery that can be recharged. The advantage is that it gives you complete freedom from a dangling power cord.

The disadvantages are that the battery does need recharging, plus the fact that the amount of tip heat is rather small. If the iron isn't used for quite a period of time, the battery will slowly discharge itself, and so quite often the iron isn't ready for soldering when you are. The recharging process is usually a matter of at least a few hours.

SOLDERING GUN

A soldering gun has a gun shape, hence its name. Unlike ordinary soldering irons, the gun heats extremely quickly, and some do have an interchangeable tip facility. Some also have dual power ratings, such as 100 watts and 140 watts. The 140-watt rating is highly useful for soldering a joint consisting of a number of thick wires. Unlike many soldering irons that must be plugged or unplugged from the power line, the soldering gun has a trigger action. Pressing the trigger turns the gun on; releasing it turns it off. The same trigger controls either 100-watt or 140-watt heat, depending on how far back the trigger is pulled. Some soldering guns come equipped with a built-in light, helpful when it is necessary to solder in dark areas.

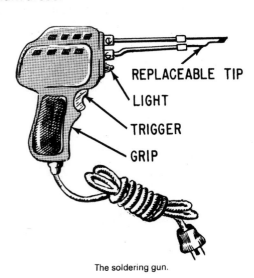

REPLACEABLE TIP
LIGHT
TRIGGER
GRIP

The soldering gun.

The tip of a soldering gun must be tinned, just as that of any other soldering iron and by means of exactly the same procedure. Some soldering guns come equipped with a pre-tinned silver tip. The silver coating on the tip makes the iron ready for use immediately. Ultimately, however, the silver wears away and then the iron must be tinned with solder.

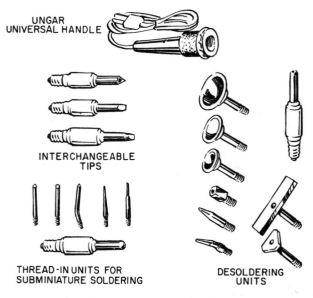

UNGAR UNIVERSAL HANDLE

INTERCHANGEABLE TIPS

THREAD-IN UNITS FOR SUBMINIATURE SOLDERING

DESOLDERING UNITS

Use a pencil iron for soldering fine wires. The soldering iron can have a universal handle so that you can use interchangeable tips. For removing solder from a joint, in the event you want to unsolder fine wires without breaking them, use the desoldering units shown at the right. They also fit into the universal handle. Typical wattage ratings of pencil irons are about 25 watts to 35 watts.

One of the advantages of the soldering gun is that it is housed in a plastic case. This means that you can put the gun down on a table when not using it for soldering. The case keeps the tip an inch or so above the table. However, you can get a soldering-iron stand made especially for the gun-type iron.

The electrical construction of a soldering gun is different from that of an ordinary iron. A regular iron uses a resistive element that gets hot when current passes through it. A gun uses a transformer, a step-down type, with the tip of the iron forming part of the secondary winding. When the trigger is closed, a heavy current flows through the secondary, heating the tip. Because of its construction, the tip of a soldering gun cools more quickly than that of a regular iron. It also heats much more rapidly, with the soldering tip ready for action just a few seconds after depressing the gun trigger.

THE PENCIL IRON

If your soldering iron supplies insufficient heat to the joint that is being soldered, the result will be a cold solder joint. The solder will form a rough, grayish mass, and while it may give an outward appearance of being mechanically secure, the electrical connection between the wires being soldered will either not exist or will be very poor.

The opposite extreme, excessive heat, produces equally unsatisfactory results. With too much heat the solder will have a tendency to roll up in the form of a ball. It will then drop away from the joint and splatter over the worktable. Excessive heat can also cause the insulation near the joint being soldered to char or possibly burn. While the insulation may not drop off, it will be considerably weakened and may ultimately fall away.

The advantage of the pencil iron is that it is light in weight and can often be used to solder in difficult-to-reach areas. You can get a pencil iron with an interchangeable-tip feature. Some of these tips can be curved, or straight but longer than usual.

There are two basic ways in which removable tips can be fastened to ir   . In one the removable tip is held in place by a setscrew. In the other, the tips have threads and are screwed into the barrel of the iron. The setscrew type is not as good as the tip that must be screwed in. With the screw-in tip, there is more intimate contact between the tip and the barrel of the iron. Since there is a transfer of heat from the barrel to the tip, it is important that the tip make good, secure contact with the barrel. With the screw-in type, turning the screw to make sure the tip is securely fastened results in pushing part of the tip away from the barrel. Further, the screw, a small slotted type known as a setscrew, is easily lost.

However, the screw-in type of tip also presents problems. There is a tendency for the heat to cause the threads of the tip to remain fastened to the threads of the barrel. When this happens, the tip is said to be frozen in position, an odd term to

PLUG-TYPE
TIP

SCREW TIP

Soldering iron.

apply to a soldering iron. To prevent this, use an "anti-seize" compound. Put a bit of it on the threads of the tip before turning the tip into the barrel of the iron. Incidentally, you can also use this iron as a light source in an emergency. Remove the tip and insert a 117-volt 6-watt type 6S6 bulb.

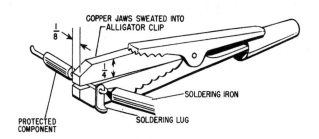

Use a heat shunt to conduct excess heat away from joint being soldered. A simpler technique is to use a pair of gas pliers for this purpose. Simply put the jaws of the pliers in the position shown above. Put a rubber band around the end of the plier handles to hold the *pliers shut and to free your hands for soldering.

Another method is to take two scrap bits of copper and force them into the jaws of an alligator clip. Mount this arrangement, as shown, on some section of the wire near the spot where you plan to solder. The mass of copper will conduct away excess heat. A still easier technique is to use a pair of gas pliers for this purpose. Put the jaws of the pliers near the soldering point. You can hold the pliers closed with a rubber band, thus freeing your hands for work with the soldering iron.

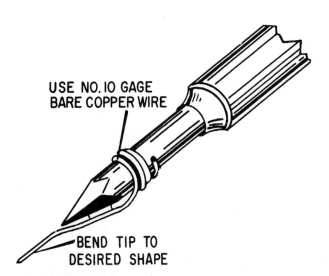

Method for making a low-wattage iron from a standard 100-watt to 150-watt iron.

HEAT-REDUCTION METHODS

While it is convenient to have a pencil iron, you can make a 100-watt or 150-watt iron do double duty and function both as a lightweight and heavyweight iron. There are various techniques for doing this.

In one method, as shown in the illustration, wrap a length of heavy, bare, solid copper conductor around the body of the soldering-iron tip. About three or four turns of wire should do, but try to make the turns as tight as possible. Let part of the copper wire extend beyond the soldering-iron tip. Because of the smaller volume of copper wire, compared to the regular soldering-iron tip, the wire tip will tend to lose heat more rapidly. You must tin the wire tip just as you would any soldering-iron tip.

THERMOSTATICALLY CONTROLLED IRONS

You can buy an iron with a built-in thermostat. When the iron reaches its operating temperature, the thermostat opens a switch, cutting current flow to the iron. As the iron cools and its temperature drops below its operating point, the thermostat switches on again and so current flows to the iron once again, raising its temperature. The advantage of an iron of this kind is that you can not only keep the iron connected to the outlet at all times, but that the temperature of the iron usually remains somewhere near its correct working range. It takes some experience in soldering, with non-thermostatically controlled irons, to know just when the iron is at the right temperature, neither too hot nor too cold.

One of the problems with the thermostatically controlled iron is that there is a time lag after the thermostat shuts off the current. Heating an iron isn't an instantaneous process, and so if you have decided to use the iron a few minutes after the thermostat has interrupted the current, you may have to wait a short time for the iron to get back to its working temperature.

To avoid this problem, some thermostatically controlled irons do not shut off current flow completely. Instead, the thermostat is shunted by a resistive element. During operation the thermostat shorts the resistive element, letting the iron get its full amount of current. When the temperature of the iron rises too high, the thermostat opens. This permits current to flow through the shunting resistor. Thus, instead of cutting off the current completely, it is just reduced. And since the iron will continue receiving current, although on a reduced current-flow basis, the temperature of the iron will decrease more slowly. The resistance of the shunting element is designed so that the iron remains more or less within its working temperature at all times.

SOLDERING-IRON HINTS

It isn't difficult to use a soldering iron. On the contrary, soldering is easy if you follow some simple rules.

1. Don't try to use a cold iron or one that hasn't reached its correct operating temperature. If you do, the solder will not melt into its liquid state, but will become a gray, plastic mass. This blob may actually separate the wires that are to be joined electrically and so the result may be an open circuit. It may be difficult to locate the problem since the blob will prevent inspection of the joint.

2. The soldering-iron tip must be tinned. If at all possible, tin the tip with silver—that is, hard-solder it. If not, tin it with rosin-core soft solder.

3. During use, the tinning on the tip of the iron wears away and so it will be necessary to tin the tip again.

4. During use, wipe the tip of the iron regularly with a cloth. The cloth should be clean and preferably have a rough texture. Do not use a cloth that has previously been used to wipe up oil spills or paint.

5. Cleanliness is the watchword in soldering. The copper wires to be joined must be clean; the soldering-iron tip must not only be tinned, but must also be clean. Grease, oil, dirt, oxidation, bits of insulating material, and enamel can and will prevent soldering.

6. When not in use, rest the iron on a stand.

7. Do not leave the iron plugged into an outlet for an indefinite period of time. Poor soldering can result if the iron is too hot as well as too cold.

SOLDERING-IRON TEMPERATURE

Most soldering irons have a tip temperature ranging from about 500° F. to 600° F. Even the small 25-watt irons, the so-called pencil irons, have this temperature, as well as the more commonly used 100-watt types. But immediately before applying solder to a joint, the iron must supply enough heat to the joint so that it can melt the solder. This means a substantial heat drain on the soldering-iron tip. However, when soldering, the iron must continue to deliver heat for a few seconds after the solder has melted. If the joint consists of two or more conductors, such as no. 16 wire, plus a machine screw, this entire mass of metal will drain heat rapidly away from the area where the iron tip is being applied. For a joint such as that just described, the 25-watt iron would not be able to continue supplying enough heat; the 100-watt iron would be able to do so.

THE SOLDERING-IRON STAND

When not soldering, you will need to rest the iron on some surface. Even if you remove the plug or release the trigger on a soldering-iron gun, the iron will remain hot for quite sometime. Under these conditions, the iron is a potential source of trouble. You may accidentally touch the exposed metal shank of the iron, resulting in a painful burn. Or, you may put the iron on some combustible surface, such as wood. Even if the wood does not catch fire, the hot iron will make a large, dark, ugly burn that will be difficult to remove.

To prevent either or both of these possibilities, use a soldering-iron stand. You can make a temporary stand by crushing a V notch into any clean tin can, but a much better stand is one made for the purpose. Such a stand will completely enclose the metal portion of the iron. Made of metal in grille shape, the metal prevents the iron from touching the table and also acts as a barrier between your hands and the hot metal. The open grille allows the heat of the iron to escape, permitting the iron to cool more rapidly.

COOL IT

Sometimes, after you finish soldering, you will be in a hurry to put the iron away. You may have a storage place for the iron and you may want to return the iron to its storage without delay. Do not cool the iron by putting it in water. The best way to get rid of the heat is to rest the metal shank or barrel of the iron on as large a metal surface as possible. The metal surface should be clean and free of paint, oil, or dirt.

THE SOLDER SUCKER

One of the problems in soldering is the tendency of people who have had no previous experience to use too much solder. It takes quite a bit of heat to maintain an excess of solder in its molten state or to get it to reach a molten state. When this happens, a large blob forms and the result is a cold solder joint. It then becomes difficult to remove the excess solder. One way of doing so is to heat the joint and then to try to brush away some of the unwanted solder with the hot tip of the iron. But there are several risks in doing this. One is that some of the solder may land on the insulation of the wires, burning it. In some cases the hot solder will bury itself in the in-

sulation, making it extremely difficult to remove. Another good possibility is that some of the solder will drop on the table or on the floor. The solder will be hot enough to leave a burn mark. The solder may also drop on your clothing and may be difficult to remove.

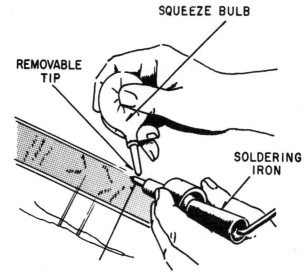

Solder sucker is excellent tool to use for removal of excess solder.

A better technique is to use a solder sucker. As shown in the drawing, it consists of a squeeze bulb and a tip. Its function is to "suck up" excess solder. Incidentally, as it does so, it also removes some of the heat from the joint being soldered. Do not use glass or plastic medicine droppers as temporary substitutes for a solder sucker. The glass tip (or the plastic tip) will be unable to withstand the heat. A Teflon tip is best.

TO SOLDER OR NOT TO SOLDER?

There is no question that soldering does produce a better electrical connection, but the modern trend is to avoid soldering, if possible. It is better to solder taps and splices, but you can use wraparound terminal connections and crimped terminals to eliminate soldering.

TERMINAL CONNECTIONS

In some instances you will need to attach a wire to a machine screw that is fastened in position, as shown at the left in the drawing. Form a loop at the end of the exposed wire and be sure that the wire makes a tight circle around the threads of the screw. Put a flat circular washer over the connection and then fasten in place with a hexagonal machine screw. Tighten the nut in position with a nut driver. Note especially that the nut, in being tightened, is turned in the same direction as the wire loop.

In the drawing to the right, a slotted machine screw is used to hold the wire in position. Make a loop of the exposed wire and put a flat circular washer right above it. Put the machine screw through the washer and the wire loop and then tighten the screw with a suitable screwdriver. Once again, note that the direction of travel of the screw is the same as that of the wire.

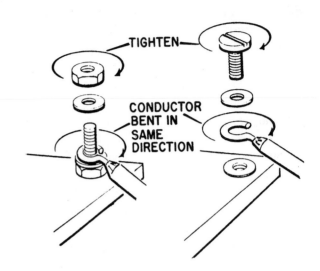

Two wire-fastening techniques: Wire loop must be clean and free of insulation. Do not close wire loop but allow a small space.

HOW TO MAKE SCREW CONNECTIONS

Screw connections are used more often for joining one electrical conductor to another than for soldering. It isn't necessarily better but it is easier and faster, and if properly done is quite satisfactory. Wrapping a wire around a screw, however, does not automatically mean a good connection.

The first step in a screw connection is to remove all insulation from the end of the wire. The insulation near the exposed wire should have a small taper, not as sharp as the taper on a pencil, but following the same technique described in the section on splices and taps.

Wrap the exposed wire around the screw in the same direction the screw will take when it is fastened. This will usually be clockwise. If you use the opposite direction in fastening the wire around the screw, the act of fastening the screw will force the wire out.

The wire under the head of the screw should not form a completely closed loop. Instead, there should be a small space. If not, as you turn the screw clockwise, the end of the wire will butt

against the body of the wire, preventing a tight circle of copper wire around the screw.

When wrapping copper wire around a screw head, make sure the wire fits snugly against the screw. Force it into position with a pair of long-nose pliers if necessary. If, as you turn the screw inward, the wire gets forced out, hold the wire in position with a pair of long-nose pliers. Tighten the screw head firmly, using the correct screwdriver. Do not connect wires to "hot" terminals—that is, to terminals that are wired to an outlet or connected to current-carrying wires.

RIGHT

TURNING SCREW CLOSES LOOP

WRONG

TURNING SCREW OPENS LOOP

Right and wrong ways of wrapping a wire around a screw.

Before wrapping the wire around the screw body, make sure the wire is clean and that no insulation threads hang over it. When using stranded conductor, twist the strands tightly together before wrapping around the screw. If the exposed copper is too long to wrap firmly around the screw, cut off enough of it so that its end does not touch the body of the wire. With stranded wire, the pressure of the closing screw head may sometimes break off one or more strands. In that event, do the job over. It is much easier to connect solid conductor to a screw rather than stranded wire.

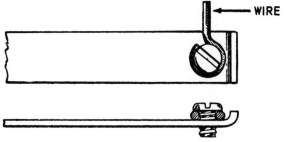

How to attach a wire to a common terminal.

CRIMPED OR SOLDERLESS TERMINALS

Sometimes a machine screw will be in such an awkward position that it will be difficult to wrap the wire around the screw. In that case you can make the work easier by attaching a solderless terminal to the end of the wire. However, this does require a special tool. Solderless connectors are satisfactory when the current flow is limited to a few amperes, preferably less. For stronger current, it is much better to use the wraparound method.

CRIMPED TERMINALS

While it is quite easy to fasten solid conductor to a machine screw, it becomes somewhat of a problem when working with stranded conductor. When tightening the connection, there is always the possibility that the pressure will force one of the wire strands out of position. Not only does this reduce the effectiveness of the contact, but the escaped strand can touch an adjoining wire or other metal, resulting in a short.

One way of avoiding this is to coat the exposed stranded conductors very lightly with solder. First, twist the strands until they are twisted tightly together. Use a pliers for this purpose, since your fingers may transfer perspiration or dirt. The trouble with this method is that it tends to make the stranded wire stiff and more difficult to handle.

A better technique is to use a crimping tool and a crimp-on terminal lug. Slide the lug onto the wire and then crimp the lug into position by squeezing on the crimping tool. The terminal of the lug will now fit easily over any machine screw.

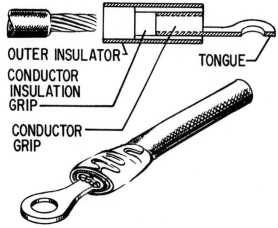

Crimp-on terminal lugs can make connections easier.

There are two types of crimp-on terminal lugs. One is the insulated type, which is preferable for home electrical work since it supplies insulation right up to the terminal lug. When crimping, use the crimping tool directly over the insulation material. If you use the uninsulated type of crimp-on lug, you may need to tape the lug after doing the work.

When using stranded wire, always twirl the wire strands together before making connection.

Chapter 6
Electrical Hardware

There is a tremendous variety of electrical hardware available and it would be literally impossible to describe each and every item without converting this book into a catalog. Yet, it is important to know about electrical hardware for various reasons. Certain kinds of hardware may be required by your local electrical codes. Knowing what hardware is available may make your home wiring or home electrical repairs much easier. In some instances, the right hardware will make your home electrical system more flexible—that is, it may give you a more desirable switching arrangement, or a more convenient outlet setup, or it may put electric power more readily at your disposal.

MALE PLUGS

A male plug, more often simply referred to as a plug, is one of the more common replacement items around the home. It looks like a simple device and it is; yet it is an important element, for it is the component that connects electrical power to your home appliances.

Some plugs are molded directly to lamp cord. Such plugs aren't removable and so if the plug becomes defective, the only alternative is to throw away the plug and its associated lamp cord.

Plug with grounding terminal.

The best type of plug is the rubber-molded type with a finger grip. The finger grip extends from the body of the plug and lets you pull the plug from an outlet easily. Never remove a plug by pulling on the wire connected to the plug. The wire may come away from the plug.

Adapter for fitting a three-prong plug into a receptacle designed for a two-prong plug. Connect the wire coming out of the adapter to ground, using the center screw terminal on the receptacle outlet cover plate.

Double-prong plub in molded-rubber housing: The finger extension at the end of the plug is a grip that makes it easy to remove the plug from the outlet. This is an excellent feature for plugs that get regular usage.

CONNECTING WIRES TO A MALE PLUG

The first step in making a connection to a plug is to strip and clean the ends of the wires to be connected. Remove the insulation about ½″ from the ends of the wires. If the wire is stranded, twirl it with your fingers to make the strands into a more solid unit. Make sure no stray strands escape your attention. A single strand can cause a short across the plug.

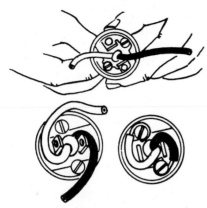

Steps in connecting wires to a plug: Bring the wires through the center hole (top illustration); bend each wire around one of the prongs (lower left); then wrap each wire around a screw (lower right) and tighten. Although not shown in the drawings, strip each wire before proceeding.

The plug may have a fiber washer covering both prongs. Remove the washer and push the wires through the center hole of the plug. Take one of the wires—either one—and put it so it is around one of the prongs as shown in the illustration. Loosen the screw to which the wire is to be connected and bend the wire around the shaft of the screw. If you have excess wire, cut it away at this time with a pair of cutters. When putting the wire around the screw, of course, follow the procedure mentioned earlier by wrapping the wire so that it is in a clockwise direction. Tighten the screw and make sure that no strands have escaped from beneath the screw head. Now repeat with the other screw. It makes no difference which wire, black or white, is connected since the connections are interchangeable.

Twist-lock plug with three prongs: A pair of screws, shown on the right in the drawing, clamp the insulated power cord and hold it firmly in position.

The kind of plug you select depends on what you expect to do with it. If intended for a lamp that will seldom, if ever, be moved, a simple plastic plug without a finger grip is satisfactory. If the plug is intended for a portable appliance that requires several amperes or more, a more suitable

type would be a twist-lock type. Plugs of this kind have several advantages. The twist feature means that the plug makes firm contact with its mating receptacle. A screw attachment at the end of the plug permits a firm grip on any kind of connecting cable.

THE UNDERWRITERS KNOT

The purpose of making connections to a plug is electrical only. It is true that twisting wires around the screws of a plug is a mechanical action, but at no time should there be a strain on the connecting wires. Even if you do not pull on the connecting cord, there is always the possibility that the wire leading into the plug will be taut. To relieve the possibility of mechanical strain, it is a good technique to tie a knot in the connecting wires. The recommended knot is the Underwriters knot, as shown in the drawing. After making the knot, fasten the respective wires to the plug terminals by wrapping them around the pair of screws and tightening.

Method of tying an Underwriters knot on line cord before connecting the wires to the plug screws.

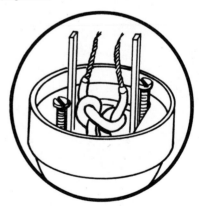

100

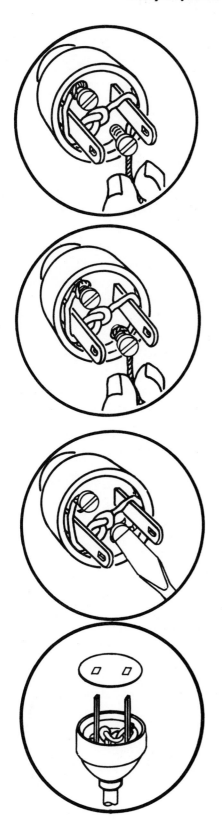

Steps in connecting a line cord to a plug using an Underwriters knot.

ADAPTER PLUGS

Plugs can have two or three prongs. A three-prong plug is the same as the two-prong type, except that the third prong is a ground connection. If, for any reason, the "hot" lead going into an appliance shorts, as, for example, to the metal case of the appliance, there will be an automatic short through the ground connection of the cable. Without this feature, the metal case would also become "hot" and anyone touching the case could receive a shock.

Ground all appliances. Use an adapter plug, if necessary, but it is much better to have a three-terminal receptacle.

Many homes are not equipped to accommodate three-prong plugs but will accept two-prong plugs only. A three-prong plug can fit into a two-prong receptacle by using an adapter. The adapter has a wire coming out of it ending in a lug. This wire is a ground and its function is to ground the appliance. Connect the wire to the center screw that holds the receptacle cover to the outlet.

An adapter provides a temporary three-hole outlet. The trouble, though, is that once an adapter is used it tends to remain in use. While an adapter is better than no adapter at all, the best arrangement is to substitute three-hole receptacles for the two-hole type.

SOCKETS

Sockets are convenient for connecting such devices as lamps and plug-type fuses. Most sockets are screw-base types—that is, they contain threads that mate with similar threads on lamps or other items. For small bulbs, such as those used in flashlights, the socket may be a bayonet type. The accompanying bulb is equipped with a small metal extension that engages a slot in the socket. With bulbs of this kind, just push the bulb in the socket, give a small twist to the right, and the bulb is then locked into position.

Still another type of socket is that used by fluorescent lamps. The fluorescent has a pair of prongs at each end. The lamp is inserted into a pair of holders, one at each end. As for the bayonet bulb, the insertion is a snap-in action, rather than a screw-in effect as in the case of threaded sockets. Fluorescent bulbs are usually two-socket types; incandescent bulbs are single-socket types.

There is no shortage of lamp sockets for just about every conceivable arrangement and use. For home wiring the advantage is that you can put some of these socket ideas to work for your convenience and comfort. A socket is simply a device for bringing electric power to a component, usually to a bulb.

CLEAT SOCKETS

A cleat socket is a completely exposed type with the wires carrying electrical current connected to a pair of machine screws, one on each side of the socket. Since the screws are exposed, it is easy to get a shock by accidentally touching both screws, or possibly just one of them. Cleat sockets, however, are convenient and are extremely easy to install. They can be held in place by a pair of wood screws inserted in holes at the base of the socket.

PORCELAIN

Cleat socket: Exposed terminals for connecting AC line results in possible shock hazard.

Like all other sockets, the cleat socket can also be used as a receptacle. You can do this by inserting a screw-type plug into the socket. Such plugs come equipped with one, two, or three female terminals. Cleat sockets are generally made of porcelain. If you have the AC line connected to such a socket, never insert a plug-type fuse. The effect will be to blow the fuse immediately, possibly opening other fuses in the branch line as well. Naturally, such sockets should be mounted so that other people, especially children, cannot reach and accidentally touch the exposed terminals.

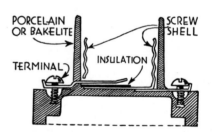

Cross-sectional view of cleat socket. The base contains a pair of through holes (not shown in this drawing) for wood screws. Sockets of this type can easily be screwed to wood support.

BASE-PULL SOCKETS

The base-pull socket resembles the cleat socket quite closely but is much safer. Also made of porcelain, the base-pull socket receives its electrical power through a connection beneath its base and so the connecting wires aren't exposed. As a further safety feature, the base-pull socket comes equipped with a pull chain, a switch that is used for turning power on and off. Base pull sockets can be mounted on metal junction boxes. The box protects the wiring and also keeps it from being touched accidentally.

Base-pull socket: Mount this socket on a metal junction box to enclose connecting wires.

The chain on such sockets is usually quite short. Just attach a suitable length of string to it. This will keep your fingers from getting too close to a hot electric bulb and makes turning the bulb on and off very convenient. Base-pull sockets are handy for basement installation. Their disadvantage is that you must be sufficiently close to the socket to be able to reach the string attached to the pull chain. For this reason you should have at least one switch-type lamp in the basement to supply some illumination.

THE WEATHERPROOF SOCKET

A weatherproof socket, as its name implies, is for outdoor use. However, such use is not permanent, but for supplying outdoor lighting on a temporary basis. The socket, made of rubber, or some synthetic, has a pair of connecting wires coming out of the base to which current-carrying wires are to be connected. Never use exposed power connections outdoors. Always tape the connections thoroughly, with rubber tape, followed by friction tape. After the lamp has served its outdoor purpose, bring the socket (or sockets) indoors. Always disconnect power going to such sockets before handling them.

Weatherproof socket.

The trouble with a phrase such as "weatherproof socket" is that it implies more than is possible. You cannot, for example, connect naked electric-light bulbs to such sockets and expose such bulbs to rain. The first few drops of rain on the hot glass of an electric-light bulb will cause it to shatter.

HIDDEN TERMINAL SOCKETS

There are various types of hidden terminal sockets, but they all perform the same double purpose. The first is to conceal the connecting wires and the other is to supply a convenient socket for a lamp or plug. Hidden terminal sockets are usually remote-switch operated—that is, the switch isn't directly associated with the socket but is located elsewhere.

Some types of hidden terminal sockets.

LAMP SOCKETS

Lamp sockets have either a pull-chain type switch or one that is knob-operated. The top part, the part opposite the threaded portion for the bulb, has various arrangements for fastening the socket in position. Some are threaded, while others are held in position by a set screw.

LAMP SOCKET ADAPTERS

You can connect a bulb having a bayonet-type base into a screw-type socket by using a lamp socket adapter. Screw the lamp socket adapter into a socket, just as though it were an electric light bulb. Then insert the bulb having a bayonet-type base into the adapter.

Screw threads in sockets are either molded or

rolled. Sockets are also designed to be used in all types of lighting fixtures, such as table lamps, floor lamps, or hanging fixtures having decorative shades or light reflectors. Sometimes a socket of the type used for household lamps is called a medium socket. It has a diameter of little more than 1˝.

BAYONET SOCKETS

Miniature bulbs, such as those used for flashlights, may be designed for a bayonet socket. To use such a socket, insert the metal bottom portion of the bulb in the socket, push in slightly, and twist the bulb clockwise. To release the bulb and to remove it, reverse the procedure. Depress slightly and then turn the bulb counterclockwise. Bulbs that use bayonet sockets are flanged types. However, small bulbs, such as panel and pilot lamps, neon glow lamps, and flashlight bulbs are available in threaded as well as flanged form. When buying replacement lamps, you should know: (1) the voltage rating of the lamp; (2) the type of base—whether bayonet or screw type; and (3) the size of the base.

Hanging sockets: pull-chain type (left) and know switch (right).

Adapter for connecting a bayonet-type lamp to a screw-type socket.

Bayonet-type socket.

SOCKET SIZES

Lamp sockets are available in a number of different sizes, and while the medium size is the most common in the home, you will also find the mogul, the intermediate, and the candelabra types. The mogul, designed for large-size bulbs, has a diameter of 1 ½˝, while the diameter of the medium socket is only 1˝. The intermediate has a diameter of ⅝˝ while the candelabra is less than ½˝, measuring about 7/16˝.

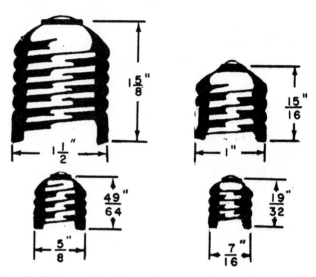

Lamp-socket sizes: Mogul (top left); medium (top right); intermediate (lower left); and candelabra (lower right). The mogul is the largest; the candelabra, the smallest. The medium is most commonly used in the home although the candelabra size is becoming more popular. Before buying lamps, make sure they have the correct base size.

Screw and bayonet bulbs. Counting from the left, the third bulb and the sixth are bayonet types; all the others are screw types.

UPSET (CAPTIVE) SCREWS

There is nothing more exasperating than removing a machine screw from some electrical part, only to have the screw fall inside a wall, or roll out of sight somewhere on the floor. Part of the problem is that machine screws used in electrical work are often no more than ¼˝ long, and so it takes just one or two turns of a screwdriver to remove them.

The upset prevents the screw from being completely removed. Such screws are sometimes called captive screws.

To prevent loss of screws, some electrical hardware comes equipped with upset screws. An upset screw has a somewhat larger diameter at the end of the screw (the end opposite the screw head). As a result the screw can be turned outward just a small distance. When turning the screw outward, the upset end will prevent the screw from being completely removed. However, enough of the screw will be turned to permit connecting a wire to it or removing a wire.

The advantage is that the upset prevents possible loss of the screw. The disadvantage is that if you do use a rather strong turning force on he screwdriver, the screw will come out, anyway, but in so doing may damage the threads in the terminal to which it was attached. This means that a replacement screw may not fit or may fit very loosely.

STRAPS AND STAPLES

While BX and conduit may look strong, and they are, the metal housing is designed just to protect wires and not to act as a support. Further, BX and conduit must be supported so there is no mechanical strain on the metal. Cables must be supported at least every 4½' whether the cable runs horizontally or vertically. You should also have a staple or a strap within 12" of every outlet box.

CABLE STAPLES

Use cable staples for anchoring BX to wood supports. There are two types of cable staples: those in which the two arms of the staple are parallel to each other, and those whose arms are offset. The straight staple or parallel-arm type is the easiest t

of the BX and then hammer the flat portion of the staple until it makes firm contact with the BX.

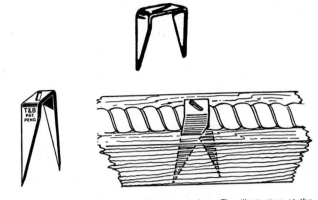

Straight BX staple (above) and offset type below: The illustration at the lower right is a phantom view showing how an offset staple holds BX cable firmly to a wooden support. Always make sure the BX is firm and flat against the wood frame and that the cable does not kink or belly.

You can handle the offset staple in the same way, but if you should later change your mind and decide to remove the staple, you will find it more difficult to remove the offset type. The offset type also supplies a more secure anchorage for the BX.

Insulated staple is suitable for low-voltage wires, undesirable for 117-volt AC lines. Insulation can fall off.

INSULATED STAPLES

Use insulated staples for low-voltage wire, but do not use it for lamp cord or for any wires carrying current from the 117-volt AC line. An insulated staple looks somewhat like a BX staple, but is much smaller and, of course, is not as strong. It has a small bit of insulating material across its top, flat portion. Homeowners sometimes use these insulated staples for tacking lamp cord to baseboards. This is not a good procedure, since the insulation on the staple can fall off and it then becomes possible for the staple to cut through and short the wires. Insulated staples can be used with bell wire.

CABLE STRAPS

While cable straps and cable staples perform the same function, they differ in the way they are mounted. Further, cable straps are available as non-metallic or metallic types. The advantage of a non-metallic cable strap is that, unlike a holding device such as the insulated staple, it will not cut through and short wires. The disadvantage of the cable strap is that it must be mounted with screws. To save some time and effort, however, there are some straps that are one-screw mounts only. A two-screw strap is sometimes called a full-strap, while those using just a single screw are termed half-straps. You can use full-straps or half-straps for BX or for conduit. The full-strap type, of course, supplies stronger and firmer support, but sometimes you will have no choice but to use the half-strap. You may not have enough room for a full-strap, or the BX or conduit may be in such a location that you will be unable to use a full-strap.

Insulated strap (top) is especially suited for supporting flat cable. Use full strap (lower left) or half strap (lower right) for BX or conduit. The two lower straps are made of metal. The mounting clip at the bottom is for mounting non-metallic cable. The difference between the clip at the top and the one at the bottom is that the one at the top is an insulated type, made of some non-conducting substance, while that at the bottom is metal.

ELECTRICAL BOXES

An electrical box has a number of uses. It helps supply a continuous ground system. Since the conduit or BX coming into the box is grounded, the physical connection also puts the box at ground potential. The box also holds either BX or conduit in position, forming a substantial holding support. However, this assumes the box is firmly screwed into position, as it should be. Finally, the box helps protect against fire in the event that a fire takes place at the splice.

Boxes are available in a number of sizes and shapes and so you can get round boxes, or those that are square, rectangular, or octagonal. Some boxes are ganged, while others are single types. Some are made to use as cover plates for switches or receptacles. Naturally, the smaller-size boxes cost less, but they are also more difficult to work with. A good rule of thumb is to use boxes that have a depth of at least 1 ½".

JUNCTION BOXES

A junction box is just one type of electrical box. Its purpose is to supply a housing for a splice. If you need to splice wires, bring the wires into the junction box and then do the splice. After taping the wires, cover the junction box with a blank plate. The junction box will then be enclosed on all sides. Try to put junction boxes where they will always be accessible. Don't plaster over them or conceal them behind walls. The advantage here is that the junction box is a natural takeoff point for a new branch, should you need to expand the wiring setup in your home.

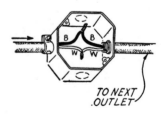

Basic setup of a junction box: The cover plate has been removed to show the interior wiring splice. The splice should be taped or covered with solderless connectors.

The illustration shows the appearance of a pair of wires forming a splice inside a junction box. The letters B and W refer to black and white. Black is the hot lead; white is the ground lead. Note that the white lead is joined to a white lead; the black lead to a black. If you were to connect a test lamp across the splice—that is from black to white—the lamp should light, assuming power is on. The lamp should also light when connected between the black and the metal housing of the junction box or between the black lead and the conduit. The lamp should *not* light when connected between the white lead and the junction box or conduit.

This illustration shows the junction box with its plate removed. The plate is generally held in place by two or more machine screws.

KNOCKOUTS

If you will examine an electrical box, you will note it is supplied with a number of small metal circles. These are known as knockouts. Push hard on any one of the circles and you will be able to remove this circle of metal and leave a hole for the connection of BX or conduit. Do not push out more knockouts than you require so as to give the wiring the maximum amount of shielding.

MOUNTING ELECTRICAL BOXES

Electrical boxes are available with screw or nail holes punched out in the back to let you mount the boxes. You can also get attachment plates so that you can set up the box in just about any position. The box also has screw holes in front so that you can support it by mounting across a pair of wood cleats. You can also use metal hanging straps for this purpose.

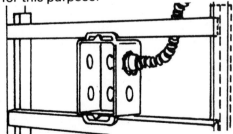

Electric box mounted across a pair of wooded cleats. The box is held to the wooden cross supports by wood screws, one at the top front of the electric box, the other at the bottom front. Note the BX cable leading into the right side of the box, brought in through one of the circular knockouts.

In older houses using lath strips, the electric box is mounted in a space cut out in the lath. The box is then fastened into position by wood screws, top and bottom. Before mounting the box, make sure you have decided on which knockout areas to use for BX or conduit and then punch out the circular bits of metal accordingly. Make all cable connections to the box before mounting it. After connecting the cables and mounting the box, you can then make the wire splices, pushing the splices into the box after you have finished.

Another way of mounting boxes is to use an offset hanger. The offset hanger may be necessary if the positioning of the box is such that it cannot be nailed or screwed into a supporting wood frame. The offset hanger comes equipped with a mounting stud that is threaded for a machine nut. Screw or nail the hanger into position and then use one of the knockout holes in the electric box, letting the stud slide through it. The nut supplied with the hanger will then support the outlet box.

You can get deep or shallow offset hangers. Select the type of hanger that will let the front box fit flush with the wall. Lath in itself does not have sufficient strength or thickness to support boxes. Boxes should be fastened to studs, and if they cannot be made to do so directly, then use an offset hanger.

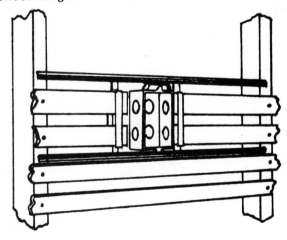

Junction box supported on metal mounting straps.

Offset hanger for supporting electric boxes. Always mount boxes on rigid support, such as a joist, or else use an offset hanger. Hanger can be attached to a pair of wooden joists.

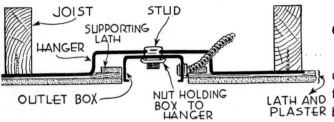

How to mount an outlet box using a hanger: Screw the hanger in position and then support the outlet box on the hanger with machine stud and nut.

Homes are sufficiently different so that each will present its own box-mounting problems. But in each case the box must be rigidly supported. When mounting a box into a plaster wall, you will find that you have knocked out more plaster than necessary. Fill in all areas with fresh plaster so that the plaster comes right up to all sides of the box. Generally, with sheetrock walls this isn't necessary since openings can be cut fairly precisely.

GROUND

The white wire in an electrical system is the ground wire, but if for some reason the ground connection should be removed from this wire, you would then have two "hot" leads. Touching either wire while touching ground would result in a shock. To make sure that the white wire is always ground (that is, at zero voltage with respect to you), some cables come equipped with a special third wire, which functions solely as a ground wire. Look on this wire as a backup for the white wire. Some BX comes equipped with such a ground wire in the form of a bare copper or aluminum wire running completely through the BX. When connecting BX to an electrical box, make sure that you also connect this bare wire to some metal portion of the box, possibly wrapping it around a

screw and tightening it. It is true that the outside shield of Bx is grounded and that the electric box automatically becomes grounded when the BX is connected to it. The ground wire is an added safety precaution. The ground wire is especially important for non-metallic cable, such as plastic-sheathed types.

OCTAGON BOXES

The shape of an electric box helps decide its ultimate use. Octagon boxes are intended for fixtures or for use as junction boxes. With these boxes you can bring in conduit, armored cable such as BX, or non-metallic cable.

These boxes are usually made of steel and can have knockouts, generally ½" in diameter; or they may come equipped with cable clamps. The cable clamps are somewhat similar to straps, but are built into the electric box and can be used to hold one or a pair of cables firmly in position simply by turning a machine screw.

RECTANGULAR BOXES

There are available steel boxes espevpally designed for switches and receptacles. You can get them with or without built-in cable clamps. You can gang such boxes—that is, arrange them to work side by side—by removing a side plate from each of the boxes. This doubles the available volume and supplies more room if you have a number of cables coming together in this box.

BEVELED-CORNER BOXES

One of the problems in doing electrical work in older buildings is the extensive use of laths, the long wooden strips used as a wall and plaster support. The newer buildings are constructed with Sheetrock nailed against wooden studs or joists. It may be easier to use a beveled box when installing a new electric box in an older home or replacing one. This box looks just like the rectangular box, except that its rear section is beveled. You can use such boxes with BX, conduit, or non-metallic sheathed cable.

SIDE-BRACKET BOXES

The side-bracket box is a square or rectangular type. It is so called since it has a bracket on one side for mounting the box. This type of box can be used for switches and receptacles, and has either ½″ or ¾″ knockouts. Use the side-bracket box with BX, conduit, or with plastic-sheathed cable.

The side bracket can be to the left or to the right of the box. Slide brackets are generally used only in new installations, since it is very difficult to install the brackets once walls are completed. The advantage of side brackets is that you can mount them so that the box is always at the correct depth, whether you use lath or sheetrock. Side brackets are also convenient for moutning boxes on wooden crossbeams in an attic or basement. Since these areas are exposed, the side brackets can be used in either new or old homes.

WEATHERPROOF BOXES

Use weatherproof boxes for outdoor installation. With newer homes they form part of the outside veneer of the house. The distinguishing characteristic of these boxes is that they are equipped with weatherproof snap covers. The covers are spring-loaded and must be lifted up to permit access to the receptacle housed in the box. When the plug is removed, the cover snaps shut, thus protecting the receptacle against the weather.

THROUGH BOXES

Some boxes are through types and are used for installing switches or receptacles on both sides of a wall. Unlike ordinary boxes, this type is open at both ends so that switch or receptacle plates can be used. The advantage of using a through box is that it is not only convenient, but more economical. Most important, such a box saves wiring time.

BOX MATERIALS

For the most part, you will find boxes made of steel, possibly galvanized, but boxes of aluminum and plastic are available also. The disadvantage of the plastic type is that plastic is an insulator and so you do not get the grounding effect when connecting BX or conduit to the box. Further, in the event of a fire, the plastic will either deform severely or may simply drop away, exposing wires to fvame. Steel boxes offer far more fire protection. Plastic boxes can be purchased in ganged form, but you cannot disassemble them to make your own ganged box, as you can with the metal type. NM cable is the only kind you may use with plastic boxes. Actually, some local electric codes prohibit the installation of such boxes.

ROUND BOXES

You may see such boxes in electrical supply stores, but they aren't ordinarily used in home wiring. Because of the curvature of the box it is difficult to fasten BX or conduit to the box and so you must use special cable clamps. Round boxes, however, are sometimes used to install ceiling lamps.

RECEPTACLES

A female receptacle is more commonly known as a receptacle or outlet or convenience outlet. The purpose of a receptacle is to allow the quick connection, and the equally quick disconnection, of electric appliances terminating in a male plug.

For permanent installations, receptacles can be mounted in electric boxes of the type just described. The receptacle has machine screws on either side for connecting wires, with the screws quite often of the captive type. Most receptacles are duplex types—that is, they can accommodate two plugs—but less common, single receptacles are also available. Receptacles are the two-, or three-hole types used in new home installations.

LIMITATIONS OF THE TWO-HOLE RE-CEPTACLE

Many modern appliances, including shop power tools and electrically operated kitchen devices, are equipped with a three-wire power cord ending in a three-prong plug. While only two wires are required to carry an electric current, the third wire connects the outer metal housing of the appliance to the third prong on the male plug. This mates with a hole in the receptacle to which a ground wire in the house-wiring system is connected. Thus, the act of connecting a three-plug into a properly wired three-hole outlet automatically grounds the outer metal frame of the appliance and any metal parts connected to it.

While it is possible to connet an appliance with a three-prong plug to a two-hole outlet through the use of an adapter, the ground wire on the adapter is often ignored, or is connected to the center screw on the plate covering the two-hole outlet. The trouble is that this center screw may not be grounded. The cover plate may be made of some insulating material such as plastic, or else the center screw may be so coated with paint that it has become an insulator rather than a conductor. The best arrangement is a three-hole outlet.

THE TWO-HOLE RECEPTACLE

Receptacles, whether they are single, duplex, or two-or three-hole types, come equipped with a pair of top and bottom metal flanges, one at each end. These flanges have openings for machine screws for fastening the outlet to its electric box. The receptacle is then covered with a plate made of metal, porcelain, or plastic. The cover plate is held in position by a single screw through the center. Cutouts in the cover plate expose only that part of the receptacle that is to receive the male plug.

RECEPTACLE POWER RATINGS

The usual in-home receptacles, such as those found along baseboards, are rated to handle a

Two-hole duplex receptacle: The center hole is used for mounting a cover plate. The receptacle is fastened to an electric box by machine screws passing through the upper and lower flanges.

Duplex receptacle for three-prong plugs: This is a more desirable type of receptacle, since it is designed for automatic grounding of appliances.

maximum of 15 amperes. To calculate its power-handling ability, multiply the existing line voltage by the maximum current. If you assume a line voltage of 117 volts, then the power is 117 x 15 equals 1755 watts or a bit less than 2 kilowatts. Since this rating is for the entire outlet, if it is a duplex type, then each one of the convenicne outlets will have a rating of 1755/2 equals 877½ watts.

Whether you will overload the receptacle or not depends on the appliances you connect to it. You can easily convert a duplex receptacle into one having six outlets by inserting a pair of cube taps into the receptacle. A cube tap is a combined plug and receptacle. It supplies additional outlets quickly, but it is easy to violate electrical common sense when using them, for with so many outlets convenient and available, the tendency is to keep plugging in more and more appliances.

DISADVANTAGES OF OUTLETS AND TAPS

Basically, an outlet does not belong in an electrical system: the plug of an appliance makes only sliding contact with the metal elements in hhe outlet. Yet, current must pass from those metal contacts in the outlet to the prongs of the plug and then into the appliance. This, then, is the weak link in the electrical system, for elsewhere in the system all connections are extremely tight, and often soldered. However, there is no alternative if we are to have the convenience of connecting and disconnecting appliances at will. We can at least make sure that plugs make firm and positive contact with the outlets.

There are several things you can do to give the electric currents a fighting chance to flow into appliances.

1. Make sure that the portion of the receptacle receiving and housing the male plug extends beyond its cover plate. In other words, the plug must go as far into the outlet as possible. with the prong end of the plug firmly up against the receptacle.

2. The plug-receptacle fit must be good and tight. Tug gently on the wire connected to the plug. If the plug falls out of the receptacle, the fit is a very poor one. You can improve the connection if you will spread the prongs of the plug slightly or twist the prongs with the help of two pliers. Howevver, bending and twisting the prongs sometimes loosens the prong supports, in which case it is better to buy a new plug to replace the old one. Don't keep the old one around for possible se at some later date. Throw it away.

3. The loose connection may be due to sprung metal contacts in the receptacle—that is, which have separated. To check, remove the plug and insert it into a different outlet. You can tell by the feel of a plug as it is inserted into an outlet whether the contact is firm or not. If you aren't sure, tug gently on the connecting wires, as described earlier. If the plug fits firmly into one outlet, but is quite loose in the other, then you have fairly good evidence of a defective outlet. Don't try to repair it. Replace it.

4. The prongs of a plug are mounted in rubber or Bakelite. After some use, either one or both of the prongs work their way loose. If you can wiggle

a prong back and forth quite easily, discard the plug and get a new one.

5. After using a plug for sometime, remove it and touch the prongs. They may be very mildly warm or barely warm. If more than that, or if hot to the touch, then the plug is making poor contact. You will notice this more with current-hungry appliances than with those that require just small currents.

TWIST-LOCK OUTLETS

Plugs, particularly if loose, have a habit of falling out of receptacles. Since this means the plug must be reinserted before the appliance will work, then there is at least the possibility of making somewhat better contact. A worse situation is a loose plug that comes part of the way out of its outlet and remains in that position. The contact area between the prongs of the plug and the metal section of the outlet is greatly reduced, increasing the resistance to the flow of current.

Single (left) and duplex (right) twist-and-turn receptacles. These are three-hole types intended to accommodate a plug carrying a ground wire.

A twist-lock plug and associated twist-lock outlet are designed to prevent this. Such plugs require a twist-and-turn push action and so the plug not only remains secure in the outlet, but also makes more positive contact.

RECESSED OUTLETS

Once you put a plug into an outlet, the connecting wires to the plug extend away from the wall holding the outlet. For many applications, such as lamps or toasters or electric shavers, this arrangement is satisfactory. There is no reason why the wire should hug the wall. But there are times when it is desirable to have a wire as close against a wall as possible. An electric kitchen clock is one example, and for such an application, we recommend that use of a special clock outlet. The unit is recessed and will hold both the plug and excess wire.

SOCKETS VS. OUTLETS

Although regarded as a separate category, the various sockets described earlier, such as the pull-chain socket and the cleat socket are directly related to receptacles and can be considered part of the receptacle family. The difference is that sockets are screw-in or bayonet types, while receptacles depend on sliding contact between the plug prongs and the metal arms of the receptacle. Because they are so closely identified, sockets are sometimes called outlets or receptacles.

COMBINED SWITCH AND CONVENIENCE OUTLET

Instead of a duplex receptacle, you can get a combined switch and receptacle. You can use the receptacle for plugging in appliances and the switch for controlling a light.

SWITCHED AND UNSWITCHED OUTLETS

The combined switch and convenience outlet can be arranged so that the switch controls power to the outlet. With outlets of this kind, the switch must be in its "on" position for power to reach the appliance plugged into the outlet. An outlet of this kind is known as a switched outlet. All other types are called unswitched.

SWITCHES

The purpose of a switch is to open or close a circuit—that is, to stop the flow of current or to allow it to flow. In the home the switch is the most visible portion of the electrical system. Switches can either be mounted on walls, be pull-chain types, or be mounted directly on appliances. Some switches control one circuit; others, a number of circuits.

The moving portion or blade of a switch is called a pole. Some switches have just a single blade, or single pole; others have two blades and are double-pole types.

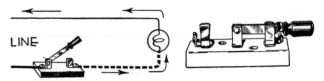

SPST switch (left) and SPDT switch (right): These are used to show switch action only and are not the type used in home wiring.

The drawing at the left shows a simple switch, known as a single-pole single-throw type. It is called single-throw because the blade or pole touches just one metal contact when it is closed. The drawing at the right illustrates a single-pole double-throw type. Note that the blade can now be made to touch two separate metal contacts. Single-pole single-throw is abbreviated to SPST, and the single-pole double-throw is referred to as SPDT.

THE SPST SWITCH

Most switches in the home are SPST types. When the SPST switch is closed—that is, when the metal blades or pole of the switch joins or mates with the metal contact—the circuit is closed. Current will now flow through the blade to the appliance. When the pole is lifted, contact is broken. We now have an open-circuit condition and current no longer reaches the appliance. Voltage, however, is still present at the pole of the switch. However, because of the open-circuit condition there is no voltage at the appliance.

The SPST and SPDT switches illustrated earlier aren't the types used in home wiring. Instead, the switch more closely resembles the one shown in our drawing. The action, however, is the same. Current cannot flow to the appliance or light until the switch is turned on. When it is turned on, the pole inside the sealed switch will touch a contact, thus closing the circuit, and allowing the current to flow. The switch is mounted in an electric box and is held in position by a pair of machine screws: one at the top of the switch, and the other at the bottom. After the switch is fastened into position, it is shielded with a cover plate. Cover plates for switches have holes, top and bottom, for the insertion of machine screws. The cover plate is fastened to the switch, but the switch is fastened to the electric box.

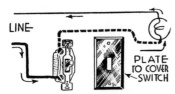

SPST switch is used to control flow of current to appliance or lamp.

HOW THE SPST SWITCH IS CONNECTED

The SPST switch is inserted in series with the "hot" lead—that is, the black wire. The wire is cut open and the two ends of the wire are then stripped clean. One wire is fastened to one machine screw in the switch, the other wire to the other screw. If the wires are transposed, the switch will still work and no damage will be done. The usual procedure is that the switch remain off when the toggle or moving arm of the switch is in the down position. An upward movement turns the switch on. With transposed wires, the reverse action takes place: the switch is on in the down position, and off when it is up.

The SPST switch does not break into the ground lead or white wire. Never connect a switch into the ground lead. At all times the ground should be continuous and unbroken.

SWITCH TYPES

There are many different types of switches, but just a few of these are found in home electrical wiring. Most of those used in home wall mounts are toggle switches housed in Bakelite. Some switches, known as mercury switches, are "noiseproof" and are usually intended for bedrooms or sickrooms. You can, of course, also get switches that are illuminated by a tiny bulb and glow in the dark. Their advantage is that they can be located quite easily and thus eliminate switch fumbling.

CONDUIT FITTINGS

Conduit can be threaded at the end that connects to an electric box. To fasten the conduit to an outlet box, put a locknut on the threaded end of the conduit and then insert the end of the conduit through the round hole obtained by removing a knockout in the box. Fit a bushing on the threaded portion of the conduit now in the box and tighten it. The conduit will now be held in place by the bushing on one side (from inside the box) and the locknut (outside the box). Keep the amount of conduit going into the box at a minimum since you will want as much available space as possible for wiring and also for other parts, such as a switch.

There are various types of locknuts and bushings, but the best are those whose outer edges are flanged. They are not only easier to tighten but can be tightened more securely.

Locknuts and bushings can be used to fasten threaded conduit to outlet boxes. The bushing shown in the lower drawing is known as a grounding bushing.

You will find condulets associated with conduit. These are boxes, somewhat like the electrical boxes described earlier, but smaller. Since wire must be pulled or fished through conduit, long lengths of wire present a problem. Condulets supply intermediate points in long conduit runs for pull-through of wire. They can also be used as junctions for inaccessible, concealed installations.

Condulets are used as intermediate points for long runs of conduit.

THREADLESS CONDUIT COUPLINGS

You can install conduit that isn't threaded by using conduit couplings. A coupling is a small section that fits over the conduit rather tightly. To avoid making a bend in conduit, you can use a conduit elbow. When you join the conduit to the elbow, the two sections of conduit will be at right angles to each other. Also, to join various lengths of conduit, you can use a conduit union.

EMT

Thin-wall conduit is more properly known as electrical metallic tubing and abbreviated as EMT. EMT has a thinner wall than regular conduit, but its interior diameter and cross-sectional area are the same. You can get EMT in sizes from ⅜″ to 2″. One of the advantages of EMT is that the inside surface is enameled. This supplies a smoother inside surface, making it easier to fish wires through the conduit. Enamel is also an insulator and so, presumably, you have some added protection in the event a wire happens to make contact with the inner wall. But don't count on it. Enamel scrapes easily and it flakes.

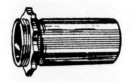

Indent-type fittings for thin-walled conduit.

Box connector for thin-walled conduit.

Coupling for thin-walled conduit.

EMT or thin-walled conduit: It is easier to handle than rigid conduit.

All couplings and connections to boxes can be threadless and are either clamp or compression types. Some fittings are similar to sleeves and you can fasten them to conduit by an impinger tool. This tool pinches circular indentations in the fitting and this holds it firmly against the conduit. Others have threaded bushings that, when tightened, force a tapered sleeve firmly against the tubing.

FLEXIBLE METAL CONDUIT

There are two basic differences between BX and conduit: BX is flexible; conduit, whether regular or EMT, is not. BX comes complete with wires; with conduit, you must fish the wires through.

One type of flexible metal conduit has some of the characteristics of both BX and conduit. It is as flexible as BX, but it does not come complete with wires. You must fish them through as you would with conduit. Flexible metal conduit is available in two types: plain and plastic covered. The plastic covered is preferable if there is any possibility that the conduit will be exposed to harmful fumes such as gasoline vapor, or to oil or chemicals.

Plain (left) and plastic-coated (right) flexible-metal conduit.

Flexible metal conduit, sometimes called Greenfield, must be supported more than regular conduit, and, in fact, as much as BX. For home use, EMT is preferable since it is just as easy to install and also costs less. However, there are some situations in which flexible metal conduit is desirable. If you must connect a power line to some component that shakes or vibrates, such as a motor, use Greenfield since conduit simply will not absorb such punishment. If you are unable to bend conduit or if you must make a very difficult bend, you may find it advantageous to use flexible metal conduit for that particular section.

Couplings and connectors for flexible-metal conduit. Unit at left is for connecting two sections of Greenfield. The coupling shown in the center is for joining rigid conduit to flexible conduit. The electrical part at the right is a box connector for joining flexible conduit to an electric box.

HARDWARE FOR FLEXIBLE STEEL CONDUIT

You can join two separate lengths of flexible steel conduit by using a screw-type coupling. Fit the ends of the conduit into the coupling and tighten the four machine screws mounted directly on the coupling. When making such a union, butt the two ends of the flexible conduit against each other inside the coupling before tightening it.

You can also use a coupling for joining a section of rigid conduit to flexible conduit. The coupling is threaded at one end to accept threaded rigid conduit. At the other end of the coupling, you will find a pair of machine screws. Insert the flexible conduit into the coupling, tighten the screws, and the union is complete.

You can also obtain box connectors for joining flexible conduit to an electric box. One end of the conductor is threaded. Insert this end into the box through any one of the knockouts and fasten it on the inside with a locknut. The other end of the box connector is open to receive the flexible conduit. A single machine screw mounted at that end of the box connector will hold the flexible conduit in place.

ARMORED-CABLE FITTINGS

Some electric boxes are made specifically for armored-cable fittings with screw clamps located immediately inside the box adjacent to knockouts. These cable fittings are clamps for holding the armored cable in position. The trouble with such clamps is that they take up room inside the box and so it is sometimes better to use a cable connector that fits directly into the knockout hole. These cable connectors slip right over the BX and are held in position with a machine screw that is part of the connector. You can also get connectors that form a sharp turn in case you want to connect BX that makes a right angle with the box, and connectors that can accommodate two cables at the same time.

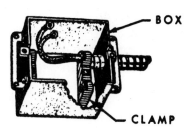

Some boxes come equipped with internal clamps for use on BX. Clamps are removable. Use a connector that fits into knockout space if you need maximum room inside the box.

Connectors for fastening BX to electric boxes, with typical connector at left top. Fit BX through connector and then through knockout hole in box. Tighten machine screw on connector to hold BX in place. Then fasten locknuts on connector, outside and inside the box to hold connector securely to box. When cable and connector are tight, you can then make wire splice of ends to be put inside box. For BX that must make right angle turn to get into box, use curved connector, upper right. You can bring two cables into box with two-cable connector (lower left). Always use antishort bushing after cutting Bx (lower right).

After cutting BX, you will find that the armor has sharp edges. Because of the inward pressure of the cutting tool when cutting BX, a part of the cable's edge will be inward and so just some slight flexing of the wire will cut it. To prevent this, use an antishort bushing. This is an insulating bushing that slides eight over the exposed wires. Push it into place between the wires and the BX.

WIRE CONNECTORS

There are three widely used methods for joining wires to each other or to some terminal: To join wires, twist them together to form a splice. To join wires to a connector, you can either solder them to a terminal or use a soldering lug, or else you can fasten the wire (or wires) to a terminal by using a screw or bolt.

There are many kinds of fastenings and so the best step is to browse electrical and hardware shops for the types you want. The fasteners we show across the top part of the illustration are just two of the many kinds available. However, they all work in much the same way. Strip the wire and insert the bare end of the wire into the fastener. The fastener will have one screw, as in the drawing at the top left; or two, as in the drawing at top right. Usually such fasteners are suitable only for solid wire, not for stranded. If you must use stranded wire, tin the exposed end of the wire all around so that it assumes the shape and appearance of solid wire. The screws used in this hardware may be setscrews, or regular machine screws. The machine screws are often flat-head types with a single slot for a regular screwdriver.

In the second row, the item at the left is a soldering lug, with an opening into which you can insert the wire. Tin the wire with solder before inserting. After inserting the wire, heat the end of the soldering lug and solder it to the wire. The lug has a circular opening at its flat end so you can slip this over a screw that may be part of the device to which you want to connect the wire.

The center illustration shows a spring-loaded connector. To connect the wire you must with your finger press down on the top of the connector, push the wire through the hole in the connector, and then remove your finger. A spring at the bottom of the connector will then push up against the wire. The advantage of such a device is that you can make connections extremely quickly. However, it does present two problems. It is very unsatisfactory for moderate or large currents—that is, for currents of half an ampere or more. Another disadvantage is that in time the spring will become weaker, thus reducing the tension and gradually making the connection a poorer one.

The drawing at the center right shows a typical wire connection to a terminal. This is a form that is commonly used. You will find such screw-fastening arrangements on light switches, on sockets, on fuse boxes, and on some electric boxes. They are quick, convenient, and effective.

The drawing at the bottom shows the slotted-bolt method of making a connection. Bare the end of the wire, put it in the slot, and then fasten with a nut or bolt. This method permits you to fasten a wire to some terminal, and also to fasten several wires at the same time. It is also a quick way of joining wires if you don't want to splice them.

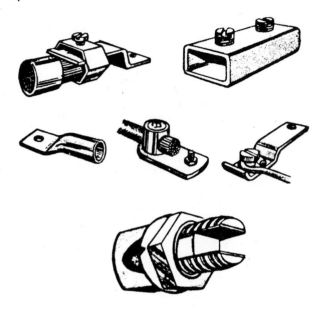

Various types of wire connectors.

REFLECTORS AND SHADES

There are various kinds of reflectors. They resemble light shades somewhat but are different from those normally used with lamps. The purpose of a lampshade is to diffuse the light and also to concentrate it within a specific area. A reflector has a hard surface, does not spread the light, but is used to focus it. Reflectors are sometimes used in work areas, particularly over a basement workbench. Reflectors are often made of metal, coated green on the outside and white on the inside. The drawing shows two types, but essentially they are the same.

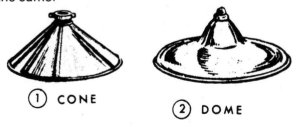

① CONE   ② DOME

(1) Cone and (2) dome reflectors: Depending on the type used, no mechanical attachment is required, and the cones and domes can be held in place by the bulbs whose light they reflect.

FLOODLIGHTS

Home wiring includes facilities for lighting outside the home as well as inside. You may, for example, in addition to the usual outside lights for front and garage doors, have occasion to use a floodlight in order to cover an outside area with high intensity light. A spotlight is a form of floodlight, and belongs to the same family, but consists of a single bulb that focuses the light on a much smaller area.

You can get both floods and spots in clusters of two or three lights, mounted on swivel holders. The swivel feature is desirable since it will let you position the lights for maximum effectiveness. Floodlights usually come equipped with some sort of reflecting shade and are mounted on a swivel. Spots, however, are generally not accompanied by shades.

There are several precautions necessary when using floods and spots. These bulbs have much higher wattage ratings than ordinary in-home electric lights and get extremely hot after working a short time. If you must unscrew such a bulb, make sure it is off long enough to cool. If you use an extension cord for floods, make sure the wire has the capacity to carry the current required by the floods. If, for example, your floods require a total of 2 kilowatts, then the current I is equal to the power (W) divided by the voltage (E). In this example, I equals W/E equals 2,000/117 equals 17.09 amperes. That's a hefty current. The connecting wire should be able to safely carry at least 20 amperes, preferably more; the usual extension cord cannot take this kind of punishment.

Floodlights may come as single units, as shown, or in clusters of two or three. They are generally mounted on swivel bases. Floods and spots require much more current than ordinary in-house bulbs.

117

TRANSFORMERS

Transformers are used in the home for operating bells, buzzers, and chimes. At one time no. 6 dry cells were used, but unlike the battery, the transformer never needs to be recharged, and normally never needs to be replaced during the lifetime of a house.

A transformer has no moving parts. The home type has two coils: a primary coil of wire and a secondary coil. These coils are wound over an iron core. One of the coils, the primary, is connected to the 117-volt power line. The other coil, the secondary, is wired to the bell, buzzer, or chimes. A switch is connected into the secondary winding. When the switch is pushed or depressed, it closes, permitting current to flow through the bell, buzzer or chime and to produce sound.

These transformers are step-down types since they reduce the line voltage to a smaller amount, usually somewhere between 6 and 12 volts, depending on the voltage requirement of the bell, buzzer, or chimes. The transformers are small, inexpensive, and can be mounted where most convenient (usually in the basement).

The input to the transformer—that is, the connections of the power line to the primary—is AC. The output voltage delivered by the secondary winding, the lower voltage, is also AC. The amount of current demanded by bells, buzzers, and chimes is quite small and is ordinarily a fraction of an ampere.

6 VOLT BUZZER LEADS

120 VOLT LINE LEADS

Bell-ringing transformer: This is just one of many different styles, but they all work in the same way. Some transformers have a built-in clamp as part of the outside metal frame of the transformer to make mounting much easier. You can mount transformers in any position—horizontal, vertical, sideways. When connecting wire leads to the primary and secondary, splice and solder the joining wires as described earlier. Transformer is quiet and there are no moving parts.

WALL PLATES

When you mount a switch or a receptacle into a wall-type electric box, the only part of the switch that should show will be the handle and the only part of the receptacle will be the plug-in surface area. To make the outlet or switch more attractive and to protect against accidental shock, the boxes are covered with wall plates. A wall plate may be metal or can be an insulating material such as plastic or porcelain. The least expensive are metal plates, made of thin steel, and covered on the outside with white enamel. More elaborate—and more expensive—plates are available in brass-coated metal or in mirror glass and some are very artistic.

Wall plates are available in numerous arrangements. You can have wall plates for single, double, or triple switches; for single or duplex outlets, or for combinations of switches and outlets. Switch wall plates are held in position by two machine screws, one above and the other below the switch handle. Receptacle plates are held in place by a single machine screw in the center of the plate.

Wall plates, also known as surface plates, are sometimes also called 2-gang plates if designed for two receptacles, and 3-gang plates if intended for three.

RECEPTACLES

Probably the most common receptacle is the type that will accommodate a pair of parallel prongs mounted on a plug. But the name of the game in electrical hardware is variety, so you will find all sorts of receptacles. There is just one requirement. The design of the plug must follow the design of the receptacle, or the plug will not fit.

SINGLE RECEPTACLE WITH TANDEM BLADES

The blades in a receptacle are the metal parts of the receptacle that mate or make contact with the prongs of the plug. The drawing (upper left) shows a receptacle with tendem blades and a U-shaped ground. This means that the grounding prong on the plug will have a U shape as well. These receptacles are available in two sizes for home use: 0 to 15 amperes, 240 volts, for small air conditioners (or similar appliances) and 21 to 30 amperes, 240 volts, for larger air conditioners.

The purpose of the tandem arrangement for the blades is to keep you from plugging in a 120-volt appliance into a 240-volt socket. Air conditioners draw substantial currents and so it is a good idea for them to have the luxury of their own outlets. In addition, these outlets are specifically designed not to permit the use of cube taps or extension cords.

 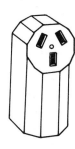

Single receptacle with tandem blades and U-shaped ground (upper left); single receptacle with horizontal and vertical blades with U-shaped ground (upper right); surface-type receptacle with L-shaped ground (lower left); and surface-type receptacle with offset blades and rectangular ground (lower right). (Courtesy, Sears).

SINGLE RECEPTACLE WITH HORIZONTAL AND VERTICAL BLADES

Another type of receptacle (upper right) uses horizontal and vertical blades and has an opening for a U-shaped grounding prong. This receptacle is intended for 240-volt equipment drawing up to 20 amperes. The plug for this receptacle will not fit the receptacle previously described, or any parallel-blade receptacle. Again, the design of the receptacle is such that plugs used with 120-volt equipment will not fit.

When buying appliafces having tandem blade plugs or plugs with horizontal and verticle blades, you should be aware that you will require corresponding receptacles. Further, these receptacles must be wired to a 240-volt branch and so there is more to buying an appliance than just making the purchase. You must be able to plug in the unit to a proper source of voltage and current.

SURFACE RECEPTACLES

The next drawing (lower left) shows a surface-type receptacle with an L-shaped ground. The corresponding plug will have an L-shaped plug to fit. This type of receptacle is often used with standard driers and is intended for 120-240 volts and with currents of 30 amperes or less.

The next surface receptacle (lower right) uses offset blades—that is, blades that are not parallel to each other, but form a small angle. The ground is a rectangular shape. This receptacle is used with high-speed driers and electric ranges and is intended for equipment using 120/240 volts and currents of 50 amperes or less.

OUTDOOR RECEPTACLES

These should always be designed for grounding of the outdoor appliance to be used and so must be three-hole types. The outlets can be mounted in the building wall and have a spring-loaded drop cover that falls into place automatically when the plug is removed. The purpose of the cap is to keep rain from entering the receptacle.

MISCELLANEOUS HARDWARE

There are so many different kinds of hardware that listing and describing them all would require a catalog. Those we show in the drawings will give you some idea of a few of the those items that are available.

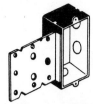

Converts fuse box into automatic circuit breaker. Just screw into fuse socket. Trips at once on overloads, but takes temporary overloads in stride. (Such as washer, etc.). Colored trip ring points out blown Circuit Saver. Simply push button to restore to use.

Octagon boxes for use with fixture or junction outlets. These are for use with conduit, or armored or non-metallic cable. Available in steel with half-inch knockouts or with cable clamps. Important hint: use bar hangers with studs wherever ceiling fixtures are to be installed. Recommended for in-home use.

Use steel boxes for switch, receptacle and bracket outlets in the home. Available with or without clamps. Gang two or more by removing one side plate on each box. Then hook boxes together.

Steel outlet or switch boxes with wall mounting bracket. Mount brackets to allow correct depth for lath (or sheetrock), plaster or paneling. Available for use with connectors or with handy built-in clamps. Warning: use only in new work.

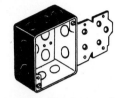

Plug and cartridge fuses with safety valves to protect wires against overloads. Fuse amperage should never exceed amperage capacity of the wire you are using.

At left: beveled corner box. Fits into wall opening in old buildings. Has clamps for loom or non-metallic sheathed cable. No connector needed. Side-bracket box (center) used with cover (right) in new work, wherever extra space is needed for wires. Used for switches, receptacles, bracket outlets. Combination ½ and ¾-inch knockouts, requires connectors. Use with armored, non-metallic or plastic cable, or with conduit.

Fuse devices—designed to protect low ampere capacity motors on appliances, power tools, etc. Fit standard switch boxes. Device on the right has fuse holder for lag fuse; also a receptacle with "U"-shape ground. Device on the left has a fuse holder for lag fuse and a toggle switch.

Bakelite toggle switch and plate fits any standard switch box. Choice of single-pole, 3-way or 4-way types, ivory or brown finish. Available too, in silent "Mercury" type, for bed and sick rooms. Also comes in illuminated type. Tiny bulb glows in the dark.

Bakelite duplex wall outlet and plate. Fits any standard flush or surface mounted switch box. Has mounting bracket for aligning with wall surface.

Clock outlet with hanger. The receptacle is recessed to hold both plug and wire. This permits electric clock to hang flush with any wall surface.

Porcelain pull chain outlet with receptacle. Fits any octagon box. Receptacle always "alive." Use porcelain to protect against rust and corrosion in damp places.

Dryer or range pigtails and receptacles are more convenient than permanent type because appliances can be moved easily for cleaning. Receptacle connects from entrance switch.

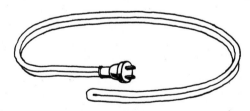

Weatherproof receptacles, switches and boxes for outdoor use. Receptacles, with weatherproof snap covers, come in single and duplex types. Switches available in single and 3-way. Boxes available with four ½-inch openings. Use these outdoor devices for decorative lighting, Christmas lighting, for temporary yard lighting, patio or garden lighting, or any other outdoor installation.

Heating cables can help prevent frozen water pipes or ice buildup in gutters. Flexible thermoplastic cables come in popular lengths.

Pipe cable comes in lengths from 6' to 30' while gutter heating cable is available in 25', 50', 75' or 100' lengths. Prevent costly repairs of frozen pipes or ice damaged gutters and ceilings.

The right kind of electrical hardware can make a repair or an installation much easier. (Courtesy, Sears.)

Chapter 7

HOW TO MAKE ELECTRIC INSTALLATIONS

There are all sorts of electrical jobs needed in the home, ranging from nothing more than replacing a fuse, to the installation of new wiring and additional appliances. You should be able to do many electrical jobs yourself; for others you may need the help of a professional electrician. But even if you must call in outside help, your knowledge of electrical work will not only enable you to understand more completely the details of a proposed change or repair, but you will be in a better position to get competing bids.

HOW TO HANDLE BX

Generally, for home-wiring changes or repairs, BX is much easier to handle than EMT or rigid wall conduit. You do not need to thread BX, you do not need to fish wires through it, and because it is flexible, it is easy to make bends with it. When you do buy BX, make sure it has a ground wire running through it, in addition to the usual white ground wire.

Just because you can bend BX does not mean there are no limits. Don't try to square off the cable—that is, to make a sharp right-angle turn. If anything, make the turn as gradual as possible to avoid damaging the armor. Once adjacent turns of armor separate, there will be no way in which you will be able to get the armor back into its original position.

SUPPORTING BX

If you are doing a new installation and want to use BX "in wall," you can drill through holes in the

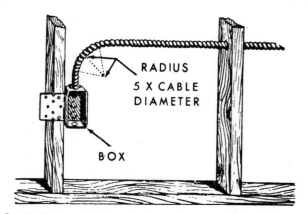

Do not make excessively sharp bends in BX cable.

joists (the studs), but make such holes at least ⅛" larger in diameter than the diameter of the BX so that you can pull the BX through without difficulty.

When running BX along a beam, you can use BX staples of the kind shown in the preceding chapter. The usual routine is to support the BX with staples every 4½', but if the BX shows a tendency to sag, double the number of staples by hammering one in about every 2'. In any event, whenever you bring BX into an electric box, make sure that BX has some support not more than 12" away from the box. The reason for this is to avoid any mechanical strain on splices located in the box.

There is just one other important precaution. For the most part, when cutting BX you will be measuring BX to connect from one electric box to another. Do not make the cable too short. If you do, you will find yourself tempted to splice and add on. Don't do it. Cut a completely new section of BX and save the piece you have presumably spoiled for a shorter run.

HOW TO PREPARE AND ATTACH BX

The easiest and fastest tool to use for cutting BX is a special BX cutter designed for that purpose. However, you can use a hacksaw and still do an effective job. When using the hacksaw, take two preliminary steps. Use a reasonably new hacksaw blade. Some blades are better and more durable than others, have sharper teeth, and are designed to cut through tough metal. Your job will be easier if you use one of these instead of "bargain-basement" type of hacksaw blade. When inserting the hacksaw blade into the hacksaw frame, make sure the teeth point away from the handle. Also make sure the blade is in tight and that it does not bend or curve along its length. Hacksaw blades can and do snap if they are not inserted or used properly.

Cut across the BX at an angle (left), and when the blade is almost through the armor (right), bend the cable back and forth until it snaps. The armor will break before the wires. You can then cut both wires with diagonal cutters.

As a first step, measure the length of BX you will need to use. Include all bends and make some allowance for the fact that the BX may not follow an absolutely straight line when installed.

Cut through the BX with the hacksaw blade at right angles to the armor. It is better to use a vise to hold the cable when cutting. This is a preparatory step to cutting the BX to the correct length.

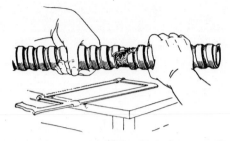

Once the BX has been cut to the right length, hacksaw a section about 8'' from the end by making a circular notch all the way around the armor. When the notching action is almost completed, grip the armor and twist and you will find that the small section, 8'' long, will come off in your hand. The wires of the BX and the paper wrapping will now be exposed.

You can cut through BX by holding it, but this is awkward, and you may get cut. Use a vise; and then cut at right angles to the armor strip.

Once you have cut the cable to what should be the correct length, you will need to use the hacksaw again, but this time just to remove the armor. Cut the armor about 8'' from the end so that you will have ample wire to go inside the electric box. This time you will need to cut very carefully or you will also cut through the enclosed wire. One way of doing this is to put the BX in a vise, with an 8'' length extending beyond the end of the vise. This time cut at right angles to the cable—that is, with the blade of the hacksaw right up against the vise. In this way you will be using the vise as a guide. Do not let the hacksaw blade cut continually at one spot but move the blade so that you cut a sort of semicircle. Make your strokes light and do not exert too much pressure. You will be able to tell when the blade begins to get through the armor since the armor will then tend to grip the blade, making it more difficult to move. Now loosen the vise, and rotate the armor. Continue cutting, again in semicircular form.

When you finish, you will have cut a circle around the armor, at right angles to the armor. Gently, keep deepening the cut. Finally, the notch in the BX will be so deep that you will be able to bend the cable back and forth, breaking the armor at the cut. If some of the armor still remains unbroken, cut it away with the hacksaw. This job isn't difficult to do, but it does take patience and practice.

After you have cut the armor, pull it off carefully so as not to cut the wires. You will find paper wrapped around the wires. unwrap the paper from the full length of the exposed wires and cut it away with the scissors.

Unwrap the paper that surrounds the exposed ends of the wire. You can cut it away with scissors.

You now have completed one end of the BX. Do the same job with the other end. When you have finished, some of the edges of the BX may be very rough. File these with a flat file. Again, you must be careful not to damage the insulation on the wires. You are now ready to insert insulated antishorting bushings at each end of the BX. Slide the bushing over the wires and then insert the bushing so it fits snugly between the wires and the inside of the BX armor.

After you have removed the paper around the wires, insert the insulated bushing. If the bushing will not fit, reach into the inside of the cable with a small pair of scissors and cut away more of the paper. The extra space will now let you put the bushing into position.

ATTACHING BX TO AN ELECTRIC BOX

Your BX is now ready for the next step. Slide a cable connector over the BX so that the threaded portion of the connector faces the exposed wires of the cable. On the connector you will find a machine screw. Tighten this screw and this will hold the connector firmly against the BX.

Slide a cable connector over the end of the BX and fasten the connector into place. The connector comes equipped with a machine screw. When you tighten this screw, you will also be tightening the connector firmly against the BX.

Knock out one of the holes in the electric box. The idea is to select a knockout that will be closest to the BX and will not require any bends in the cable. Push the wires through the hole and also the threaded portion of the connector. Put a locknut over the wires that are now inside the box and attach it to the threaded connector. Turn the locknut with your fingers until it is right up against the inside of the electric box.

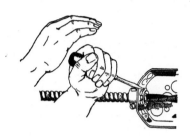

After the locknut on the inside of the box is partially screwed onto the threaded position with a screwdriver. Put the blade of the screwdriver against one of the extensions of the locknut and tap the end of the screwdriver with the palm of your hand.

The locknut isn't smooth and round but has small metallic protrusions or fingers around its outer edge. Put a screwdriver against one of these protrusions and strike the end of the driver. This will tighten the locknut firmly on the cable connector

The BX cable is now fastened to the electric box.

INSTALLING NON-METALLIC SHEATHED CABLE

You can connect non-metallic sheathed cable to an electric box even more easily than BX, while using the same connection method. Strip the ends of the cable so that the wires are exposed, and attach a connector to the cable. Unlike connectors for BX, connectors for non-metallic cable often have two screws. Tighten both of these and then push the connector through the previously prepared hole in the electric box. Unlike BX, there is no paper insulation to remove and there is no need to use an insulated bushing.

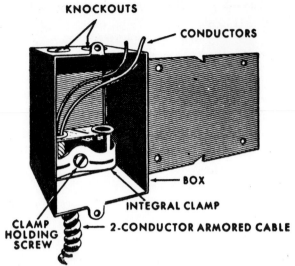

KNOCKOUTS

CONDUCTORS

BOX

INTEGRAL CLAMP

CLAMP HOLDING SCREW

2-CONDUCTOR ARMORED CABLE

You can use an electric box with a built-in clamp to hold one or two lengths of BX.

After you have pushed the cable connector through the hole in the box, put on a locknut. Rotate the locknut with your fingers until it makes contact with the inside of the box, and then use a screwdriver to fasten it more tightly, following the procedure described earlier. Connect the ground wire of the cable to a ground clamp inside the box or to any screw terminal inside the box that is part of the box. If you are using BX, you should also connect the wire to a ground terminal in the box.

HOW TO USE INTEGRAL CLAMPS

An easier way of connecting BX to an electric box is to select a box having an integral clamp. This type of clamp is built into the box. Bring the BX directly through a knockout hole in the box so that the metal armor of the cable fits into the clamp, as shown. The two conductors can fit through a hole right above the clamp. You can fasten the BX into place by tightening just one screw. Integral clamps are made to hold either one or two BX cables. Their disadvantage is that they take up room inside the box. You must also use insulated bushings at the end of the BX, whether you use integral clamps or external cable connectors.

COMBINED BX AND CONDUIT

You can intermix BX and conduit if you want, with both types going to the same box. Thus, for a short run having a bend you might want to take advantage of the flexibility of BX. For a longer, straight run, you might decide to use EMT.

LIGHT SWITCHING METHODS

The most common switch in the home is the SPST type. It can be used to control a single light,

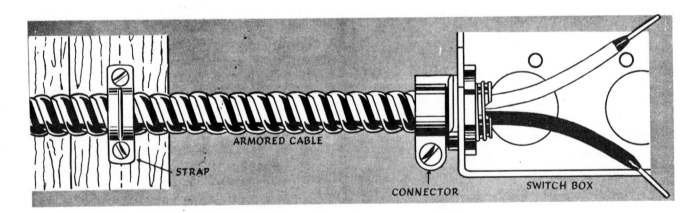

ARMORED CABLE

STRAP

CONNECTOR

SWITCH BOX

Details of armored cable fastened to an electric box: Note support (at left) for the cable. There are various kinds of connectors for joining the cable to the box. The one shown here is typical. BX is intended for indoor use only and may only be joined to steel electric boxes, not plaxtic. Be sure to insert fiber bushing at end of cable inside box. Cable support, shown at left in drawing, should be within 12″ of the box. (Courtesy, Sears.)

or a group of lights connected in-parallel. The illustration shows an SPST switch controlling three lights marked a, b, and c. The lights are independent of each other—that is, any one or more can be removed and the remaining light or lights will not be affected. When the switch is open, none of the lights will glow. When the switch is closed, all three will burn, assuming they are all in good condition and are in their respective sockets.

With this arrangement, the amount of current flowing through the switch will depend on two factors. The first is the number of bulbs being controlled; and the second, the wattage rating of the bulbs. If each bulb is rated at 100 watts, and all three are burning, then the total power consumption will be 100 times 3 equals 300 watts. Divide the wattage by the voltage to get an estimate of the current flow. 300/117 equals 2.56 amperes. This is the current required by all three lamps. Each takes only one-third this amount.

In the series arrangement, shown in the next drawing, each light is controlled by a separate switch. The bulbs are still independent of each other and you can have one or all bulbs working. In the shunt arrangement, however, the only way you can get independent operation is by removing a bulb. Essentially, that is what you do when the switches are in series with the bulbs, except that it is easier to open and close a switch than to remove bulbs.

In the next drawing we have a combination of the first two arrangements. Switch A controls bulb a and that is the only light bulb it does control. Switch B controls five different lamps but switch B must be closed before any of these five will light. Switch C is the same arrangment as switch B, while switch D is the same setup as switch A. Thus, the way in which you connect bulbs to switches will determine your control. The best thing to do is to make a sketch or circuit of just how many bulbs you want to control and then determine just how many switches you will need for that purpose.

HOW TO REPLACE A SWITCH

This is one of the easiest electrical jobs you can do around the house. You may want to replace an old-style pushbutton type switch or the existing switch may have decided to call it quits. Whatever the reason, you should be able to tackle this job with confidence.

Shut off power to the switch. Do not rely only on turning the switch to its off position, for voltage is available at the switch whether it is on or off. If you cannot locate the fuse that controls voltage to this branch, simply open the main switch or main breaker in the fuse or breaker box.

Unscrew the two machine screws that hold the face plate in position. If the plate is on a wall that has been painted, you may find the paint holding the plate even after the screws are out. Just cut around the edges of the plate with a small knife to loosen the paint.

After you have removed the face plate, you will see the switch in its box. It is held in place with two screws, one at the top and the other at the bottom. Remove these screws. You should now be able to pull the switch out of the box. It won't fall because it will be supported by its connecting wires. Examine the wires and note just how they are connected. If you can't rely on memory, make a small sketch.

Loosen the screws holding the wires. The screws may not turn all the way, since they may be captive types. In that case, unscrew them as much as possible, and then, with long-nose pliers, undo the loops at the ends of the wires.

You can now remove the switch. To replace it, follow the same procedure, but in reverse order. Loosen the screws on the side of the new switch and connect the wires. The wires should have the same positioning as on the old switch.

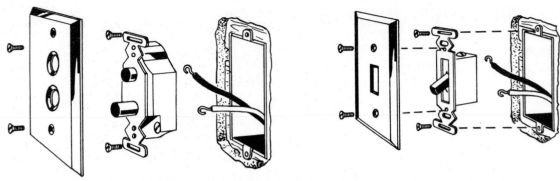

Remove 2 screws to disconnect switch plate; then remove 2 screws holding switch to box. Install new switch, using same wire hook-up as before

How to replace a toggle switch. (Courtesy, Sears.)

After the wires are connected and you have tightened the wire-holding screws, push the switch back into its box. You will have new screws for holding the switch in position, and these will fit through slotted holes at the top and bottom of the switch. Tighten these screws, but not all the way—just enough to hold the switch in position. With the help of a flashlight, examine the switch and make absolutely sure that none of the wires or side screws on the switch touch the metal sides of the electric box. Also make sure the switch is vertical and doesn't tilt to one side.

If you are satisfied, turn power on by putting back the fuse or closing the circuit breaker in the main fuse or breaker box. Try the switch. With the toggle of the switch in the down position, the light it controls should be off; in the up position, the light should be on. If, however, the reverse situation applies, it just means you have transposed the wire connections to the switch. If that is the case, you can do either of two things. You can ignore it, for the switch will work equally well if its toggle-operating conditions are reversed; or, you can shut the power off once again, unscrew the switch, and transpose the leads.

If you simply want to replace the face plate on a switch, there is no need to shut off the power. Remove the two screws holding the old plate, take off the plate, and put in a new one.

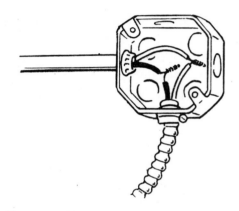

In this setup, conduit is brought into the left side of the box; BX is brought into the bottom. Note that inside the box the black wire of the conduit is spliced to the black wire of the BX; the white wires of both are also connected.

SHUNT CONNECTIONS

The words shunt or parallel were used earlier in connection with batteries as a means of connecting them for maximum current output. Shunt (or parallel) are also used for wiring and loads, but with a completely different meaning.

The basic power line feeding electricity to your home consists of a pair of wires. Any device or component attached across these wires is in shunt with the power line. The connections to a light bulb, for example, consist of a pair of wires. One of these wires is somehow joined to the black wire of the power line; the other, to the white wire. When this is done, the electric light bulb is then said to be shunted across the power line. Of course, this also applies to all electrical devices you have in your home: other lights, radio sets, a television receiver, broiler, toaster, electric heater, electric shaver, and so on. This means, then, that every convenience outlet in your home is connected to the power line so that it is in shunt with it.

There is a very good reason for having this basic electrical arrangement. You can shunt as many appliances across the power line as you want. You can connect or disconnect an appliance any time you wish without affecting any other appliance. Thus, with the shunt setup, each appliance is independent of any other appliance.

The purpose of a shunt connection is to deliver electrical power to a load. For this reason you would never put a fuse in shunt with the power line. A fuse is not a load, but when shunted across the line, represents a short circuit. A short circuit, incidentally, is also a shunt connection. For the same reason you would never connect a switch in shunt with the power line. When the switch is in its closed position, it would represent a short across the power line. With this information on hand, we can now set up some rules that will help in wiring and in making electrical repairs.

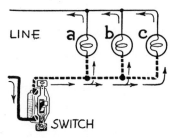

The three lamps are in shunt or parallel. The single switch is in series with all three lamps. This single switch can turn all three lamps on or off at the same time.

SHUNT RULES

1. Never connect a fuse in shunt with the power line.

2. Never connect a switch in shunt with the power line.

3. Never connect a wire or any other current-carrying conductor (such as a bit of scrap metal) in shunt with the power line.

4. All appliances, regardless of how much or how little current they draw, are put in shunt with the power line.

5. When an appliance is plugged into a convenience outlet, it is automatically put in shunt with the power line.

6. Since all appliances are in shunt with the power line, they are also in shunt with each other.

7. The larger the number of active appliances that are plugged into convenience outlets, the greater is the total load, and the greater the total amount of current taken from the line.

The drawing shows three lamps shunted across the AC power line. This is a simplified illustration, for the lamps might be in some sort of fixture, each of which might be controlled by a switch, not shown in this picture. Instead of lamps, you could have appliances or a combination of appliances and lamps.

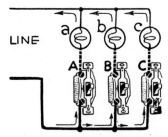

Each switch is now in series with each individual lamp and so each lamp can be turned on or off, independently of the other lamps.

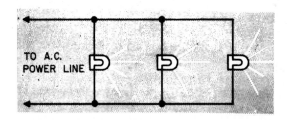

The shunt wiring system is used for supplying electrical power to all in-home lamps and appliances.

THE SERIES CONNECTION

Series connections were also discussed in the section on batteries as a means of wiring batteries to get more voltage. The series connection is also used in electrical wiring, but in a different context.

In a series connection, one side of the line is opened and the load—three lamps in this example—are inserted. If any one of the lamps is removed, current flow is stopped and all lamps go off.

In a series connection, one leg of the power line is opened and the load, an appliance or one or more lights, are inserted. But if any one of these are removed, the flow of current is interrupted and all appliances and bulbs are turned off. Thus, in a series connection, all the components, bulbs, and appliances are interdependent. They must all work, or none. With such a connection you cannot turn on one bulb, or two, and have the othrs remain off. Your electric sewing machine, broiler, refrigerator, washer, vacuum cleaner would all need to be on at the same time. For house wiring, then, the series connection is impractical, yet it does have some uses.

Switches and fuses are inserted in series with the hot line of a two-wire system. Note the difference between an outlet and a switch. An outlet is shunted across the two-wire line. One wire of the outlet is connected to the white ground wire; the other wire of the outlet is connected to the black "hot" wire. But the two leads of the power line are not broken open. With a switch, however, the black or "hot" lead is opened and the switch is inserted. One terminal of the switch is connected to one of the open ends of the black lead; the other terminal of the switch is connected to the other end of the black lead. The white or ground lead is not opened, and, if anything, every effort is made to have the white ground lead a continuous run.

SERIES RULES

1. Never wire appliances in series.
2. Do not wire electric lights in series. One possible exception could be Christmas tree lights, but these come already wired in series.
3. Wire fuses and switches in series with the "hot" wire of the power branch.

HOW TO CONNECT A DUPLEX CONVENIENCE OUTLET

If you will examine an outlet, you will see that it has one or two pairs of screws to which wires are to be connected. One of these screws will be brass colored; the other white or nickel colored, or with a nickel finish. Connect the hot lead coming out of the cable to the brass-colored terminal screw on the outlet. Connect the other lead, the white lead of the cable, to the other screw. This screw most often has a nickel finish.

After you have connected these two wires, push the outlet into the receptacle box (electric box). Near the top and bottom of the receptacle, you will find a pair of captive screws. Use these to fasten the receptacle into the box. You can adjust the receptacle so that it is perfectly straight. As a final step, fasten the wall plate to the receptacle. Use a single small machine screw that passes through a center hole in the wall plate. The screw fastens the wall plate to the receptacle.

The arrangement just described is for a condition in which the two wires of the cable terminate at the convenience outlet.

Assume, however, that the cable is to continue on to some other section, possibly another convenience outlet. If you will examine the convenience receptacle, you will see it has not two, but four screws. Examine the screws carefully and you will see that each pair on each side is joined by a strip of metal. The receptacle may have the word "white" stamped on the back, near the screws having a nickel finish. Be sure to connect the white lead to either of these screws. Now connect the black lead to either of the brass-finished screws on the other side.

You will also find a grounding screw on the bottom of the receptacle. Connect the grounding wire that accompanies the two-wire power line to this screw.

Most convenience outlets are made with four screws, two on each side. You can use such an outlet as a termination type, or a line-continuation type. For line termination, use just two screws, one on each side. For continuation, use all four screws.

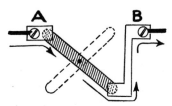

Action of a single-pole, single-throw switch. The pole connects point A to point B, or opens the circuit between these two points.

SWITCHING CIRCUITS

The most commonly used switch in the home is the single-pole, single-throw type. The drawing shows how this switch is connected into the black or hot wire. Point A is one end of the hot wire; point B, the other end. The shaded connection shows how point A is connected to B. Point B is attached to a length of metal and when the switch is closed, the end of this metal conductor and the metal piece at point A are connected. When the switch is opened, the pole moves into the position represented by the dashed lines. There is no connection between A and B and the black wire is then effectively open and no current can flow through the switch.

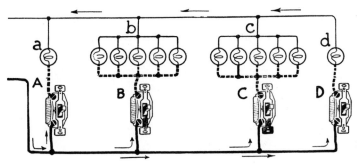

A switch can control one or more lamps. The switches and bulbs can be transposed. Thus, switch A and bulb a can exchange places and the circuit will work in the same way.

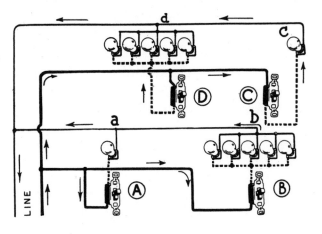

This drawing is exactly the same circuit arrangement as the preceding one.

In the next drawing we have four SPST switches, marked A, B, C, and D. Lamp a is a single unit as is lamp d. Examine that part of the circuit consisting of lamp a and switch A. There are several things you should note about this switch-bulb setup. First, the top, unbroken, thin horizontal line represents the ground wire. Not only is bulb a directly attached to this wire, but all the other bulbs as well. Also, note that none of the switches—A, B, C, or D—is connected to ground. The thick horizontal line across the bottom is the "hot" lead.

One terminal of switch A is wired directly to the hot line. The other terminal of switch A is connected to one wire of the lamp. Finally, the other lead of the lamp is wired to the ground wire of the two-wire power line. Lamp a is in a terminating receptacle. This receptacle can have either two or four screws; if four, just two are used.

Note particularly what happens when switch A is closed. This has the effect of connecting lamp a directly to the hot lead of the power line. But the other lead of lamp a is already attached to the ground wire of the power line. Thus, when switch A is closed, lamp a is put directly in parallel or shunt with the two wires of the power line. But what about switch A? It is in series with an extension or wire coming from the hot lead of the power line. And when switch A is closed, it can be represented by a solid connection directly across it.

Now consider the next circuit, consisting of switch B and five lamps, identified by the letter b. Each of these lamps is plugged into a convenience outlet. These are *not* terminating types since there are a pair of wires connecting each of the outlets to each other.

Examine the connection going across the top of each of the five lamps. This is the ground wire and permanently connects the ground screws of the receptacles to the ground wire. The dashed line beneath the five bulbs represents the hot lead. Note that this hot lead runs from one convenience outlet to the next. However, it also connects to switch B. The other side of switch B is wired to a branch wire connected to the hot lead. When switch B is open, none of the lamps will light. When it is closed, they will all light.

Circuits C and D are repeats of A and B. This is true of most home electrical wiring, for it consists of nothing more than the same circus repeated over and over again. If you can understand and set up one, you can do two; and if you can do two, you can do as many as you wish.

The next drawing shows one possible arrangement for an in-home switching circuit. It looks a little complicated, but it is exactly the same as the preceding illustration. Once again we have four switches. The heavy black line is the hot lead of the two wire line; the thinner line is the ground or cold wire. Four switches are used—A, B, C, and D—and these switches control single lamps or groups. The purpose of showing you this drawing is to let you see that a wiring plan can be made to look very complicated or can be quite simplified as in the first drawing of the same circuit setup.

HOW TO CONTROL A LIGHT AT THE END OF A RUN

If you have a lamp, possibly a wall or ceiling fixture, and want to be able to turn it on and off, you can follow the same wiring procedure described earlier in connection with switch A and light a. The feed wire, shown in the next drawing, is a branch to an existing two-wire line. The feed wire is a cable containing two, preferably three wires, one of which should be a bare grounding wire. The drawing shows only two wires, but there is a third, connect it to the grounding terminal on the electric box holding the wiring for the fixture. If you will examine the drawing, you will see one wire inside the box that has a splice. This is the ground wire or white wire. One lead of the hot wire is opened and is connected to one wire of the lamp. The other lead of the lamp is wired to a screw terminal on the switch. The other terminal of T e switch is connected to the white or ground wire.

HOW TO CONTROL A LIGHT IN THE MIDDLE OF A RUN

You can add light fixtures at any point in a run. The only advantage of switching at the end of a run is that there will be fewer wires inside the electric box, but if you follow the wiring color code, you should have no difficulties. The next drawing shows how to connect anywhere along the length of a run.

Inside the BX or conduit between the lamp's junction box and the switch you will have a pair of wires, or possibly a pair of wires plus a grounding wire. The grounding wire usually does not have insulation. Connect the black wire to the brass-finished screw on the switch, and the other end of that black wire to the black wire inside the lamp's junction box. Note that this black wire is not connected to either of the two wires coming out of the lamp.

The two wires of the lamp have not yet been connected. Now connect one of the lamp's leads, either one, to the white wire inside the lamp's junction box. Connect the remaining lead of the lamp to the white wire of the cable and the other end of this white wire inside the cable to the remaining machine screw on the switch. Finally, attach the grounding wire to the grounding screw on the lamp's receptacle and the other end to the receptacle for the switch.

Wiring, and that includes wiring of a switch to a single lamp, can be confusing. If so, go back to the earlier drawing showing a single switch A controlling a single light a. Now, looking at this diagram, here are the steps you have taken:

1. You connected one lead of the lamp to the ground wire inside the lamp's receptable.

2. You connected the other lead of the lamp to a wire going off to the switch.

3. Finally, you connected the other terminal of the switch to the hot wire of the two-wire cable; and, incidentally, you then connected the grounding wire inside the cable to both electric boxes: the one for the light and the one for the switch.

The procedure is exactly the same as for wiring a switch at the end of a run. The only difference is that you will have a cable connected to the electric box going off somewhere in some other direction.

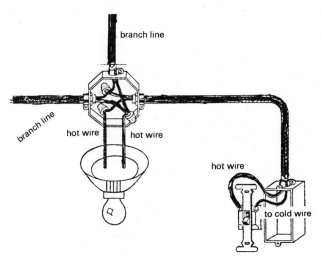

Method of connecting a switch to control a light anywhere in a run.

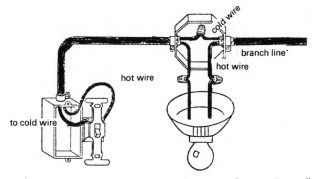

Method of connecting single-pole, single-throw switch for controlling well or ceiling fixture.

HOW TO CONTROL TWO OR MORE LIGHTS WITH ONE SWITCH

To control two or more lights either at the end of a run or anywhere along the run, follow exactly the same procedure recommended for controlling a single light at the end of a run. The first thing to remember is that the two lamps will be wired in shunt—that is, the black lead of the first lamp will be directly connected to the black lead of the other. Similarly, the white leads of both lamps will be joined. Now run the white wire from either lamp (not both) to a terminal on the switch, and connect the other switch terminal to the black wire in the cable.

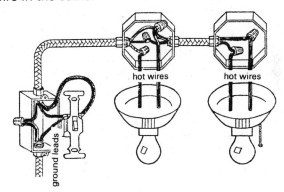

How to control two lamps with a single switch.

Since both lamps will go on and off simultaneously, you may find it convenient if one of the lamps is a pull-chain type. This will give you the option of having both lights on at the same time, or just one. However, for the pull chain to be effective, the main switch will have to be in its "on" position.

HOW TO CONTROL A LIGHT
AND A CONVENIENCE RECEPTACLE

You can control a light and convenience receptacle with a single switch by using the same wiring arrangement as you would for two lamps. Instead of a second light, however, substitute a receptacle. The receptacle will then be a switched type with power available at the receptacle when the switch is on, and only then.

HOW TO INSTALL THREE-WAY
SWITCHES

The SPST switches described so far are easy to install, but they do present one minor difficulty. If, for example, you turn the light on in a particular room, you must return to that room to be able to close the light. Sometimes this can be inconvenient. For example, you may want to turn on (or turn off) the light in an upstairs hall from downstairs or vice versa; or you may want to be able to turn on garage lights at one end of the garage and turn them off from the other end. The switch that will permit you to do this is the single-pole, double-throw type described in the preceding chapter.

The drawing shows how the three-way switch works. The pole of the switch has two possible positions. The shaded section shows how the pole connects point A to point B. An alternative position connects point A to point C. The dashed lines show the pole in this other position. Thus, point A can contact B or C, depending on the setting of the switch.

If you will examine the drawing, you will see it has three connection points compared with just two for the single-pole, single-throw switch. Also, just like the SPST switch, the SPDT switch is connected in series with the hot wire of the line. This hot lead is always attached to screw terminal A. This means, then, that the hot line will also be connected to terminals B or C, depending on the position of the pole at any moment.

There is one more difference, an important one, between installing the regular single-pole, single-throw switch and the three-way type. For the three-way type you need two switches, one in each location. If you plan, for example, to control a downstairs hall light from upstairs, you will need one switch down and the other upstairs.

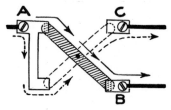

Basic operation of a single-pole, double-throw (SPDT) switch.

The drawing shows how three-way switches work. Here we have a pair of three-way switches marked S1 and S2. Points a and b at the left are connected to any branch carrying power. Switch S1 is in one location; switch S2 is in another. With the circuit as shown, the lamp will light since there is a connecting wire, 1-3, between the two switches. If the pole of S1, however, is moved so it touches point 2, the circuit will be opened, and the lamp will be off. It can be turned on again, from either the location of S1 or that of S2. To turn the lamp on again at location S1, simply press the switch so that the pole moves back to point 4. If the pole of S1 is at point 2, and you are at location S2, just press the switch so that the pole is on point 4.

This leads us to another difference between this type of switch and the usual SPST type. With the SPST, "off" is usually with the switch in the down position; "on," with it in the up position. But with the three-way switch, either up or down can be on or off, depending at any moment on the position of the pole of the second switch. Consequently, panels for such switches do not carry "on-off" designations.

Examine the illustration once again and you will see that the lamp is on when S1 is at 1 and S2 is at 3. It is also on when S1 is at 2 and S2 is at 4.

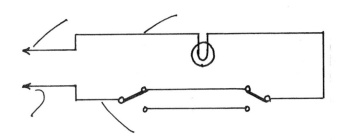

Three-way switches are used to control a light from two different locations.

CONNECTING THE THREE-WAY SWITCH

The three-way switch has three terminals on it, one of which is called the common. In the drawing, the letters A and B identify the common terminals of the switch. These correspond to terminal A in the preceding drawing. Terminals 3 and 4, and 1 and 2, also correspond to similarly identified terminals (B and C) in the preceding drawing. Connect the two switches as shown in the drawing. If you transpose the wires to 3 and 4, or to 1 and 2, the only effect will be to change the position of the switch handle, but since these switch handles can represent on and off when up or down, it doesn't make any difference.

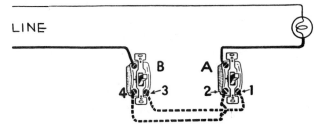

Method of connecting a pair of three-way switches.

FOUR-WAY SWITCHING

You may sometimes want to control a device, usually a light, from three different locations, and so for this you will require a four-way switching system. For this type of arrangement you will need a total of three switches: Two of these will be three-way switches and the other will be a four-way type.

The drawing shows the four-way switch in its two possible positions. As a start, examine the drawing at the left. Point A is connected to point B and so current can flow along this route. Point C is connected to point D and so we have another current path. These are the connections for the first position. When the switch is changed, the current will flow as indicated in the drawing at the right. Current now moves from A to C and there is also a current path from B to D.

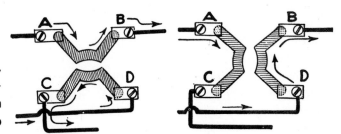

The four-way switch can occupy two possible positions: that shown at the left and that at the right. At the left, A connects to B, and C to D. After switching, A connects to C, and B to D.

The next drawing shows the four-way switch at work. Assume switch X is in its up position, and that switch Z is also in its up position. If you adjust the four-way switch so that A connects to B, the lamp will light. If you now turn any of these switches off, the lamp will go out. This same situation prevails when switches X and Z are in their down position. As far as the four-way switch Y is concerned, not only is A wired to B, but C connects to D, and so once again the circuit is complete. Once again the light can be turned off by any of the three switches.

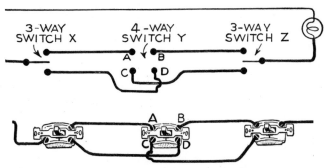

The upper drawing shows the wiring of a pair of three-way switches, identified as X and Z; and a four-way switch, marked as switch Y. The lower drawing shows the way in which you can wire these switches. Although the four-way switch is shown in the center, the switches can have any physical positioning, provided you follow the same wiring scheme.

Assume, though, that the four-way switch is set so that A connects to C. Under these circumstances, B will also connect to D in the same switch. If switch X is in its up position, current will flow from A to C in the four-way switch over to switch Z. The lamp will light if switch Z is in its down position. It will not light if switch Z is in its up position. In that case, all you will need to do is to put switch X in its up position.

The best way to understand the way a switching circuit of this kind works is to start at the left side of the drawing and assume that the switches are set to turn the lamp on. Follow the path of current, going from left to right, through the bulb, and then back along the ground wire, going horizontally across the top of the drawing from the lamp.

HOW TO CONTROL A LIGHT FROM FOUR DIFFERENT POSITIONS

It is very rarely necessary to control a light from more than two positions. The most common application is the need to turn on an upstairs hall light from downstairs, or vice versa. Controlling a light from three different positions is sometimes done between buildings, as on a farm or in a camp. However, should you have to do so, you can control lights from as many different points as you want. Just add more four-way switches as shown in the drawing. Use three-way switches at the beginning and end of the circuit. In the drawing, the line coming out of the right of the three-way switch will connect to one side of the lamp socket. This line is a hot wire and will be the black lead. The other wire coming from the lamp socket will be a ground wire and will be connected to the ground wire of the two-wire system.

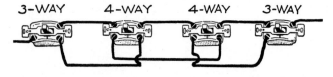

3-WAY   4-WAY   4-WAY   3-WAY

Switching arrangement for controlling light from four different locations. Lead coming out of the right of the three-way switch must be connected to one side of lamp socket. Lead coming out of the left three-way switch is attached to hot side of branch wiring.

At the left in the drawing, the wire coming out of the three-way switch is to be spliced or attached to the hot lead of the two-wire system. No matter how many switches you may have, they all follow the rule of being wired into the hot wire.

HOW TO CONTROL TWO LIGHTS WITH ONE SWITCH

Sometimes you will want to control two lights with a single switch. For example, you might have a rather big and dark basement and you might want to have more light over the entire basement area. It is true that you could have a single light with a higher wattage rating, but separate bulbs will spread the illumination. You might also wish to turn lights on in separate rooms simultaneously.

These switching arrangments not only apply to lights, but to convenience outlets as well. You might, as a further example, want to keep a toaster, coffee maker or percolater, and pilot light turned on and off simultaneously. You could arrange a switch to control the convenience outlets for these appliances and the light. The pilot light would be a constant reminder that the toaster and percolater were turned on. In some household wiring arrangements, a pilot light is used in conjunction with an electric garbage-disposal unit. A single switch controls both. When the light comes on, this is an indication that the garbage disposal unit is working. Yes, it is true that an appliance such as a garba e disposal does make enough noise to alert you to the fact it is working, but to protect the appliance, it is useful to have the pilot light. This is an arrangement often followed with electric ranges. When any one of the bur ers of an electric range is turned on, a warning light comes on simultaneously. With such appliances you do not need to wire in the pilot light since it is supplied, completely wired, as part of the range. Because there are so many different situations in which you would want to control two or more lights, or a light and a convenience outlet, or an appliance and a pilot light, you should add this to your growing repertoire of home-wiring abilities.

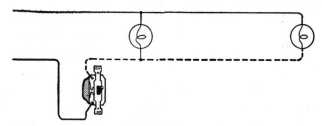

Circuit arrangement for controlling two lamps, or a lamp and a convenience outlet, or a pair of outlets, with a single switch. The dashed line is the hot lead connecting the switch to the lamps. The two leads at the left are to be attached to the power lines. The lower lead is to be wired to the hot line; the upper lead to the ground or cold line.

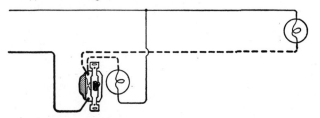

This wiring arrangement is exactly the same as that shown in the preceding drawing. Sometimes it is more convenient to use the screws on the switch as a wire-connecting point.

The drawing shows two bulbs connected to a single-pole, single throw switch. The lead coming out of the left side of the switch is to be connected to the hot side, the black-wire side, of the branch power line. The other lead of the switch leads to the sockets of two lamps. Instead of a socket, you can substitute a convenience outlet. The remaining lead of the two lights (or the light socket and receptacle) is connected to the ground lead or white-wire lead, of the branch circuit. It's as simple as all that.

The two bulbs shown in the drawing need not have the same wattage rating. One can be a small warning pilot lamp, possibly rated at about 10 watts. The other could be a 75-watt or 100-watt lamp. The lamps can be as far apart as you want, or as close together as you deem necessary.

The next illustration shows another way of wiring the two lamps. The only difference is that the two wires of the lamp sockets are connected at the switch. Circuitwise, the two setups are identical and both will work in the same way.

There is a very good reason for connecting both lamps at the switch. Whenever you connect or splice or tap one hot lead into another, they must not only be covered by tape, but the joint or splice must be housed in an electric box. The switch, however, is always housed in an electric box, and so if you make your lamp connection in the box you will benefit in two ways: First, you will not need to splice, but instead simply connect an additional wire to one of the scr4ws on the switch. This screw will be the connecting point for two wires; one going to one lamp, the other going to the second lamp. The second reason is that you will not need to supply an electric box. However, if both lamps are the type that are already mounted on electric boxes, it would probably be just as convenient to connect right at the lamp sockets.

DIMMER SWITCHES

The switches described so far are go-no go devices. This means the device, whether a lamp or appliance, is either on or off. A dimmer switch, unlike these other switches, is a variable control unit. You can have light full on or off, or any level of illumination in-between; and so the light can be made to vary from off, through dim, to bright.

Dimmer switches are two-part devices. One part is a switch that turns the light on or off. The other is the dimmer control, generally a rotary type so that turning the knob one way increases the amount of light, and turning it the other way decreases the light.

There are various types of dimmers, especially designed for use with incandescent bulbs or with fluorescents. One type of dimmer switch has a high-low control that supplies two levels of illumination; full brightness at the top position; half-brightness at its bottom position. The switch is a special dual type. When it is in the "low" position, a silicon rectifier is put in series with the hot lead going to the lamp. The rectifier reduces the current by about 50 percent and so the light becomes dim. In the high position, the switch shorts the rectifier and the lamp receives full current, hence glows at full brightness.

There are a number of advantages in using a dimmer. The first, of course, is the savings in energy costs. If the dimmer controlled bulb is rated at 150 watts, and you cut the illumination in half, the bulb will then be using only about 75 watts. You might want to do this, for example, while watching television. With ordinary lighting and switching your only choices are full light on, or the room in total darkness. With the dimmer you can reduce the light just enough to be able to see objects in the room but without annoying interference with the light coming from the TV picture screen.

Before buying a dimmer, decide on how many lights it is to control. You may, for example, want it to control a light fixture having a number of light bulbs. Add the wattage rating of the individual bulbs to get the minimum wattage rating of the dimmer. If the fixture has six bulbs, each 50-watt types, then the dimmer should have a minimum rating of 6 x 50 equals 300 watts.

You can install a dimmer in just the same way as you would an ordinary in-home type of wall switch. The dimmer control itself generally is housed in a small sealed box. Just connect the existing wires to the two terminal screws on the dimmer and put the dimmer in the electric box that originally held the switch. Put on a standard face plate, held in position by two machine screws. The final step is to fasten the round knob to the central shaft protruding from the dimmer. This central shaft works as a switch by pushing the knob in and it is this action that turns lights on or off. Push in to turn on. Push in again to turn off. To control the amount of light, rotate the knob to the right (clockwise) for maximum light; rotate it to the left (counterclockwise) for minimum light.

TIME-DELAY SWITCH

The time delay switch, as its name implies, allows a certain amount of time to elapse, generally about a half-minute, before it turns a light off. You might find it more convenient to install a time-delay switch instead of a two-way lighting system. For example, if you have a garage a short distance from your home, closing the garage-door light with a time-delay switch would provide enough light to let you get to your front door. It would then turn off automatically. With a two-way lighting system, you would need to turn the light off from a switch inside the house. Whether you use a time-delay switch or a two-way lighting system depends entirely on what you personally want in the way of switching and lighting convenience.

You can install a time-delay switch in exactly the same way as you did the usual SPST switch. If there is an existing switch, remove it and substitute the time-delay type. The wiring and connections are the same.

MERCURY SWITCH

Most ordinary switches make some sort of clicking noise whether moving into the "on" or "off" positions. During daytime hours the slight noise is barely noticeable, but at night, when ambient sound is quite low, the click may be disturbing in an infant's room or in a sickroom.

The mercury switch contains a small hollow cylinder filled with mercury. Mercury is a liquid metal and can conduct a current, just as a copper wire does. When the switch is in its "off" position, a small metal contact is removed from the mercury, but is immersed in the mercury when the switch is closed.

Electrically, the mercury switch works in exactly the same way as the usual toggle switch. However, just before installing it, read the manufacturer's instructions that accompany the switch The mercury switch must be mounted so that it is level. However, the connections to the switch are just the same as for the toggle type.

The mercury switch isn't the only silent type. You can get mechanical types, similar to the usual toggle switch, but designed to be quiet. With these you do not need to worry about correct positioning and they, like the mercury switch, can be substituted for or used in place of ordinary toggle switches.

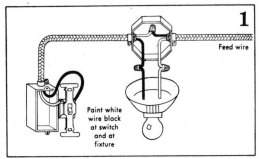

To add a wall switch to control ceiling
light at end of run

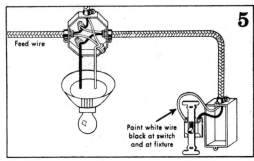

To add wall switch to control ceiling
light in middle of run

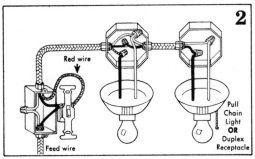

To install two ceiling lights on same
line; one controlled by switch

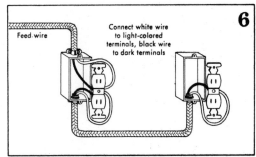

To add new convenience outlets beyond
old convenience outlets

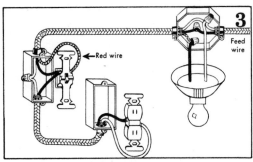

To add a switch and convenience outlet
beyond existing ceiling light

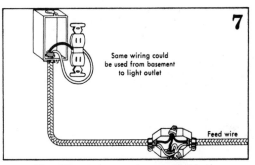

To add a new convenience outlet from
an existing junction box

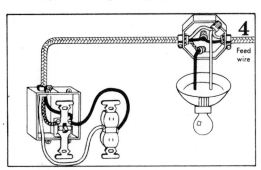

To add a switch and convenience outlet
in one outlet box beyond existing ceiling light

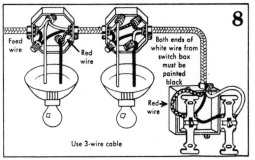

To install one new ceiling outlet and
two new switch outlets from existing
ceiling outlet

Various switch and outlet arrangements. (Courtesy, Sears.)

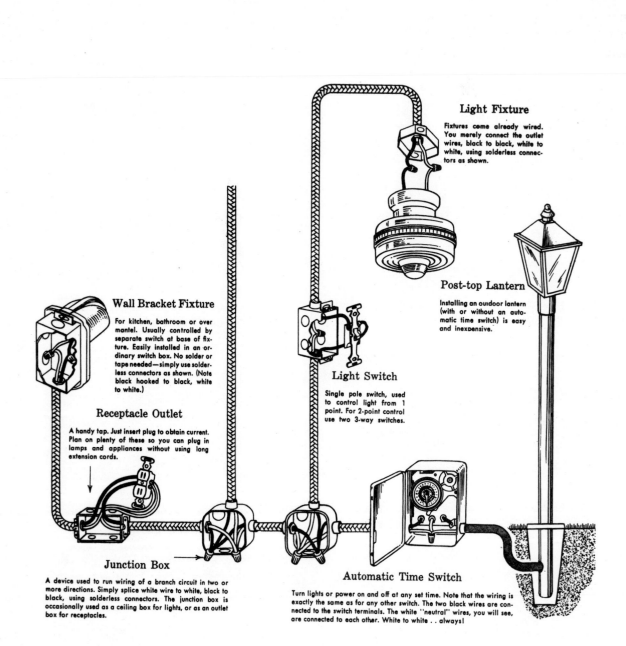

Light Fixture

Fixtures come already wired. You merely connect the outlet wires, black to black, white to white, using solderless connectors as shown.

Post-top Lantern

Installing an outdoor lantern (with or without an automatic time switch) is easy and inexpensive.

Wall Bracket Fixture

For kitchen, bathroom or over mantel. Usually controlled by separate switch at base of fixture. Easily installed in an ordinary switch box. No solder or tape needed—simply use solderless connectors as shown. (Note black hooked to black, white to white.)

Receptacle Outlet

A handy tap. Just insert plug to obtain current. Plan on plenty of these so you can plug in lamps and appliances without using long extension cords.

Light Switch

Single pole switch, used to control light from 1 point. For 2-point control use two 3-way switches.

Junction Box

A device used to run wiring of a branch circuit in two or more directions. Simply splice white wire to white, black to black, using solderless connectors. The junction box is occasionally used as a ceiling box for lights, or as an outlet box for receptacles.

Automatic Time Switch

Turn lights or power on and off at any set time. Note that the wiring is exactly the same as for any other switch. The two black wires are connected to the switch terminals. The white "neutral" wires, you will see, are connected to each other. White to white . . always!

ADDING SWITCHES AND OUTLETS

Even in a brand-new home, you can be sure that a new outlet or switch will be needed somewhere. While builders, electrical contractors, and potential home owners may try to anticipate every possible electrical need, there is only one way to really discover them and that is to live in a new house for awhile. Then, and only then, will come the full awareness of how many more outlets and switches are required. Part of the reason for this is that the positioning of desk and floor lamps cannot always be predicted in advance. Of course, light switches often occupy a time-honored position at the door entrance, but it is sometimes equally convenient to have switches elsewhere in a room.

The numbered drawings, 1 through 8, show a few of the possible variations in switch and outlet setups for greater convenience. While these may not represent your particular switch or outlet problem, the ways in which these wiring situations are handled should give you some clue to help with your wiring.

HOW TO PLAN WIRING

For some home repairs, no planning is needed. If you intend replacing a switch or a light bulb, obviously the solution is to remove the defective item and replace it. But even here you do need to do some thinking. If you are going to replace an electric-light bulb you must at lease decide on its wattage rating, whether it is to be clear or frosted, on the base size, and the purpose for which the bulb is to be used. When replacing a wall switch, make a simple sketch of how the wires were originally connected. Do this before removing the wires. Quite often, there will be only two wires coming into the switch box, but even then you should know which wire connects to the upper screw and which to the lower one. You may also have additional wires coming into the switch box, your clue that the switch is being used as a junction point. To avoid problems th switches and outlets elsewhere in your home, make a drawing showing just how the wires were connected. Don't depend on your memory.

If you intend rewiring, or if you want to add more wiring to old or new rooms, it would be best to start with a sketch. This will help you decide on the best location of the switches. Never mount a switch so that is is behind a door. Since more people are right-handed, place the switch so that you can operate it with your right hand as you enter a room. Door hinges are generally put at the left as you face a door, so mount the switches on the side opposite the hinges.

You can also have one or more doors inside a room, such as doors leading to closets. Again, it is better to follow the rule of putting switches to the right of the door, that is, on the side opposite the hinges.

Begin your wiring drawing with rectangular boxes to represent the rooms, since most rooms are rectangular rather than square. Position the boxes so that they are in proper relationship to each other.

Start with a pair of lines to indicate the two wires of the power system. You will find it helpful to make one of these lines thicker or blacker than the other, or, if you prefer, use two different colors. One of these lines will be the ground line and will represent the white wire; the other will be both the hot wire and the black wire.

The drawing shows a first effort. The thin line is the ground line; the thicker line the hot wire. There is no need to draw switches, for you can indicate them by the large letter X. If you will examine the drawing, you will now see that we have a ground wire coming from each lamp. Each of these wires is regarded as part of the branch wiring, and since we have four lamps, there are four branches. Note also that the thin line, or ground wire, is unbroken. No parts are inserted in series with the ground wire and so from each lamp you can trace the ground wire directly back, without interruption, as far as the main power line.

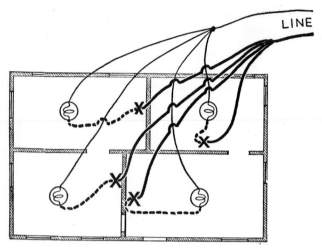

Preliminary sketch of a wiring installation.

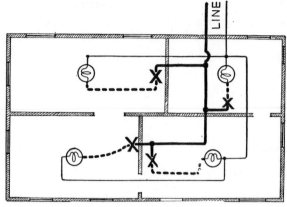

Final sketch of a wiring installation.

Finally, examine the hot leads. Instead of having separate hot leads, we have these tapping off a single hot wire.

Now examine the thicker lines. Each of these (and there are four, since there are four branch circuits) is connected to a switch X. From the switches, each hot line continues, and we have done one for each lamp. The hot wires from the switches to the lamps are represented by a dashed line.

The arrangement shown in this first drawing will work, and if the lamps and switches are in good working order, will function well and properly. With this arrangement only one junction box will be needed, and this will be at the point where all the ground wires from the lamps will need to be spliced to the main ground wire. It will also be the point where all the hot leads will be spliced to the main wire as well. The only question that remains, then, is whether some wiring could not possibly be eliminated, or even made shorter.

Now examine the next drawing. This is exactly the same wiring problem, but note what has been done. Examine the ground lines first. Instead of all going directly back to the main power line, we have a ground line running from lamp to lamp, and so there is a reduction in the amount of ground-line wiring.

Clearly, by making a sketch and with some planning, you can reduce your costs, as well as the amount of work you will have to do. However, there is one way in which planning can make matters a bit difficult for you. When you make a wiring plan, you know just what you want to do and the final wiring setup will be the results of your efforts. On the other hand, when you move into a used house or apartment, or into a new one for that matter, you will not be familiar with the wiring plan, unless you can persuade the electrical contractor who did the wiring to supply you with one. That is why you will often find outlet boxes, switch boxes, and junction boxes with a number of wires, all going in different directions. To complicate matters, fuse boxes and circuit-breaker boxes often do not identify the branches they protect; that is, there is no paper pasted in or near the box that will tell you which fuses or breakers are which. This applies to new as well as to used homes and apartments. The only thing you can do is to try to trace the wiring to the best of your ability. With a fuse box or circuit-breaker box, opening the switch or removing a fuse while keeping lights on throughout the house will soon tell you the fusing arrangement. The only way you can work out junction-box and switch-box or other kinds of box wiring is to remove one wire at a time and see which light or lights or appliances are affected by the removal of that wire.

Electrical contractors do not always make wiring diagrams. An experienced electrical contractor installing wiring in similar homes may become so experienced that he will know just what to do without making a wiring plan, hence will not do so unless he must in order to meet some legal requirement.

ADVANTAGE OF PULL-CHAIN FIXTURES

Pull-chain fixtures are commonly used in closets, basements, and attics. The advantage of such fixtures is that the switch and receptacle for the light are mounted in a common housing. This eliminates the need for a separate switch box, and the wiring to the switch box. The disadvantage of the pull chain is that it is unsightly, but it is suitable for closets,or other areas where it is not in the way of normal house traffic.

OTHER SWITCHES

You will find a tremendous variety of switches. Some do not even look like switches, since they do not have a protruding toggle arm. Instead, they consist of decorative plates that can be made to move up and down. You can have foot-operated switches, switches that glow in the dark, switches that are combined with outlets, and so on. These are all types designed for particular applications. For the most part, in-wall switches are used to control lights, although they can be and are used to control receptacles as well.

Appliances are ordinarily switch equipped, although there are some exceptions. Electric fans, vacuum cleaners, and electric drills are just a few of the many that are switch equipped. The switches used on these components are single-pole, single-throw types and work in the same way as wall-mounted switches.

Some appliances aren't switch equipped and are turned on simply by plugging into an active outlet. These could include electric toothbrushes, electric shavers, and similar items. Generally, de-

vices that require very little power may have the switch omitted. Power tools are always switch equipped, and they should be.

OUTLETS AND SWITCHES

Outlets and switches, and the accompanying wiring, represent the installation problems of in-home wiring. The basic idea is very simple. From your fuse box you have various branches going to different portions of your home. These branches supply electrical power to a number of outlets and to lamps. Mostly, the lamps are controlled by switches and generally the outlets are not switch controlled. By using the right size of wire, by using BX or conduit, as required, and by installing electric boxes correctly, you can meet all your electrical needs.

TWO-AND THREE-WIRE CIRCUITS

The wiring that comes into your home is called service entrance. Service entrance can consist of two wires or three. If it has two wires, one of these will be the black or hot wire, the other will be the white or cold or ground wire. These wires will enter your kilowatt-hour meter, so that your power usage can be measured, and from there will go into your fuse box or circuit-breaker box. From either of these boxes, various branches will go off to different parts of your home. Like the service entrance, each branch will consist of a pair of wires, one white and the other black. Theoretically, we could have a single pair of wires going to the most distant point in your home—that is, the point farthest away from the fuse box or circuit-breaker box. This would then be the main power line, or simply the main line. Connections to the main line would consist of branches from the various service outlets. However, it is customary to have a number of branches moving directly from the fuse or circuit breaker so as to distribute the amount of current flow. Thus, one branch might carry current to all appliances in the kitchen. Another branch would carry current for all the lights, and so on. The number of branches running from the main service wires depends on how big your house is, how old it is, and the intentions of the original builder. As a general rule, most homes are inadequately wired. This isn't because the original builder skimped on wiring, but rather can be attributed to the tendency in the past decade to use more and more electrical power. Television sets have moved in, and so have a host of kitchen appliances and power tools. This means a greater current demand on wires not originally designed to carry such a heavy load.

Some service entrances use three wires instead of two. One of the wires is the neutral or ground wire, while the other two are hot wires. The voltage from either one of the hot wires to the ground wire is approximately 117 volts. The voltage from one hot wire to the other is 2 x 117 equals 234 volts. The ground wire is usually white, while the two hot wires can either be black, or may consist of one black and one red wire.

The three-wire system has a number of advantages. Some appliances—kitchen ranges and clothing driers, for example—are designed to work from 234 volts. Using 234 volts instead of 117 means that such appliances can work on smaller amounts of current. Another advantage is that the total current demand can be split between the two hot leads of the three-wire system. Thus, part of the house can be wired to one branch consisting of a black wire and a white wire; and the other part wired to a branch consisting of a red wire and a white wire. The white wire is common to both—that is, it is the ground wire for the two hot leads.

Your fuse box or circuit-breaker box is located close to the service-entrance wires. Since these carry the total house current, it is advisable for these wires to be as short as possible so as to keep possible heat losses in the wires at an absolute minimum. Heat losses that are after your kilowatt-hour meter are your problem and you pay for them. Heat losses in wiring preceding the kilowatt-hour meter are the problem of your local utility.

HOW TO ADD ADDITIONAL WIRING

Installing additional wiring in a home that is an older type or even a newer one that is finished is more difficult than putting in wiring during the construction of a home. You may need to drill through floors and you may be forced to find your way between existing joists. But even if you cannot or will not do the job yourself, understanding the problem will make you a better and more selective buyer if you have an outside electrical contractor do the work. You can shop among contractors just as you would for any other service or materials. If you show yourself to be a more knowledgeable customer, you are less likely to be overcharged.

As a start, assume you want to install a junction box somewhere near your fuse cabinet or circuit-breaker box in your basement. Your first problem is to decide whether to use thin-walled or rigid conduit. Why conduit and not BX? Many local electrical codes now prohibit the use of BX in new homes or in additional wiring in older homes. With rigid conduit you will use threaded fittings so connecting the conduit at either end will be easier. This means, though, that you will need to buy a die for cutting the conduit threads, unless you can buy threaded conduit cut to your required size. However, if you use thin-walled conduit, you will find it easier to bend and you will be able to use compression-type fittings. Remember, when you buy conduit, make sure it is interior waxed to let you fish the wires through more easily.

Most conduit is either ½" or ¾" in diameter. The size of the conduit will be determined by the size of the wires you plan to fish through. The following table shows the number of wires in conduit, and the minimum size of conduit that is permitted.

Size Wire	Number of Wires in One Conduit 1	2	3	4	5	6	7	8
	Minimum Size Conduit Permitted							
14	½"	½"	½"	½"	¾"	¾"	1"	1"
12	½"	½"	½"	¾"	¾"	1"	1"	1"
10	½"	¾"	¾"	¾"	1"	1"	1"	1¼"
8	½"	¾"	¾"	1"	1¼"	1¼"	1¼"	1½"
6	½"	1"	1"	1¼"	1½"	1½"	2"	2"
4	½"	1¼"	*1¼"	1½"	1½"	2"	2"	2"
2	¾"	1¼"	1¼"	2"	2"	2"	2½"	2½"
1	¾"	1½"	1½"	2"	2½"	2½"	2½"	3"
0	1"	1½"	2"	2"	2½"	2½"	3"	3"
00	1"	2"	2"	2½"	2½"	3"	3"	3"

If, for example, you decide to use two no. 10 wires, then you will need ¾'' conduit.

The tricky part is in measuring the distance between your starting point, the fuse cabinet or circuit-breaker box in this example, and the position of your first junction box. One technique you might try is to take a scrap length of BX and tack it temporarily into position in place of the conduit. Put a mark with a red felt-type pen at the start and end of the run of BX. If the run is to be curved at one or more points, make sure that the BX is placed in the exact path the conduit will follow. Remove the BX and since it will now be straight you will be able to measure its length. Be careful, though. BX can have slight curvatures, so put the BX on a flat surface and put a yardstick against it to make sure the BX is straight. You will now be able to measure it and will then have the length of the conduit. Make an allowance for the fact that the conduit will extend slightly into the fuse cabinet or circuit-breaker box and also into the first junction box.

Now that you have the length of the conduit, bend it into the shape it should have. For this you will need to rent or buy a conduit bender. Don't try bending by hand or by putting the conduit in a vise. The bends of the conduit must be gentle. The drawing shows that the conduit in this installation has two bends (yours might have two, or one, or possibly none) and that these two bends are actually 90°.

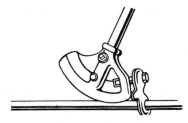

Thin wall conduit is easy to bend with the help of a conduit bender. (Courtesy, Sears.)

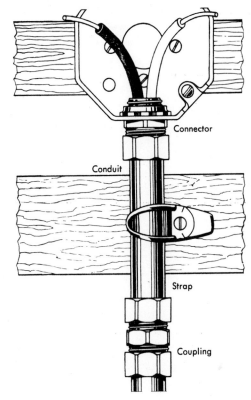

Details of thin-wall conduit installation: Connect only to steel box, never to plastic types. Conduit is available in 10' lengths, but is easy to cut to exact size with hacksaw. After cutting, ream the ends (on the inside) and then taper with a file. Conduit bender will help you make bends. Force connector over end of conduit, insert into electric box, and tighten with locknut. Conduit inside walls bust be supported. Coupling shown in drawing is used to connect one section of thin-wall conduit to another. (Courtesy, Sears.)

Before you fasten the conduit into position, mount a locking nut at each end. Insert one end into your fuse or breaker box and the other end into the junction box. Do not fasten the junction box into position just yet.

Now put a lockwasher on the inside of the junction box so that the box becomes fastened to the conduit. You can now mount the conduit against joists or other wooden supports.

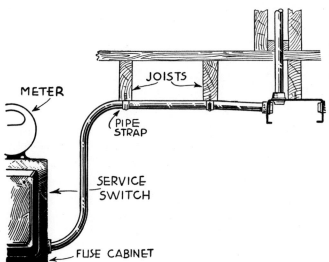

How conduit can be installed between fuse box and first junction box.

There are two more steps you must take. The first is to put a locknut over that section of conduit that extends into the fuse or breaker box. Fasten the junction box into position by using wood screws going into a wooden support behind or above the box. As a final step, tighten all locknuts. There are two at the fuse or breaker box (one inside, one outside) and two at the junction box (one inside, another outside). If necessary, add more pipe straps to support the conduit. You should have one at least every two feet. The finished job (without wires) will look as shown in the drawing.

You now have the conduit fixed into position and so you are ready to fish your wires through it. You know the length of the conduit, so cut your wires accordingly. It's a good idea to allow about 6" to 8" extra length at each end. If the conduit is relatively short and if the bends are very gradual, you may be able to push the wires through. Before you try it make sure the wires are straight, have no kinks, and that the ends of the wires being pushed into the conduit aren't knotted or curved. If this proves difficult or impossible to do, you can buy fish wire at an electrical shop. It is available in different thicknesses and lengths, so here you will need to use your judgment. A thickness of about ⅛" should be adequate, and as for the length, that will depend on how long the conduit will be overall.

Push the fish wire through the conduit, attach both wires (or three wires if you are planning a three-wire line) and then pull on the fish wire. If the fish wire is sold to you with a hook at one end, then just strip the ends of the wires, form a hook, attach one to the other, and that will be that. If, however, the fish wire does not have a hook at one end, try bending one into position with a pair of gas pliers. You may not be able to do so if the fish wire is too springy. In that case, take the two or three wires, and place them along the fish wire so they overlap by about 1 ". Then take a small section of plastic tape (not friction tape) and tape the wires together as tightly as you can. Coat the plastic tape with some lubricant such as petroleum jelly, or use cold cream or any other oily substance. The whole idea is to make the joint between the wires and the fish wire as non-bumpy, as smooth and as friction free as possible.

Should you fish the wires through before or after putting the conduit into position? That's up to you. With the conduit in place, you will have eliminated one item that needs to be held. On the other hand, the conduit may be in a location that makes inserting the wires rather difficult. Do what is easier for you to do.

INDOOR PLASTIC-SHEATHED CABLE

You can avoid using conduit and the problem of getting wires through it by using indoor-type plastic-sheathed cable instead. Be sure to get "ground-type" cable, cable that carries a grounding wire. However, first check whether your local electrical code will permit you to use such wire in place of conduit.

MAKING THE CONNECTIONS

You now have your conduit installed and the wires fished through it. If you plan to use the electric box as a service outlet, all you will need to do will be to connect the wires to the receptacle, attach the receptacle to the electric box, and then put on the cover plate. Alternatively, you may decide to use the box as a junction box for future use. In that case, cover each wire with a solderless connector and then put a plate over the box and screw it into position.

Finally, you may prefer, as shown in the drawing, to use the box as a junction type and from this junction to have two branches—One going upstairs, and the other continuing along in the basement. The drawing shows this possibility.

KNOCKOUTS

It is easy, particularly for those with limited experience, to drive out more knockouts than they really need. A knockout, as explained earlier, consists of a circular bit of metal that can easily be pushed out of an electric box to leave a round hole. However, if you do have one or more such holes and you do not use them for inserting cable connectors, then you must cover them.

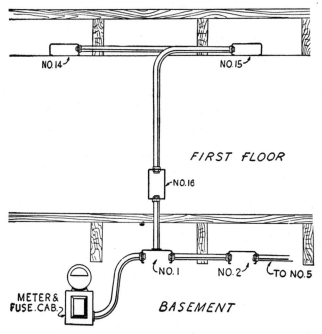

FIRST FLOOR

NO.16

NO.14   NO.15

NO.1   NO.2   TO NO.5

METER & FUSE.CAB.

BASEMENT

Make a written plan, as shown here, and identify each electric box by number. On the plan indicate the size of wire used inside the conduit. This will help in the future when you install more appliances. Adequate wiring and planning is also helpful when selling a house.

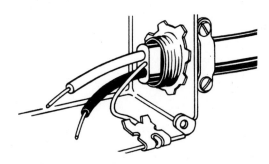

Connectors are available for clamping plastic-sheathed cable to electric box. Note connection of ground wire to grounding clamp in the box. Plastic-sheathed cable is much easier to work with than conduit or BX. (Courtesy, Sears.)

There are two ways in which you can do this. You can buy knockout covers in an electrical store and use these to close the knockout holes, or you can supply a homemade alternative. Use two circular washers whose diameter is a bit larger

than that of the knockout holes. Put one washer inside the electric box and another on the outside so that they cover the entire area of the knockout hole. Fasten the washers with a machine screw and nut. With the head of the screw inside the box, put the screw through the center hole of the washers. This center hole should be just about large enough to let the screw pass through. Fasten the nut against the washer on the outside of the box. If too much of the screw protrudes, cut it off with a hacksaw. Make sure the nut is tight. A nutdriver will help you do this.

There are a number of valid reasons why knockout holes should be covered. The first is that in case of a fire inside the box, it will be confined to that space. Another is to keep immature, inquisitve little fingers from poking around inside. If you have a fire outside the box, the box will offer protection for some while and will keep short circuits from adding to the miseries of an unexpected fire.

The drawing shows how the conduit is continued from the basement to the first floor. Along the length of the conduit you can add more boxes for switches and outlets. Note that what you will be doing will be to add conduit in sections. If you can do one, you can do two; if you can do two, why not the whole house?

Some professional electricians prefer to install all conduit first, and then to fish the wires through. In that case they allow a little wire slack in each electric box, as shown in the drawing, cutting the wires at the time they are ready to connect outlets or switches. An easier way is to cut the wires to the approximately correct length, allowing extra for making connections.

All the various lengths of conduit can be installed, and then the wire for the entire job can be fished through.

TESTING THE INSTALLATION

You now have two wires, one black and the other white, pulled through the conduit. You have joined black wire to black wire, white to white, inside any junction boxes. You have wired in switches and convenience outlets. You have attached the ground wire that accompanied the white and black wires to grounding terminals on all electric boxes. Question: Will it work?

There are various ways you have of testing. Note that you cannot as yet plug in any test lamps, for one crucial step has been omitted. The wires have not as yet been connected in the fuse box or circuit-breaker box. All you really have is a pair of wires hidden inside miscellaneous lengths of conduit.

There are various ways you can test. You could, for example, join the exposed wire ends closest to the fuse or breaker box and then test with an ohmmeter. Go the most distant point and put the ohmmeter terminals across the two exposed ends of the wire. You should read practically zero resistance.

But you may not have an ohmmeter. An alternative method would be to attach the two wires nearest the fuse or circuit-breaker box to a two-wire line ending in a male plug. Use solderless connectors and then insert the plug into the nearest active outlet. Your two-wire line will now be "alive." Connect a lamp into each outlet to see if you get power.

There is a better way (still using the arrangement just described), and that is through the use of a small 117-volt neon tester. These are inexpensive and you should have one. When inserted into an outlet they will glow if the outlet supplies power. But there is one more test you should try. Connect the neon tester from the black to the white wire. The lamp should glow. Now connect the tester from the black wire to the bare grounding wire. Again, the lamp should glow.

Finally, repeat the test once more, this time from the black wire to the conduit. Once again the lamp should glow. The advantage of the neon tester is not only that it is economical, lightweight, and easily portable, but that it lets you make a number of checks.

To test a switch with the neon-lamp unit, connect between the terminal holding the white wire and that holding the black wire. If you are across the input terminals—that is, you are checking across the cable bringing power in—the neon lamp should glow regardless of the setting of the switch. Now transfer the lead from the screw holding the hot input wire to the one holding the wire leading to the appliance. We can call this the output wire. When the switch is turned on, the lamp will glow; when turned off, the lamp will extinguish.

CONNECTING TO THE FUSE OR BREAKER BOX

For the amateur electrician, the most difficult part of an installation such as that just described will not be the conduit or installing switches and receptacles. It will be connecting the wires to the fuse or circuit-breaker box. You will find quite a few wires here and so matters can get a bit complicated. Usually these boxes have spare fuses or breakers. If a breaker box, select a switch that will carry the current you expect to impose on your new line. If it is a fuse box, all you will need to do will be to insert a fuse having the correct current rating.

To keep from getting hurt, trip the main circuit breaker to its "off" position. If you are using a fuse box, you may have a handle on the side of the box for opening the switch to the service leads. Do not try to work with the main power turned on. If you do not have enough light, use a flashlight. Connect the black lead to one side of the fuse or breaker. The other side is probably already connected to the main service wires, even if the fuse or breaker has not been in use. Connect the white or ground wire to the white wire in the box.

If the fuse or breaker box looks too confusing, if you are unable to remove the cover plate to get in at the wiring, don't hesitate to call in an electrician. Watch him while he is at work; you may learn something from the way he handles his assignment. Some professional electricians do have an attitude of contempt toward "do-it-yourselfers," but don't let it bother you. Just get someone else. Don't let an electrician talk down to you or patronize you. The world is full of ignoramuses and the trade has its proper share.

GROUND

Of all the aspects of home electrical wiring, ground sounds the most mysterious and is often most misunderstood. Of the two wires that carry current to your appliances, one is called the ground, but it need not be that way. Both could be "hot" wires and your appliances would still get the current they need. Ground is just a reference point. We use reference points all the time. The end of a ruler is such a reference. If you say something is 3' in lenght, you mean it measures 3' starting at the left or zero end of a yardstick. If you say a mountain is 8,000 feet high, you mean it is 8,000 feet above sea level. If you say a wire is at 117 volts, you mean that the electrical pressure is 117 volts when measured with respect to another wire. That wire is the ground wire. If you touch a ground wire, you do not get a shock because you and the ground wire are at the same potential or voltage. If you touch a "hot" wire, you will get a shock because you are still at ground-potential level and the hot wire is 117 volts above zero or ground potential.

All of the current that flows into your home is supplied by an electric generator. There is no way in which that current can be consumed or destroyed or used up. If, at any particular time, 100 amperes of current flow from the service wires into your home wiring, then you can be sure that 100 amperes will flow out. That current will flow through two wires: One of these is the hot wire, and the other the ground or cold wire.

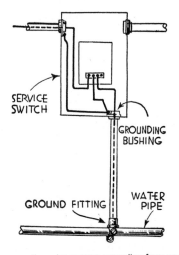

SERVICE SWITCH

GROUNDING BUSHING

GROUND FITTING

WATER PIPE

You will find a grounding wire or strap extending from your fuse or breaker box to the water pipe near the entrance to your home. If this connection is on the "house" side of the water meter, you may need to jump the water meter with a grounding strap. Make sure the ground connection from the fuse or breaker box to the water pipe is unbroken and isn't corroded. If it is, don't remove it but make another connection from a ground bushing on the box to the water pipe.

The ground wire or white wire in your wiring system is physically connected to earth or ground. If you did not have a water system in your home, you would actually need to bury a rather larger copper plate in the earth and connect your white wire to it. Fortunately, you have an alternative. The pipe that delivers water to your home is buried in the ground, makes intimate contact with it, and so is the starting point of your ground system.

In many homes (not all) there is a water meter to measure water usage, just as you have a kilowatt-hour meter to measure your power usage. The trouble is that this meter often represents a very poor electrical contact between the incoming water pipe and the water pipes you have in your house. To overcome this problem and also to make sure that the water pipes in your home are actually grounded, it is helpful to jump the meter with a water-meter jumper. For this you can use a short length of no. 6 copper wire. Scrape the water pipe clean of all rust and dirt on both sides of the meter. Use a screw-type clamp and attach the wire tightly. Instead of wire, you could use wire braid for a more effective connection. Of course, if your home-wiring system already has such a jumper, you need not be concerned about it. However, do look at it, just in case it is broken or damaged.

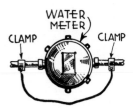

Method of jumping a water meter to assure a good ground.

SURFACE WIRING

There's no doubt that cutting into a wall and trying to install wiring behind it is work and invariably requires a cleanup, painting, or wallpapering after the job is done. It is also well worthwhile in terms of added electrical convenience, something to keep in mind as plaster dust starts floating through the air.

However, if you want to add an outlet or a switch in an attic, a pantry, a recreation room, a workshop, a closet, your garage or basement, then meticulous attention to decor may not be all that necessary. For such installations you can use surface wiring. You can get cable made especially for this purpose in a gray or ivory color. In some areas, however, surface wiring is not approved by local electrical codes.

You can also get electrical devices made especially for use with surface wiring, such as a bulb receptacle, a switch, or a duplex receptacle. A bulb receptacle, as its name implies, looks somewhat like a receptacle but has a socket mounted on its surface for inserting a bulb. The unit comes equipped with a pull-chain switch, and is fastened to the wall with a pair of wood screws. The bulb receptacle has a pair of through holes to accommodate the screws.

A wall switch for surface wiring is just an ordinary toggle type, but like the bulb receptacle, has a pair of holes for wood screws. The duplex receptacle can also be wall mounted in the same way and has two receptacles for male plugs.

If the room in which you plan to use surface wiring has a baseboard, remove the board to see if it is grooved. Some baseboards have a groove permitting you to use surface wiring so that it fits in the baseboard groove. This helps conceal most of the wire and makes the wiring installation less obvious.

Flat shape and gray or ivory color of plastic cable make it very inconspicuous in Surface Wiring of homes.

Especially suitable for barns, garages, workshops, where approved by local codes.

You can use dual-purpose cable for surface wiring. This type of installation is much less work than behind-the-wall wiring. (Courtesy, Sears.)

DUAL-PURPOSE CABLE

Dual-purpose cable is so called because it can be used either indoors or out. You can bury it in plaster inside or in the ground outside.

The first illustration (top left) shows Dual-purpose cable used beneath ground. Dig a narrow trench about 2' deep. Remove any stones or objects that could cut into the cable. Do not cover the cable until you have tested the installation to see if it will carry current between the

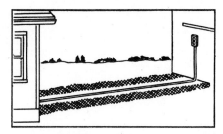

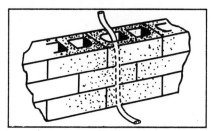

Easily buried underground. Dig trench to depth of 2 feet or more . . . deep enough to avoid injury by shovels, picks, etc. Lay in cable and replace soil.

Use Dual-purpose plastic cable in the air holes of outside masonry block walls. Dampness and condensation have no effect whatever on this cable. It's economical, too.

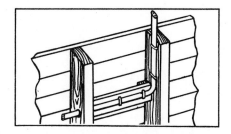

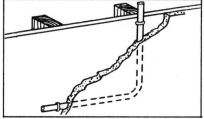

For new work this cable can be run in partition through studding, the same as ordinary sheathed cable. Ideal in damp, wet locations, flexible and easy to work.

Dual-purpose cable — so named because it can be used indoors or out, buried in the ground—or in plaster. If there is danger from nails, use a protective strip.

Various applications of dual-purpose cable. (Courtesy, Sears.)

points you have designated. Then cover the cable and stamp the soil in hard.

You can also run Dual-purpose cable through the air holes of cinder block or similar types of masonry-block walls. While cinder block can become damp, this will have no effect on the cable. The drawing at the upper right shows an installation.

For basement wiring (lower left) you can use plastic-sheathed cable, but in humid areas where there may be water condensation in basements or if your basement is usually damp, it might be preferable to use Dual-purpose cable. You can support the cable by drilling through studs or by fastening it against joists and other wooden supports.

Finally, you can put Dual-purpose cable right

into plaster walls by cutting a groove, inserting the wire, and then plastering over the groove. You need not run the cable in straight lines, since no one will see the wire after you have plastered over it. Make as direct a run as you can. See the drawing at the lower right.

FIRST-FLOOR WIRING

Wiring a first floor, if that first floor is directly above a basement that doesn't have a finished ceiling, can be much easier than wiring upper floors. Locate a space in-between studs and then cut the wall for the insertion of the new electric box (box #1 in the drawing).

One of the more difficult aspects of this job is to locate the place on the floor for drilling the hole for the cable. A way of doing this is to remove the baseboard in the room in which the new outlet is

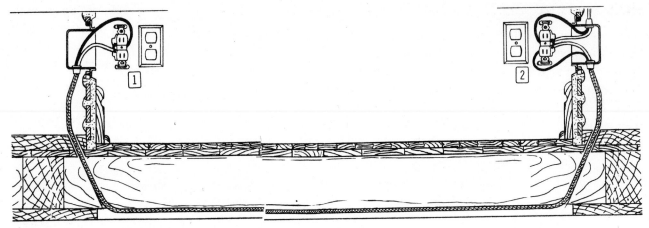

Method of connecting first-floor outlets from one room to another. (Courtesy, Sears.)

to be installed. Cut away a small section of the wall between studs and put a strong light near the opening. The flooring may be sufficiently rough to let some of the light shine through to the basement. Another way could be to put one or two nails in the open space and then use a stud locator in the basement, moving it around on the basement ceiling until you find the spot directly below where the nails have been placed. Another method you can use is to have someone tap the floor area inside the wall opening with a small hammer. While this is being done, run your hand along the basement ceiling until you can feel the direct blows of the hammer.

After you have located the drill areas, use a wood drill and bit to drill the holes. Holes must be large enough to accommodate the armored cable or sheathed cable. Push the cable through both holes and then cut the cable to its proper length. Before connecting the wires to the existing outlet, turn power off by removing the fuse that controls the outlet. At the new outlet, connect the black wire to the brass terminals of the outlet and the white or neutral wire to the light-colored terminals. The cable must not suspend by its own weight. Instead, use cable straps every three feet, fastening the cable to the wooden ceiling of the basement or to any other available wooden support.

HOW TO INSTALL
BASEMENT CEILING FIXTURE

This procedure is almost identical to the one just described. Drill through the basement ceiling using a long-shank bit so that a hole is made in the floor, in-between studs and inside the wall behind the baseboard. Push a short length of fish wire through the hole and you will be able to use it to pull the cable through. Since the new basement fixture will not be switch controlled, use one having a pull chain.

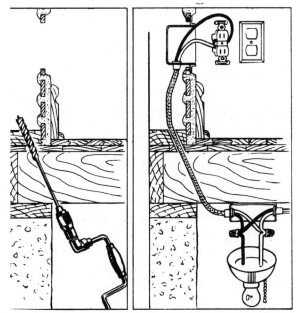

How to install a basement light by tapping off first-floor receptacle. (Courtesy, Sears.)

152

HOW TO GANG METAL BOXES

You can group any number of metal electric boxes by ganging. To gang two boxes, remove adjacent walls and then fit the boxes together. They can be held together with screws. This technique applies to metal boxes only, and not to plastic types. Boxes must be covered with metal plates after wiring is completed. Use a ganged double-box arrangement to avoid excessive wire crowding. Ample room inside the double box makes connecting wires much easier.

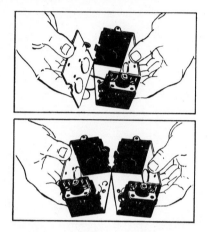

How to gang metal electric boxes. (Courtesy, Sears.)

HOW TO RUN A CABLE AROUND A DOOR FRAME

You can be sure of one thing whenever you try to do behind-the-wall wiring. Everything will seem to conspire to keep you from completing the job. You may run into unexpected studs or headers. A stud is part of the vertical wood framing of a house; a header is a horizontal section of framing. Headers are usually mounted between studs. A pair of studs and a header sometimes look like the letter H.

Doors can sometimes be a nuisance when you want to wire in a new outlet, for you must either run the cable under the door flooring or over and around the door. Over and around is usually easier. To do this job, remove the baseboards on both sides of the door. Also remove the door trim. Headers are commonly used to supply additional support for the door. The two lower drawings

indicate methods of installing cable when a header is present. Run the cable around the header (drawing at lower left), or drill hole through header large enough to permit cable to pass through.

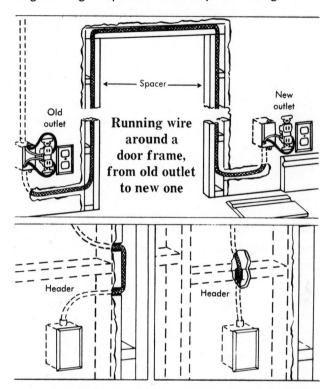

Running a cable around a door may meet with interference from header. Two lower drawings show methods of solving this problem. (Courtesy, Sears.)

HOW ELECTRICAL POWER COMES INTO YOUR HOME

Your local utility delivers power to your home by means of heavy wires, usually three, consisting of two hot lines and one neutral or ground wire. If you have a private house, quite possibly the wires will be connected to three conductors housed in a pipe running alongside the dwelling. The top of this pipe consists of a curved fitting and is shaped to prevent water from entering. The three wires continue on to a kilowatt-hour meter. For apartments and older homes, the meter is indoors, but the trend in newer houses is to mount the meter on the outside. The advantage here is that the utility can read the meter at any time and will not require access to the house to do so. From the meter the three wires enter a fuse box or circuit-breaker box, passing through a pair of main fuses. Immediately preceding the fuse is a switch capable of opening both hot leads, but not the neutral or ground wire. On older fuse-type boxes, this switch is controlled by a handle directly on the outside of the box, generally to the right. Pull this handle to shut off all power throughout the house. Become acquainted with the location of this control and try it once or twice *before* you have any electrical problems, so that you will become familiar with the position of this switch and its function.

With a circuit-breaker box, there will be no outside handle. Instead, you will find a lever-type control, possibly two, identified as "main circuit breaker." This performs the same function as the outside switch on the fuse box. Both fuse box and breaker box have a metal-front cover panel. Keep this panel closed unless you are changing fuses or setting breakers.

The drawing is a diagram of the switching arrangement in a fuse box. The neutral or ground wire is not fused but continues uninterrupted from your utility throughout your home.

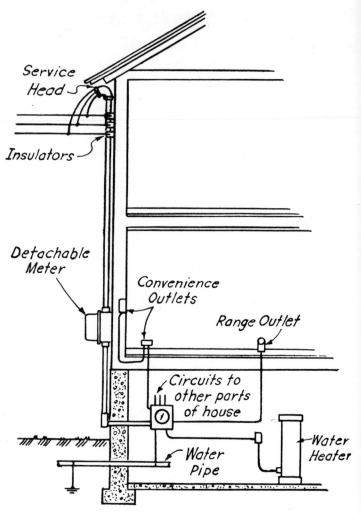

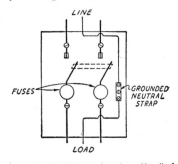

Switching arrangement for input to fuse box: Handle for controlling switch is mounted outside box. Note that neutral or ground wire is not fused. Each hot wire (there are two) is 117 volts "above" ground. The two main fuses must carry the total current demand. These fuses, rated from 30 amperes to as much as 200 amperes, rarely need replacement. Should this become necessary, substitute fuses having current ratings identical with the original. The only exception occurs when the house is rewired to carry a heavier current load.

To understand further how power comes into your home, look up at the three wires going into the entrance head or service head outside your house. This head is mounted at the top end of a

Wiring on the outside of the house follows the same pattern as inside wiring. Three wires—red, black, and white—are fished through galvanized rigid conduit and brought out through a service head at the top of the conduit. The three wires are then spliced onto the utility-company power lines.

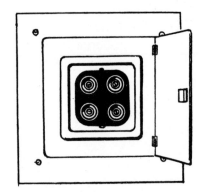

Fuse cabinet of type used in apartments. These are often mounted in a clothes closet. This type of box does not have a main fuse or a main switch. The fuses are only for branches extending into the apartment.

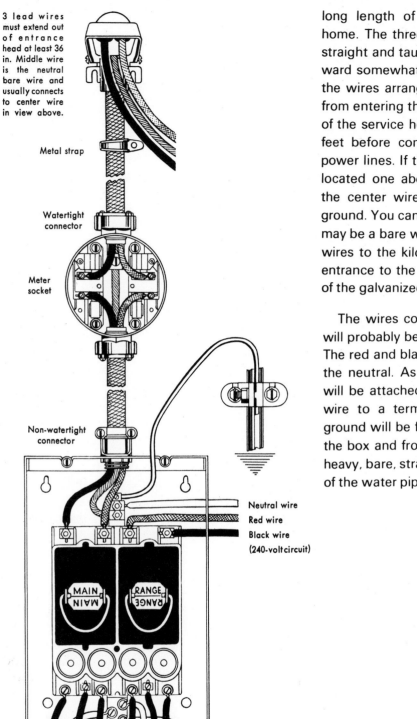

3 lead wires must extend out of entrance head at least 36 in. Middle wire is the neutral bare wire and usually connects to center wire in view above.

Metal strap

Watertight connector

Meter socket

Non-watertight connector

Neutral wire
Red wire
Black wire
(240-volt circuit)

long length of conduit running alongside your home. The three wires entering the head are not straight and taut, but form loops that hang downward somewhat. These are called drip loops with the wires arranged in this manner to keep water from entering the service head. The lead wires out of the service head must extend for at least three feet before connecting to the utility company's power lines. If the three utility-company wires are located one above the other, in vertical fashion, the center wire will probably be the neutral or ground. You can also recognize it by the fact that it may be a bare wire. The conduit carrying the three wires to the kilowatt-hour meter and then to the entrance to the fuse or breaker box must be rigid of the galvanized type.

The wires coming into the fuse or breaker box will probably be color coded red, black, and white. The red and black wires are hot, the white wire is the neutral. As you face the box, the black wire will be attached to a terminal at the left; the red wire to a terminal to its right. The neutral or ground will be fastened to a ground connector on the box and from that point the neutral, usually a heavy, bare, stranded cable will run to that section of the water pipe that precedes the water meter.

BRANCH FORMATION

After passing through the main fuses or circuit breakers, the hot leads are connected to a variety of fuses (or breakers). Some of these may be 10-ampere fuses; others 15, 20, or 30 amperes. Only the hot lead is fused. The neutral lead and a wire connected to either one of the black leads or red leads forms a branch. The number of branches depends on the original design by the electrical contractor. You may have just a few branches, or quite a number. Each branch, also called a circuit, consists of two wires: a ground or neutral and a hot wire. The procedure is the same, whether the branches or circuits come out of a fuse box or circuit breaker. The branches connected to the fuse box are housed in either rigid or thin-walled conduit, although newer dwellings are beginning to use indoor-type plastic-sheathed cable.

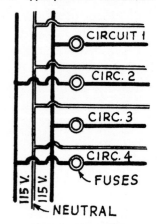

This drawing shows circuits or branches connected to the main power lines. The hot leads of circuits 1 and 3 are connected to the red wire; of circuits 2 and 4 to the black wire. All the branches shown here form 117-volt power lines that then go to various outlets and switches throughout the home.

HOW TO LOCATE BLOWN FUSES

Whether you have a circuit-breaker main box or a fuse type, the first step in checking for trouble is to look. Don't touch, just look. If you have a fuse box, examine each fuse carefully, using a flashlight. The blown fuse may have a dark smear across its top (on the inside). On some fuses, the conducting element is held in position near the top so you can see it. If it is no longer there, the fuse is open.

One of the easiest ways for locating a blown fuse is the substitution test. You should keep a box of known good fuses just for this purpose. Replace fuses, one at a time to see if power is restored to the open branch. Do *not* replace all the fuses at the same time, for if you do you may not learn which branch opened.

Once power is restored, buy another fuse to replace the one you have taken out of your box of fuses you keep just for substitution purposes. Get rid of the old blown fuse at once. Throw it away, put it in the garbage, but do something. It can be a troublemaker if you let it get into your box of substitute fuses.

If you have a circuit-breaker box, the work is easier. Examine the trip handles of each switch. When up, the breaker switch is on; when down, it is off; and the breaker is "blown" when the switch is in an intermediate position. If you cannot decide from the setting of the handle, open and then close each breaker switch until power is restored.

FUSE OR BREAKER PROBLEMS

Theoretically, you should never have to replace a fuse or reset a circuit breaker. But if a particular fuse or breaker keeps opening, you are being given a warning signal that something is wrong. Don't ignore it.

Remove the fuse and examine it. Is it the right size for the branch? Does that branch call for a 20-ampere fuse and have you replaced that 20-ampere fuse with a 10-ampere unit just because it happened to be handy and you didn't have a 20-ampere replacement? When you insert the fuse in its socket, do you make sure it is tight and secure?

Examine the "window" of the blown fuse. Is it discolored severely? Is there a black smudge across its face? If yes, then there is a short circuit somewhere in the branch it protects.

Your next procedure is to locate the cause of

the short. It could be in the branch feeding the outlet or in an appliance. Remove all connections to the receptable (or receptacles) being fed by that power branch. Replace the fuse with a known good fuse of the proper current rating. If it does not blow, the trouble isn't in the line but in one of your appliances. Replace each appliance one at a time. Do not use more than one appliance at a time and remove it before connecting the next appliance.

If one of the appliances "blows" the fuse, then you have a short inside the appliance. If, however, none of the appliances produces a short, then you are overloading the line. You are asking the branch to deliver more current than it should.

If the fuse blows with no appliances inserted in any of the convenience outlets fed by that branch, then you have a short in the line. Open each receptacle electric box and examine the wiring carefully. Look for evidence of a short, such as a black smudge, or charred insulation.

Chapter 8

HOW TO INSTALL AND MAINTAIN
WALL AND CEILING FIXTURES

Just as most homes are inadequately wired, so too do many homes use poor lighting. There is, however, an important difference. Poor lighting doesn't always mean inadequate lighting; it can also mean excessive lighting, lighting that is too concentrated, or not soft enough. It is possible to have a large room with a strong light at one end with the rest of the room practically in darkness. Basements and attics, particularly in older homes, are usually so poorly lighted that they are often accident traps. All of this is unfortunate because it is so unnecessary. Good lighting is easily obtainable. Further, compared to some power-hungry appliances, good lighting can be your best electrical buy. A toaster will gulp 1 200 watts; a 100 watt electric-light bulb, less than 10 percent of this amount.

HOW YOU SEE

The light your eyes receive moves along nerve passageways to the brain, where it is interpreted and possibly stored as information. You can see in two ways: by direct light and by reflected light. If you look straight into the lighted bulb of a flashlight, you have an example of direct light. For the most part, though, we see by reflected light. Light shines on some object, bounces from it, and this reflected light reaches our eyes and then our brains. If objects did not reflect light, we would not be able to see them. If you have a chair or table in your room, you see them only because they can reflect light. If they did not have this capacity, you not only would not see them but you would probably fall all over them. Obviously, then, part of good lighting is to make sure that objects reflect enough light to become visible.

Four factors that determine your ability to see:
1.   ize: The larger an object is, the more it can reflect light. Drop a button on the floor and you may have trouble fi nding it. It just doesn't give back enough light. But you'll be able to see the dresser from which the button dropped. A larger reflecting surface means greater visibility.

2. Contrast: An object that is uniformly dark in color may not be seen as easily as one that is made up of contrasting colors.

3. Reflectibility: Some colors reflect light better than do other colors. A white wall in a room will reflect light, if there is any light available, better than a black wall.

4. Time: It takes time for your eyes to adapt to light. In darkened room your eyes adjust to receive the maximum reflected light. When you are out in the sunshine, your eyes adapt once again. When you go from a well-lighted room to one that is in darkness, close your eyes for a few moments and they will be better adapted to seeing in the dark room.

STEPS TO BETTER-QUALITY LIGHTING

Getting the right amount of light into your home is just one step. You also have the problem of light comfort. You can use a 50-watt electric-light bulb for reading, for example, and yet one such light setup will be uncomfortable, producing eye strain, while another arrangement, also using a 50-watt light will let you see easily and well.

To make sure light is comfortable as well as adequate, the light in the room must be well distributed, free from glare, with no bright spots and deep shadows. Light affects color. When you select a particular wall paint, or wallpaper, or wall fabric, examine it in two ways. Get as large a sample as you can, and look at it under working lighting conditions. A sample of wallpaper or fabric will have one color in the showroom and possibly another in your room because the lighting conditions are different. If you plan to paint, don't do an entire room. Try some on a section of wall and then consider it under two conditions: the first, with natural light from windows; the other, with artificial light from your lamps. The color of the paint, its reflectibility—that is, whether it is a gloss type, such as enamel, or a flat paint such as most latex types—will make a big difference in overall room illumination.

There is still another factor to consider. Your room lighting may be controlled by a dimmer switch. With incandescent lights, increasing the dimming action—that is, reducing the overall light level—has the apparent effect of changing the light of the bulbs from white light to yellow. This doesn't mean it's not good. Yellowish light can be soft and pleasing. That's not the question. The question is whether this is the color of light you want.

White in a room will give you the greatest amount of reflectibility. A room with white ceilings and white or near-white walls means you will be able to use lights with a lower wattage rating. This is also true if much of the furniture is either white or close to it in color. A child's room, particularly a nursery, may be done in a shade of white, a favored arrangement. But if unnecessarily higher wattage-rating bulbs are used, there may be too much glare, and in a nursery, the infant can complain but not communicate.

The colors you use in a room depend on the amount of light. If a room has substantial amounts

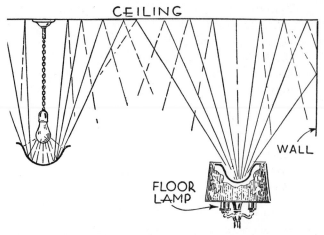

Principle of indirect lighting: Light from bulb (or bulbs) is directed toward ceiling and is then reflected downward with the help of an opaque reflector in the lamp. With this setup, ceiling and walls should be light colored for maximum reflectivity.

of daylight, then you can use strong colors. Strong colors, though, may make the room look smaller; use light tints on a wall to make it appear larger.

APPROXIMATE REFLECTANCE VALUES

The following table supplies the approximate percentage of reflection of light by various colors:

Color	Approximate percent reflection
Whites:	
Dull or flat white	75–90
Light tints:	
Cream or eggshell	79
Ivory	75
Pale pink and pale yellow	75–80
Light green, light blue, light orchid	70–75
Soft pink and light peach	69
Light beige or pale gray	70
Medium tones:	
Apricot	56–62
Pink	64
Tan, yellow-gold	55
Light grays	35–50
Medium turquoise	44
Medium light blue	42
Yellow-green	45
Old gold and pumpkin	34
Rose	29
Deep tones:	
Cocoa brown and mauve	24
Medium green and medium blue	21

Medium gray_____	20
Unsuitably dark colors:	
Dark brown and dark gray_____	10–15
Olive green_____	12
Dark blue, blue-green_____	5–10
Forest green_____	7
Natural wood tones:	
Birch and beech_____	35–50
Light maple_____	25–35
Light oak_____	25–35
Dark oak and cherry_____	10–15
Black walnut and mahogany_____	5–15

This will give you a basis for comparison of the different colors and the percentage of light they reflect. If your preference is for darker tones, such as walnut or mahogany in woods, and a deep tone such as medium blue, remember that you have selected wall and furniture colors that have low reflectibility. In such a room you should have ample natural light, and you should expect to need more wall and ceiling lighting, plus more occasional lamps.

But no matter what the room size may be, the safest course to follow is to try to strike an average: keep furniture, ceiling, and wall colors in about the 30-percent to 60-percent reflectance range. The usual routine is to have ceilings painted white, while floors are much darker. This is a good procedure since light can reach the ceiling from a ceiling fixture and is then reflected downward. The ceiling acts as a large reflecting surface and also diffuses the light, making it softer. Further, it helps spread light over an entire room. However, there are interior-design arrangements in which the ceiling is covered by paper or fabric. Invariably these reduce the amount of reflected light, and while this problem can be overcome by adding more lights or higher-powered bulbs, the fact remains that such rooms can look gloomy if this isn't done.

AMBIENT LIGHT

In any room you will have two basic kinds of light: direct light, light from incandescent bulbs and fluorescents; and ambient light, light reflected from walls, ceilings, furniture, and lampshades. Ambient light also includes light coming in through windows or any other access to outside light. The total light in a room is a combination of direct and reflected light.

SOURCES OF LIGHT

You have two basic sources of light: natural and artificial. Sunlight is natural light. Light from incandescent and fluorescent lamps, or from candles, or a fireplace is considered artificial.

INCANDESCENT BULBS

You can buy incandescent bulbs in just about every conceivable style, size, and shape. Some are designed to flicker, simulating the light of a candle; others may supply light in a number of different intensities. But most commonly, the general household bulb has a wattage range from about 10 watts to as much as 300 watts, has a standard-size base, and is available in three different finishes: clear, frosted, and white.

CLEAR BULBS

A clear bulb is so called since you can look into it and see the filament. Not all bulbs supply the same amount of light. The clear type gives the most light for a given wattage rating. Thus, a 30-watt clear will furnish more light than a 30-watt frosted or a 30-watt white. Such bulbs are used where maximum illumination is demanded at lowest cost. Thus, you might decide to use them in basement, attic areas, or garages. However, if you have a workbench in such a section of the house, it would be advisable to have supplementary lighting.

Clear bulbs are also used in specially designed shapes, such as torch lamps, for crystal-type chandeliers, particularly those that are dimmer controlled. The advantage of a clear bulb is that it not only supplies more light, but a light that has more sparkle to it. Clear bulbs do not give diffused light.

If you will look inside a clear bulb, you will see a wire arranged in the form of a loop or the letter V.

This wire is the filament and produces light when a current flows through it. One side of the filament is attached to the grooved metal around the base of the bulb. The other lead of the filament connects to a small metal section on bhe base. When you screw a bulb into a socket, you automatically connect the filament to the black and white wires of the power branch line. And because a current must flow into the filament, the bulb must be secure—that is, reasonably tight—in its socket. If not, the bulb may flicker, may not glow, and may cause interference to radio and television reception.

Electric-light bulbs get hot very rapidly. The heat is incidental, isn't wanted, but is there just the same. If you want to remove a bulb that has been on for some time, switch it off and give it a chance to cool first, or else wear a pair of gloves, or use a bit of scrap cloth when removing it.

DIRT AND ILLUMINATION

After being in use for sometime, bulbs get dirty. The dirt forms an opaque surface coating, and while it doesn't cut out the light completely, it does reduce the amount. However, if you are using a 75-watt bulb, and it is coated with dirt, you will still be paying for 75 watts of power. Thus, a dirty 75-watt bulb might supply only the equivalent of a clean 50-watt unit. The first step to getting more illumination in the house is to clean the bulbs.

Use a dry cloth. Moisture on the surface of a light bulb will cause it to crack as soon as the bulb gets hot. There is no harm in removing bulbs and washing them, provided the bulb is completely dry before putting it back in its socket.

The wattage rating of a bulb is indicated in two ways. It will be on the packing box holding the bulb, and should also be on the glass end of the bulb.

Keep extra bulbs on hand. If a fixture uses two or more bulbs, replace defective bulbs at once. Do not mix defective bulbs in with good ones. The reason for replacing a burned-out bulb without delay is that it is easy to get accustomed to a lower, and quite possibly inadequate, amount of illumination.

Selection Guide for Incandescent Bulbs

Activity	Minimum recommended wattage [1]
Reading, writing, sewing:	
Occasional periods	150.
Prolonged periods	200 or 300.
Grooming:	
Bathroom mirror:	
1 fixture each side of mirror	1–75 or 2–40's.
1 cup-type fixture over mirror	100.
1 fixture over mirror	150.
Bathroom ceiling fixture	150.
Vanity table lamps, in pairs (person seated)	100 each.
Dresser lamps, in pairs (person standing)	150 each.
Kitchen work:	
Ceiling fixture (2 or more in a large area)	150 or 200.
Fixture over sink	150.
Fixture for eating area (separate from workspace)	150.
Shopwork:	
Fixture for workbench (2 or more for long bench)	150.

[1] White bulbs preferred.

CLEAR BULBS

A clear bulb is so called since you can look into it and see the filament. Not all bulbs supply the same amount of light. The clear type gives the most light for a given wattage rating. Thus, a 30-watt clear will furnish more light than a 30-watt frosted or a 30-watt white. Such bulbs are used where maximum illumination is demanded at lowest cost. Thus, you might decide to use them in basement, attic areas, or garages. However, if you have a workbench in such a section of the house, it would be advisable to have supplementary lighting.

Clear bulbs are also used in specially designed shapes, such as torch lamps, for crystal-type chandeliers, particularly those that are dimmer controlled. The advantage of a clear bulb is that it not only supplies more light, but a light that has more sparkle to it. Clear bulbs do not give diffused light.

If you will look inside a clear bulb, you will see a wire arranged in the form of a loop or the letter V. This wire is the filament and produces light when a current flows through it. One side of the filament is attached to the grooved metal around the base of the bulb. The other lead of the filament connects to a small metal section on bhe base. When you screw a bulb into a socket, you automatically connect the filament to the black and white wires of the power branch line. And because a current must flow into the filament, the bulb must be secure—that is, reasonably tight—in its socket. If not, the bulb may flicker, may not glow, and may cause interference to radio and television reception.

Electric-light bulbs get hot very rapidly. The heat is incidental, isn't wanted, but is there just the same. If you want to remove a bulb that has been on for some time, switch it off and give it a chance to cool first, or else wear a pair of gloves, or use a bit of scrap cloth when removing it.

DIRT AND ILLUMINATION

After being in use for sometime, bulbs get dirty. The dirt forms an opaque surface coating, and while it doesn't cut out the light completely, it does reduce the amount. However, if you are using a 75-watt bulb, and it is coated with dirt, you will still be paying for 75 watts of power. Thus, a dirty 75-watt bulb might supply only the equivalent of a clean 50-watt unit. The first step to getting more illumination in the house is to clean the bulbs.

Use a dry cloth. Moisture on the surface of a light bulb will cause it to crack as soon as the bulb gets hot. There is no harm in removing bulbs and washing them, provided the bulb is completely dry before putting it back in its socket.

The wattage rating of a bulb is indicated in two ways. It will be on the packing box holding the bulb, and should also be on the glass end of the bulb.

Keep extra bulbs on hand. If a fixture uses two or more bulbs, replace defective bulbs at once. Do not mix defective bulbs in with good ones. The reason for replacing a burned-out bulb without delay is that it is easy to get accustomed to a lower, and quite possibly inadequate, amount of illumination.

Sizes and Uses for Three-Way Bulbs

Socket and wattage	Description	Where to use
Medium: 30/70/100____	Inside frost or white.	Dressing table or dresser lamps, decorative lamps, small pin up lamps.
50/100/150____	Inside frost or white.	End table or small floor and swing-arm lamps.
50/100/150____	White or indirect bulb with "built-in" diffusing bowl (R–40).	End table lamps and floor lamps with large, wide harps.
50/200/250____	White or frosted bulb.	End table or small floor and swing-arm lamps, study lamps with diffusing bowls.
Mogul (large): 50/100/150____	Inside frost_____	Small floor and swing-arm lamps and torcheres.
100/200/300__	White or frosted bulb.	Table and floor lamps, torcheres.

FROSTED AND WHITE-FINISH BULBS

Bulbs of this kind diffuse the light and help avoid excessive bright spots. For a given wattage rating they do not yield as much direct light as clear bulbs. These bulbs should also be kept clean to get the maximum amount of light per dollar.

THREE-WAY BULBS

These bulbs have two filaments and use a special socket known as a three-way socket. They are called three-way because each filament can be operated separately, or both together, supplying three different levels of illumination. Thus, one light will be 30 watts, another 70 watts, and the combination will be the sum of the two, or 100 watts. The two filaments, of course, are different. In the example just supplied, the first filament is a 30-watt type, the second is a 70-watt type, and when both are joined, the output is 30 watts plus 70 watts equals 100 watts.

Three-way lamps use either medium or mogul (large) bases. The mogul size is used for larger levels of light. The following table supplies recommendations for sizes and uses of three-way bulbs:

SELECTING INCANDESCENT-LIGHT BULBS

It is impossible to give absolute guidelines for electric-light bulbs. A room that will seem adequately illuminated for one person will seem dim to another. Nevertheless, the following table does carry recommendations and will give you some suggestions on selecting incandescent bulbs for different areas in the home.

TINTED BULBS

You can get electric-light bulbs that glow with all sorts of colors; red, blue, pink, yellow, blue, green, and so on. Some of these are intended for decorative effects; others have practical uses. Red bulbs are often used to supply light in photographic darkrooms and above exit doors; yellow bulbs simulate candles; and lamps of other colors give a particular kind of atmosphere. The color is produced by a tinted silica coating inside the bulb. The coating, however, reduces light output and so such bulbs supply less light than clear or frosted types.

SILVER-BOWL BULBS

These bulbs have a silver coating applied inside or outside the rounded end. The purpose of the coating is to work as a reflector, directing light upward toward the ceiling, or toward another reflector. Spotlight and floodlight bulbs belong to the silver-bowl family. Spotlights are used to direct a narrow beam of light on some object, while floodlights are used to cover a much wider area.

PAR BULBS

PAR is an abbreviation for parabolic and describes the shape of certain types of bulbs designed for outdoor use. These bulbs are rain- and snow-resistant.

DECORATIVE BULBS

You can buy light bulbs in a wide variety of shapes, including globe, flame, cone, mushroom, and tubular. In some types, the enclosing glass is designed with a non-smooth finish to diffuse the light.

HEAT LAMPS

Not all lamps are intended just to supply illumination. There are in-home appliances that use lamp yielding infrared heat to help soothe sore muscles and to help the skin absorb cosmetic creams. Heat lamps are available in different sizes and shapes and are not interchangeable. When buying a replacement, take along the part number of the original heat lamp, and the name and model number of the original appliance.

SUN LAMPS

A sun lamp is a high-pressure mercury lamp and may be made of special quartz to filter out harmful violet rays. Such lamps are intended to supply artificial "sunlight." These are also available in various sizes; some are tubular and others look like enlarged, clear electric-light bulbs, but contain a small pool of mercury that vaporizes when the bulb is turned on. Again, for replacement you will need to know the part number of the bulb and the model number of the appliance.

Some appliances are dual-purpose units, containing both heat lamps and sun lamps.

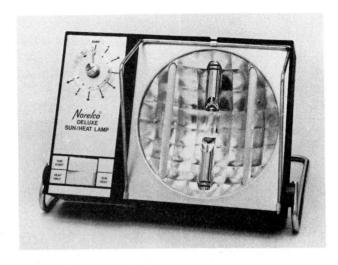

FLUORESCENT TUBES

The incandescent bulb delivers light only when its filament is heated. The light is actually just a by-product, for about 90 percent of the electrical energy delivered to an incandescent bulb turns to heat. In other words, the filament must be made hot enough to glow.

A fluorescent tube, so called because of its shape, is a much more efficient light-delivering device. They are available in various lengths, commonly from 15" to 60", although longer tubes are made for commercial use. You can also get them as straight tubes or in circle form. The circular type are commonly used in kitchens.

At each end of the fluorescent tube you will find a cap with a pair of terminals or prongs. These connect to oxide-coated filaments inside the tube. The tube may be filled with an inert gas such as argon, and in addition the bulb may contain a drop of mercury. The inside surface of the tube is coated with a fluorescent phosphor. This phosphor is somewhat like the phosphor you have covering the inside front surface of your television-picture tube.

Basically, a fluorescent tube is an arc lamp. When the tube is turned on, an electric spark or current flows from the filament at one end to the filament at the other. This arc supplies ultraviolet light. If the tube were a clear type, you would see a faint glow having a purple color. The ultraviolet light, though, strikes the inner coating of phosphorescent material, causing it to fluoresce (accounting for the name, fluorescent tube).

The two filaments inside the fluorescent work quite unlike the filaments inside incandescent tubes, for they remain on only for a second or two, when the tube is first turned on. After their momentary current flow, the filaments have no further current flowing through them.

As part of the fluorescent-light setup, there is also a "starter" and a "ballast." The starter, as its name implies, is a device for starting the flow of current from one end of the fluorescent tube to the other. Look on the starter as an automatic switch that turns itself off after passing a current for a moment or two. The ballast is a coil that has numerous turns and is wound around an iron core. When the flow of current through such a coil is interrupted a very high voltage develops across the coil. The greater the number of turns, the more quickly the current is turned off; and the greater the size of the core (and the kind of material of which it is made), the higher the voltage, often called a kickback voltage.

When you first turn on a fluorescent tube, current flows through the ballast, through one filament, through the starter, and then through the other filament. A second or two later, the starter opens. When this happens, a very high voltage is impressed across the tube, causing an arc to exist between the two filaments. Once the arc is established, current flows with the usual 117 volts AC applied to the ends of the tube.

When the fluorescent tube is turned off, the gas in the tube is a nonconductor of electricity. When the filaments are lighted they each emit some electrons. Because the voltage applied to the tube is alternating (AC), the electrons would like to surge back and forth between the filaments, but cannot do so because the voltage (117 volts) is too low. The ballast momentarily supplies a very high voltage, and so some electrons dash back and forth between the filaments. In so doing, they ionize the gas atoms inside the tube, changing some of them to ions. An ion is an atom that has been stripped of one or more of its electrons, or which may have added one or more electrons to its usual collection. In either case, the ions form an excellent conducting path from one end of the tube to the other. Once the path has been established, a current can oscillate back and forth between the ends of the tube at normal line voltage.

No, you do not need to know exactly how a fluorescent works to be able to install them. But knowing how a fluorescent functions will take you a step above being a "cookbook" electrician, an electrician who works with electricity, making repairs by the book but without understanding what is happening.

STANDARD AND DELUXE FLUOR-ESCENTS

White fluorescent tubes are available in two general types: standard and deluxe. The letter X is used to indicate the deluxe type. White fluorescents are sold in two "colors": warm white and cool white. The letters WW represent warm white; CW, cool white. A deluxe fluorescent would be either WWX or CWX. The first is warm white deluxe; the second is cool white deluxe.

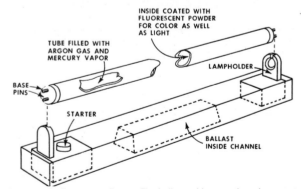

Basic setup of a fluorescent fixture: The ballast seldom needs replacement. The starter fits inside the metal housing of the fluorescent and is easily replaceable.

You can intermix WW and CW, or fluorescents with incandescent lamps to get various shades of white. You can use a CWX tube to get a daylight effect. For home use deluxe fluorescents are best. Whether you should use cold or warm fluorescents depends on your personal taste and the sort of coverings you have on your walls, and the whiteness (or lack of whiteness) of the ceiling.

Fluorescent tubes cost much more than incandescent bulbs having the same wattage rating. However, they have two important advantages: First, they have a much longer life than incandescent bulbs, but equally important, they supply much more light per watt—that is, they give much more light for less money than incandescents. Incandescent lamps behave more like point sources of light, but with a fluorescent tube, the light is spread out.

Fluorescent lamps are efficient when compared with incandescent bulbs. A 40-watt fluorescent lamp produces approximately 2800 lumens. If you divide this by 40, you will get a figure of 70 lumens per watt. The lumen is a unit of light, and the more lumens you get for each watt of electrical power, the more efficient the lamp. The 40-watt fluorescent just described produces about six times as much light per watt as a comparable 40-watt incandescent lamp. Put another way, you can turn on a 40-watt fluorescent for six hours or a 40-watt incandescent for one hour, and pay the same price.

Fluorescent lamps behave like miniature transmitters and indeed they are just that. The small current circulating rapidly back and forth inside the tube produces waves, just like a radio station, and they do travel some small distance. Fluorescent lamps in the same room with radio receivers or television sets can cause noise in the radio or streaks of light across a picture tube. The cure is to move the fluorescent tube and the radio or television set away from each other.

One other problem of fluorescents is that they can produce a sort of flicker. All lights go on and off when operated from the AC power line, but they do this so rapidly that the effect isn't noticeable. It may be helpful to use fluorescent tubes in groups of two or three (or even four). Since they will not all flicker in step, the result will be an average that will not be apparent. Another method is to have the fluorescent light come through white-tinted glass, or to enclose the fluorescents in a covering that resembles the white glass of incandescent bulbs.

The chart that follows is a selection guide for fluorescent tubes. Look on these as generalized suggestions, for the kind of fluorescent fixture (and tubes) you should use depends on the size of the room, the reflector (if any) used with the fluorescents, and the reflection factor of the room.

Fluorescent tubes require some special consideration. With incandescents, for example, a 50-watt bulb looks very much like a 75-watter, and quite often you will need to look at the designation at the base of the tube to know just what the wattage rating is. You can substitute a 100-watt bulb for a 50-watt type without concern about the socket. Both fit the same socket. However, the wattage rating of a fluorescent determines its size. Thus a 15-watt tube will be 18" long; while a 40-watter will be 48" long. You cannot substiture one tube for the other, for they will simply not fit. Further, the starter must be designed for a particular type of fluorescent.

Selection Guide for Fluorescent Tubes

[All are T12 (1½ inch diameter) tubes]

Use	Wattage and color [1]
Reading, writing, sewing:	
Occasional	1 40w or 2 20w, WWX or CWX.
Prolonged	2 40w or 2 30w, WWX or CWX.
Wall lighting (valances, brackets, cornices):	
Small living area (8-foot minimum)	2 40w, WWX or CWX.
Large living area (16-foot minimum)	4 40w, WWX or CWX.
Grooming:	
Bathroom mirror:	
One fixture each side of mirror	2 20w or 2 30w, WWX.
One fixture over mirror	1 40w, WWX or CWX.
Bathroom ceiling fixture	1 40w, WWX.
Luminous ceiling	For 2-foot squares, 4 20 w, WWX or CWX 3-foot squares, 4 30w, WWX or CWX 4-foot squares, 4 40w, WWX or CWX 6-foot squares, 6 to 8 40w, WWX or CWX.
Kitchen work:	
Ceiling fixture	2 40w or 2 30w, WWX.
Over sink	2 40w or 2 30w, WWX or CWX.
Counter top lighting	20w or 40w to fill length, WWX.
Dining area (separate from kitchen)	15 or 20 watts for each 30 inches of longest dimension of room area, WWX.
Home workshop	2 40w, CW, CWX, or WWX.

[1] WWX=warm white deluxe; CWX=cool white deluxe; CW=cool white.

Fluorescent tubes also present a disposal problem. Some apartment houses have regulations against dumping fluorescents into incinerator chutes. Wrap them in heavy kraft paper (not newspaper) and seal them securely; or hand them personally to your local garbage collector. Cuts received from broken fluorescent lights can be very nasty and difficult to heal. Children (and adults) and broken fluorescent tubes do not mix. While you were encouraged to store incandescent lamps, the same is not true of fluorescents unless you have a safe place away from busy inexperienced fingers.

The chart shown below indicates the ballast needed for various types of fluorescents.

Type of Tube For Ballast Used

[Fluorescent tube wattages vary with length of tube and are not interchangeable]

Length of tube (inches)	Wattage	Diameter of tube	Ballast marking [1]
	Watts	*Inches*	
15------	14	1½ (T12)---	Preheat start.
18------	15	1 (T8)-----	Trigger start or preheat.
		1½ (T12)---	Trigger start or preheat.
24------	20	1½ (T12)---	Preheat or rapid start.
36------	30	1 (T8)-----	Rapid start.
		1½ (T12)---	Rapid start or dimming.
48------	40	1½ (T12)---	Rapid start or dimming.

[1] Only preheat ballasts require starters and use standard-type tubes.

HOW TO WIRE CEILING-DROP FIXTURES

A ceiling-drop fixture is any lighting fixture supported by a chain link. Before you try to get at the wiring of such a fixture, remove the fuse controlling the light. Make sure power is off by turning the switch that controls it and do this several times, just to make sure. Right above the lamp and up against the ceiling, you will find a small covering held in position by a locknut. This covering is called a canopy. Loosen the locknut by turning it counterclockwise. You should be able to turn it with your fingers; if not, use a pair of pliers. Turn the locknut until it slides down and you will be able to lower the canopy. You will find two

white wires joined by a solderless connector. Similarly, there will be two black wires, also joined by a solderless connector. One black wire and one white wire go into the fixture. The remaining white and black wire go into conduit or BX that fits into an electric box in the ceiling, directly above the fixture. If you want to replace the fixture, substitute the white and black wires from the new fixture for the old one. Follow the same procedure if you are putting in a fixture for the first time.

There are various ways in which the fixture is mechanically held to the ceiling. In older fixtures you will find a stud in the ceiling box. A hickey connects this stud to the stem of the drop fixture. It sounds a bit complicated, but when you get a chance to look at it, you will see how really simple it is. A stud, a hickey and a stem are devices that fit into each other by threads cut into them. In newer fixtures, the hickey is replaced by a double-threaded holder. One end of the holder screws onto the stud that is attached to the ceiling box; the other end of the holder fastens to the threaded stem of the fixture. The stem is mechanically attached to the fixture.

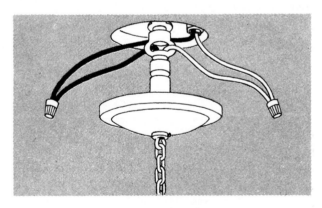

How to install a ceiling-drop fixture. (Courtesy, Sears.)

After you join the two wires of the lamp to the correspondingly colored wires that are coiled in position above the canopy, fasten solderless connectors on them, rotate the hickey onto the stud and the stem of the drop fixture onto the hickey.

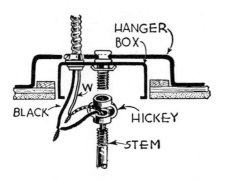

This is a detailed drawing of the preceding illustration. The hickey is used for joining the stem to the threaded stud coming out of the electric ceiling box (also called a hanger box). The hickey is now being replaced by a similar device, much lighter and more open. It still does the same job, however.

There is even an easier way to learn how to do ceiling fixture replacements: After you turn off the power to the fixture, lower the canopy; then carefully examine the way in which the ceiling-drop fixture is held in place. Disassemble these parts, and observe how they fit together. After you have taken them apart, put them together again. With this very little bit of experience, you will be able to install a new fixture.

What you have just accomplished is the mechanical side of installing a fixture. Electrically, all you need is connect the two wires of the lamp to two wires, one black and the other white, which you will find in the canopy. Incidentally, the two wires in the lamp aren't critical. Connect either one to the white wire in the canopy, and then the other to the black wire.

After you have made your electrical connections and put on the solderless connectors, replace the fuse and try the fixture with the help of an electric-light bulb. Do this *before* replacing the canopy, just to make sure that what you have done is correct. Then, turn the switch off, tuck the wiring into the ceiling hole protected by the canopy, push the canopy up, and fasten the locknut.

The advantage of putting in a new ceiling-drop fixture or replacing one is that if you can do one—and there is no reason why you shouldn't be able to do so—you can reasonably and confidently expect to be able to replace all the drop fixtures in your home, or in other homes. A little experience here will go a long, long way.

HOW TO INSTALL FLUSH-MOUNTED CEILING FIXTURES

In some cases the ceiling fixture does not have a drop chain but is directly up against the ceiling. The wiring of the fixture remains exactly the same; all that changes is the mechanical method of fastening the fixture into position. Such fixtures are usually mounted in kitchens, bathrooms, and walk-in closets. If you will examine the illustration, you will see that the black wire and white wire coming out of the ceiling electric box are fastened to a pair of wires of the fixture. Coming out of the electric box is a fixture stud, just a threaded bit of hardware that looks like the end of a small pipe. Put the strap over the stud and then fasten it into position with one ⅜" locknut. If you will examine the strap, you will see it has a pair of holes. These are intended to accomodate a pair of screws to hold the fixture to the strap.

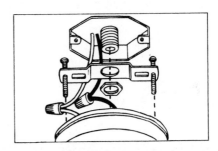

Method of attaching a fixture directly to ceiling: The threaded center piece coming out of the electric box is the stud. Directly below it is the metal mounting bracket. The metal mounting bracket is fastened to the stud with a locknut, usually a ⅜" type. The two screws at the end of the metal mounting bracket are used for holding the fixture. (Courtesy, Sears.)

What should be the order of work? Which of these steps should you do first? Should you connect the wires and then make the mechanical connections? Actually, it makes little difference. If you find you have taken a step that prevents you from doing the others, just retreat. Undo what you have done and start over again. If, for example, you fasten the fixture to the ceiling without having joined the wires, you will need to undo the fixture

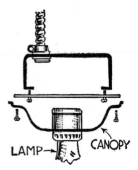

so as to make the connections. This is an extreme case, of course, but it has happened, and it has happened—you guessed it— to professional electricians.

If the fixture to be suspended is a small one, it may be held in place by a strap attached to the ears of the ceiling box.

Before fastening the fixture to the strap, insert a light bulb in the fixture, put the fuse for the fixture back into position, and try the light switch, just to make sure that the light will work. Turn the light switch off and fasten the fixture to the strap.

With each lamp you buy you will probably get the necessary hardware for attaching the lamp, either as a ceiling-drop or as a directly attached type. There will be variations in mounting hardware. Some manufacturers are even farsighted enough to supply printed mounting information with their products.

THE STUDLESS CEILING BOX

It is entirely possible that your ceiling electric box will not have a stud. However, the box will have a pair of ears. An ear is a bit of metal bent in toward the open area of the box. The ears are normally used to help hold a cover plate over the box. You will find a center hole drilled through each ear. The ears may be tapped—that is, they may be threaded. If that is the case, you will be able to fasten the metal strap to the ear with a pair of machine screws, as shown in the drawing. If not, put a machine screw through each ear, with the head of the screw inside the electric box. The screws will now be extending downward. Let these screws pass through the metal strap, and then use a pair of nuts to fasten the strap into

position. Once the strap is tightly in position, all you need do is to put two machine screws through the ends of the strap, let these extend directly into the fixture itself, and then, with the help of a pair of nuts, fasten the fixture into position. Before you do so, however, make sure you have made the electrical connections.

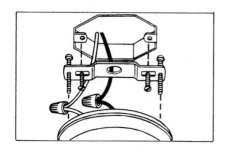

If the ceiling electric box does not have a center stud, fasten the metal mounting bracket to the ears. The drawing shows the use of threaded ears. If the ears are not threaded, simply reverse the position of the screws shown in the drawing. The two screws shown on the ends of the metal mounting bracket are for holding the fixture in position. (Courtesy, Sears.)

HOW TO INSTALL GLASS-ENCLOSED CEILING FIXTURES

Glass-enclosed ceiling fixtures are commonly used in bathrooms and kitchens. You can mount such fixtures following the techniques just described, but with one small modification: A metal mounting bracket is unnecessary as the fixture is attached and supported by the stud coming out of the ceiling electric box. With the fixture, you will receive an adapter or cap. This adapter is threaded completely through its center hole. Screw the adapter onto the stud. As part of the hardware accompanying the fixture, you will get a nipple, a length of metal that is threaded. Insert the nipple into the adapter by rotating the nipple in a clockwise direction. Make the nipple as tight as you can.

You will find there is a hole right in the center of the fixture. Now slide the fixture up over the nipple so that a small portion of the nipple extends into the fixture. Slip a washer over this part of the nipple and then put on a nut. Don't tighten the nut as yet. You now have the fixture supported, somewhat loosely. Make your electrical con-

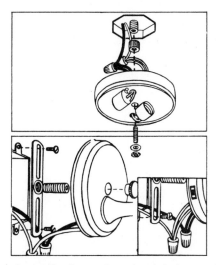

Method of mounting a ceiling fixture using a threaded adapter and a nipple (upper drawing). Method of mounting a wall fixture using a nipple and a threaded cap. (lower drawing). (Courtesy, Sears.)

nections, insert a bulb (or bulbs) into the fixture, and test to make sure the fixhure works. Turn off the switch and fasten the fixture into place by rotating the nut on the nipple in a clockwise manner.

THREADS

Threads are a succession of grooves cut into metal. A machine screw is a cylindrical bit of metal, with threads cut around its outside; hence is said to be outside threaded. You could also have a cylindrical length of metal with a hole cut through its entire length. The outside of the metal will be smooth but the interior of the longitudinal hole will be threaded, and so is referred as inside threaded. Of course, you can have similar bits of metal with threads both inside and outside. The only thing mysterious about inside, or outside, or double-threaded hardware are the names used. One may be called a stud, another an adapter, still another a machine screw. Basically, they are all alike. The names are different because they are used for different purposes.

It is easy to damage threads, and once you do, you will need to replace that particular bit of hardware. Since this is a nuisance, it is much better to be careful. Do not use tools on exposed threads. If a nut or other threaded hardware will not turn easily and smoothly onto a nipple or a stud, don't force it. The result will be "cross-threading," an undesirable situation in which the threads of one object do not properly mesh with the threads of another.

It is possible that you may receive a bit of hardware with damaged threads. If so, your solution, and possibly the only solution, is to return it to your electrical shop with a request for replacement. If you buy lamps, or other electrical devices that use threaded items, examine the threads to make sure they are continuous, not bent or otherwise damaged.

HOW TO INSTALL A WALL FIXTURE

It's just as easy to install a wall fixture as a ceiling type; actually simpler since you won't have to bend your neck or work in an awkward position.

Most wall fixtures are fastened to the ears of a wall-mounted electric box. Use a metal mounting bracket that has a threaded center hole. Mount a nipple by rotating it clockwise into the threaded center hole and then fasten the metal mounting bracket to the electric box. Do this with the help of a pair of machine screws and nuts. The metal mounting bracket has two longitudinal cutouts in the metal, and so it is not at all difficult to align the bracket so that the screws go through easily. Tighten the two cutouts and screws and you will now have the metal mounting bracket tightly in position.

You will find the wall fixture has a center hole. Slide the fixture over the nipple so that it extends through this hole. With the fixture you will have received a cap nut. A cap nut is threaded like an ordinary nut, but does not have a through center hole. Instead, there is a bit of metal over one end; hence the name cap nut.

At this point you may have a bit of a problem. After tightening the cap nut, you may find the

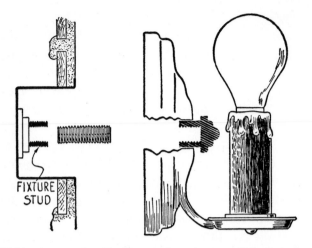

Wall-bracket mounting: The fixture stud may be mounted directly in the electric box. The threaded nipple fits into the stud. The canopy of the fixture is pushed over the nipple and the entire lighting fixture is then fastened into place by a capping nut.

fixture is somewhat loose instead of being tight against the wall and that it is impossible to turn the cap nut further. All this means is that the nipple extends too far into the fixture. Adjust the nipple so that less of it is in the fixture, replace the fixture on the nipple, and try to fasten the fixture into position with the cap nut once again.

If you can now make the fixture really tight, undo the cap nut so that you can make your electrical connections. Before finally tightening the fixture, however, insert a bulb and test to see if the fixture works.

HOW TO INSTALL
OLDER-TYPE WALL FIXTURES

If you are preparing to paper or paint a wall that has wall fixtures, you may find it more convenient to remove the fixture and then to replace it after the decorating work is finished. Or, you may need to remove the fixture to do some repairs, or you may want to install an older-style fixture to match others already in the room.

Electrically, old-style fixtures and the most modern units are identical. You will find a pair of wires in the wall electric box and these wires are to be connected to the wires of the wall fixture. You may find the old wiring was taped. If so,

remove the tape and discard it, for it has undoubtedly outlived its useful life. In place of the tape, use solderless connectors. Remember, the connectors must not only cover the wires, but must extend over the insulation of the wires. Do not try to cover bare wires with tape at the end of the connectors. Instead, cut away some of the excess metal with a pair of diagonal cutters.

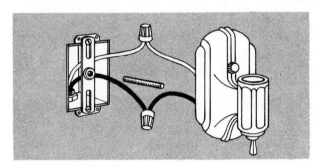

Method of installing an older type of wall fixture. (Courtesy, Sears.)

You will find connected to the wall electric box a metal mounting bracket; it will be fastened to the box by a pair of machine screws at the top and bottom of the bracket. You will find a threaded nipple coming out of the threaded center hole of the bracket. The nipple extends into the fixture with the fixture held to the nipple by a cap nut. That is all there is to it.

With older fixtures, however, you may have a problem. Some of these come equipped with small pull chains extending from the bottom of the fixture. This means they have a built-in switch. If the switch is defective, finding a replacement may be difficult. Since you will want matching fixtures in the room, one solution would be to replace the old-fashioned fixtures with more modern types.

HOW TO INSTALL
A TUBE-TYPE FLUORESCENT FIXTURE

Installing a fluorescent fixture follows the same general procedure you use for incandescent fixtures. The usual tubular fixture consists of a metal chassis with all wiring completed—that is, the starter, ballast, and fluorescent are already connected. The ballast is fixed in position and will require no attention on your part. Somewhere on the chassis you will find a small circular cutout for the starter. You may receive a starter with the fixture, or it may be missing. If the starter is not included, be sure to get one designed to handle the wattage rating and the type of fluorescent you buy. To install the starter, just insert it and then twist it in a clockwise manner. It should click into position.

If your ceiling electric box does not have a threaded stud, insert one. You can do this by getting a metal mounting bracket with provision for a stud center mount. Attach the metal mounting bracket to the ears of the ceiling outlet with a pair of machine screws and nuts.

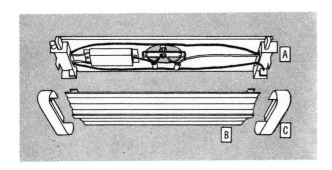

Method of installing a tubular type of fluorescent fixture: Tube support (A), light diffuser (B), and finishing end caps(C). (Courtesy, Sears.)

You can buy studs in various lengths, so be sure to get a size that will extend into the fixture. If you have an existing threaded stud and it isn't long enough, either replace it with a longer one, or use an extension nipple. The chassis of the fluorescent has a center hole. Mount the fixture so that the stud coming from the electric box passes through it. Now all you need do is to fasten it securely with a locknut. If this seems to you to be exactly the same procedure that you follow in mounting an incandescent-type ceiling or wall fixture, then you are abolutely right. Once you learn something in electrical work, it becomes applicable to many different kinbs of jobs.

TABLE LAMPS

Before you buy a table lamp, consider that the lamp will (on the average) have two openings: one at the top so that the light will be directed toward the ceiling, and the other at the bottom so that the light will be directed downward. If you plan on sitting next to the lamp, the bottom edge of the lampshade should be at least an inch or two below your eye level. If not, you will find yourself staring directly into the bulbs of the lamp. Your eye height depends on your own height and the height of the chair or sofa on which you will be sitting. An average eye height is about 42", but it can be more or less than this, depending on how small or big you are, and the kind of chair or sofa that is adjacent to the table lamp. The illustration shows various kinds of table lamps and tables. If the table is the type that has its surface area rather close to the floor, then you will need a lamp having a rather high base.

Buying a table lamp is more than looking for one that will be the most attractive. Lamps are and can be decorative, but function comes before form; the most important fact about the lamp is that it will supply light.

To eliminate the possibility of eyestrain, some table lamps come equipped with reflectors so that no matter what the positioning may be, the light is directed toward the ceiling. The problem with these, and similar types of lamps, is that the diffused light received from the lamp may not be adequate. It may also require using bulbs having a higher wattage rating.

When you plan to use the lamp for activities that require considerable use of the eyes—reading, sewing, or studying—select a shade that has a diameter of at least 16" across the bottom and a diameter of 9" across the top. The shade should also be at least 10" deep. Of course, this isn't a hard and fast rule, but at least it is a guideline.

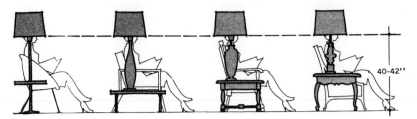

TYPICAL HEIGHTS OF LAMPS AND TABLES FOR SHADE AT EYE LEVEL

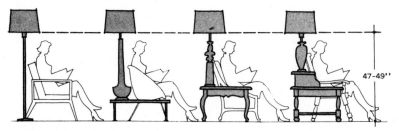

TYPICAL HEIGHTS OF LAMPS AND TABLES FOR SHADE ABOVE EYE LEVEL

A good arrangement is to have the lampshade about an inch or two below eye level, as shown in the row of drawings across the top. If the base of the shade is above eye level, looking directly at the bulbs can produce eyestrain. The lower row of drawings indicates improper lamp arrangements.

If the lamp has just a single socket, consider that the bulb will probably need to be 100 watts; possibly more. Do not use a clear type, although these do supply more light. Experiment with bulbs having different wattage ratings until you find the one most suitable for your eyes and the kind of work you plan on doing. For some, a 150-watt bulb is more desirable.

If the lamp is a multiple-socket type, you will probably need to use 50 watt bulbs or more. A good rule to follow is to allow at least 100 watts minimum. Thus, if the lamp has a triple socket arrangment, try three 40-watt bulbs as a start.

Finally, if the table lamp isn't on a separate table, but is actually on the table on which you are doing your reading or studying, keep the lamp to your left if you are right-handed, and to your right, if you are left-handed. Position the lamp so that it is about one foot away from your work, either to the left or to the right. The bottom of the shade should be such that you are unable to look directly at the light bulbs.

FLOOR LAMPS

The suggestions made with reference to table lamps apply to floor lamps as well. If possible, use a floor lamp that is an adjustable type so that the light comes from behind your shoulder, either at the right or the left, but not from directly behind the chair. A good starting point for floor lamps, as with table lamps, is to begin with a minimum of 100 watts.

THREE-WAY LAMPS

Some lamps, both floor and desk types, have a three-way feature that permits you to get three different levels of light. These have the considerable advantage that they can be used to add to the ambient light in a room, or the light can be increased for reading and studying purposes. A good three-way combination would consist of a

174

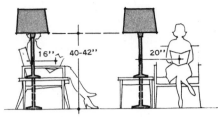

PLACEMENT DIMENSIONS FOR SHADE
AT EYE LEVEL

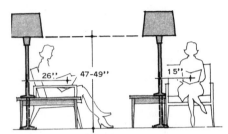

PLACEMENT DIMENSIONS FOR SHADE
ABOVE EYE LEVEL

Upper drawings show proper positioning and heights of floor lamps. Lamps shown in lower drawing can cause eye fatigue produced by looking directly into lighted bulbs.

50-watt and a 100-bulb. You could then get 50 watts, 100 watts, and 150 watts of lighting.

FLUORESCENT LAMPS

Some desk-type lamps use fluorescent bulbs, either small tubulars or circle types. With fluorescents, though, you must be careful that there is no flicker. Also, some fluorescent fixtures can produce an audible hum caused by current flowing through the ballast. You can also get lamps that consist of a combination of incandescent bulbs and fluorescents. The advantage here is that you get a mixing of light, producing a softer kind of light, plus the fact that any flicker may not be seen in the overall light combination.

BED LAMPS

Some inexpensive bed lamps are designed to be supported on the wooden or metal frame of the bed, and so are suspended directly above the head of the individual. These lamps are made to reflect all light downward, thus concentrating the light. The positioning of such lamps more often makes

them inadequate sources of light. They should be covered with a diffuser so that the light bulbs are shielded.

Proper positioning for a table lamp used as a bed lamp.

A better light source is a lamp put on a night table. The lamp should be the double open type, that is, open at the top and bottom of the shade so as to increase the ambient light in the room and still provide enough light for reading purposes. The bottom of the shade should be slightly below eye level.

LAMPS FOR DRESSING TABLES OR VANITIES

Shades for lamps of all kinds—table lamps, floor lamps, etc.—can be opaque or translucent. The disadvantage of the opaque types is that they concentrate the light exclusively in up or down directions. A translucent shade allows light to diffuse through it. This has the effect of increasing the amount of ambient light, but more important, it supplies a soft light around the area of the shade. Translucent shades are necessary for lamps on dressing tables or vanities. Select lamps that are tall enough so that the center of the shade is about 15″ above the table.

The shape of a lampshade also affects lighting. Shades having straight lines are preferable to those that have extreme curves. Since lamps of all kinds come equipped with their own switches, no special wiring is needed; just plug the lamps into the nearest convenience outlet. Some floor lamps have foot switches, but there are no more convenient than the hand-operated types, plus the fact that the base of the lamp can become dirty from shoes. Do not put the cord from lamps under rugs but make sure that the cord is out of the way and isn't where it can be stepped on or tripped over.

DIFFUSERS AND SHIELDS

Always shield incandescent bulbs to avoid the necessity of looking at such bulbs directly. A shield for a fluorescent is also helpful when these are used above or around a medicine cabinet. Some medicine cabinets come equipped with bare-type tubular fluorescents, and while such tubes are coated inside, it is better to use those that are shielded. The shield will help reduce glare, supply a softer light, and will help avoid strong shadows.

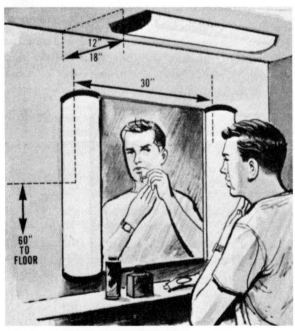

Medicine cabinets sometimes come equipped with built-in fluorescents. These should be shielded to soften the light and shadows and to prevent glare.

KITCHEN DIFFUSERS

When you first walk into a store that specializes in selling electric-light fixtures, you may well become bewildered by the tremendous variety of sizes, shapes, styles, and colors available. Buying a light fixture is often a compromise between the beauty of the unit, its practicality, and its price.

When selecting a fixture, make sure that all the other fixtures in the store surrounding if are off. Then, turn "your" fixture on and off. Will it supply enough light? Does it produce glare? Is the upward light it throws so strong that it produces heavy ceiling shadows? Is it relatively easy to get at the light bulbs for replacement? Does the light flicker?

Some fixtures look like solid brass, an expensive metal, but are brass finish only. This finish is usually extremely thin and wears away whether it is cleaned or not, exposing black metal underneath. The gaudiest finish is not always the most durable. Once brass finish disappears, it does so in spots, leaving large black areas about which you can do nothing.

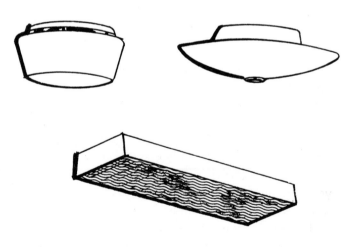

Representative kitchen fixtures: The unit at the left is a closed-globe type. White glass supplies good light diffusion. The drawing in the center shows a shielded fixture. A shallow, wide-bowl type is most desirable. Tubular fluorescents (drawing at right) should have a diffusing shield. The average kitchen uses two to four tubes, 4" long.

You must consider also whether replacement bulbs will be unusual and expensive types? Equally important, will the fixture fit into the space you have assigned to it?

Buying a fixture is like buying anything else. The rule that the buyer must beware still holds. Above all, don't buy on impulse. Think about it and deliberately delay before buying.

You will find three basic types of diffusers for the kitchen, although there are many variations. One of these is the closed-globe type. This was popular in kitchens for many years, but fashions come and fashions go. The closed globe, though, is still an excellent diffuser for it is fairly inexpensive, diffuses the light on all sides, and is easy to clean. For a kitchen, get a diffuser closed-globe that has a minimum diameter of 14". With a closed-globe unit, you will need to experiment with bulbs having various wattage ratings. The fact that a closed-globe kitchen diffuser uses a 100-watt bulb when you see it in the store means little or nothing. The size of the store is entirely different from that of your kitchen, and there is probably more ambient light.

The shielded fixture is a popular type. It is generally designed for use with three or four bulbs. Select one that ranges from about 14" to 17" in diameter. Some shielded fixtures are deep types; others are shallow. Pick one that is shallow. Since the shielded fixture is open at the top, unlike the closed-globe unit, more light reaches the ceiling and is reflected from it. The closed-globe type does not produce shadows on the ceiling; the shielded fixture may. It all depends on the color of your ceiling—that is, its reflectivity—the wattage rating of the bulbs you use, and their positioning and distance from the ceiling. The shadows may also be covered by the fixture, so when you assess a fixture in your kitchen, make your final determination after the shield is in position, not before.

There is one other disadvantage of the open-type shielded fixture. Kitchens invariably attract insects and these often move to the light and warmth of the ceiling fixture. You may find that your fixture has become a nesting place and a cemetery for bugs. Some shielded fixtures are closed types and do not have this disadvantage. In this sense, then, they more closely resemble the closed-globe type, but differ from it in styling. Closed globes are generally made only of white glass; shielded fixtures may be in various colors and also highly ornamented.

When using closed-globe or shielded fixtures, you will get more light by using clear bulbs. There isn't much point in using frosted bulbs in a fixture that already supplies excellent diffusion. If you want maximum light softness, however, frosted bulbs are clearly your choice.

Fluorescent fixtures can be a good selection for the kitchen. Here you have a choice of two basic styles: the circle type and the tubular. The circle type is often mounted on a round metal canopy made of metal having high reflectivity. Since fluorescent bulbs supply "spread-out" light rather than the point-source light furnished by incandescents, shielding is often more of a token gesture rather than effective. Circle-type fluorescents are available in cool white and warm white. Which type you decide on depends on your own personality and the kind of kitchen you have or want. Some home owners compromise and intermix, using one warm white and one cool white.

Circle fluorescent fixtures often have a center-mounted diffuser that fits into the area surrounded by the lamps. Such a diffuser may be decorative, but a diffuser it is not. When you select such a fixture, check to make sure that the diffuser extends over the bulb area. All fluorescent bulbs are interior coated and, unlike incandescent bulbs, are not available as "clear" types. Thirty-two watts is a common rating for kitchen fluorescents, but for adequate lighting get a fixture capable of holding two such fluorescent circle bulbs at the same time. Some circle fluorescents use two different sizes of bulbs, with both forming circles with one inside the other. When the bulbs are of the same size, you will find one mounted above the other.

Tube-type fluorescents are also used in kitchesn. While circle types are more compact, and are regarded by some as more attractive, the tube type will spread the light over a greater area. If you have a rather large kitchen, it is possible that a tube-type fluorescent might provide more adequate lighting. Tubular kitchen fluorescent fixtures come equipped with a diffusing shield, generally at the bottom of the fixture and at the ends. For a fluorescent fixture with a diffusing shield, you will need from two to four fluorescent tubes, 48″ long. For very large kitchens, you may need a pair of circle-type fixtures, suitably spaced away from each other, or a pair of tubular types. Inadequate kitchen lighting is not only depressing but can make the tastiest food look unpalatable. To get maximum light, all kitchen fixtures, regardless of type and their associated bulbs, must be cleaned regularly.

DINING-ROOM DIFFUSERS

The same variety you can find in kitchen fixtures also applies to the dining room. Some dining-room fixtures use cut glass. They are not only beautiful, and not only diffuse the light, but break light into its constituent colors. Cut-glass fixtures are much more expensive than ordinary types. Cheap imitations are available, but the cut glass looks tawdry and has little or no sparkle. When assembling such a fixture, particularly if it is a quality type, use gloves when mounting each individual bit of cut glass. These fixtures are not supplied assembled. Fingerprints on the glass can spoil the appearance of the fixture. Cleaning such fixtures is much more of a job than with ordinary lights, but instead of polishing each individual glass segment, you can now buy a cleaning spray.

The lantern-style pulldown lamp usually comes equipped with a three-way socket and takes a 50/100/150-watt bulb. The bulbs are covered

with a glass chimney made of frosted glass, with the chimney working as a diffuser. There is also a

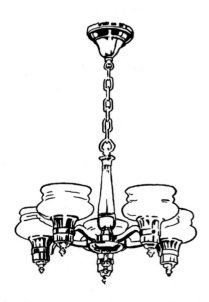

These fixtures make use of the principle of semi-indirect lighting. The diffusers permit some light to go through, supplying downward light. The diffusers also act as reflectors, sending light up to the ceiling. Light is then reflected downward. These are hanging-type fixtures and can be adjusted for proper height above the floor by removing one or more links from the supporting chain. Wires carrying current come down from the canopy at the top of the fixture, and are intertwined around the links. The surface on canopy, links, and decorations is often made of "bright finish." This may look attractive when new, but plating is very thin and reveals black areas where it is worn away. Diffuser at left is held in position by a single capped screw. Diffusers at right, one for each bulb, are supported by the fixture and are not usually fastened into position. In some fixtures you may find small thumb screws holding the diffusers.

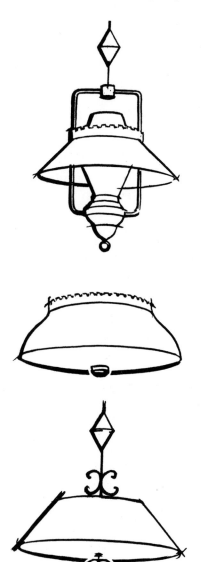

Dining-room diffusers: Unit at left is lantern-style pulldown, often equipped with three-way socket. Center drawing is ventilated ceiling fixture; diffuser is held in place with threaded cap. Pulldown fixture (at right) is ventilated unit with three-way single socket or three sockets, and white glass diffuser.

tually. However, metal shades can have high reflectivity; just make sure that the inside of the shade, the part you see when the lamp is in position, is in some off-white color. Pull-down lantern style shades aren't toys, so keep them high enough to be out of the reach of children.

Another type of dining-room diffuser is the ventilated ceiling fixture. The diffuser is of glass and may be in two parts: a round secton that surrounds the fixture, and a circular bottom section. It is called ventilated since it is open at the top. A fixture of this type is often held in place by a single cap screw fastened to a threaded nipple. Since the glass-diffuser bottom portion is held in place only by the cap screw, make sure the screw is tight.

Ventilated fixtures are also available as pull-down types. This ventilated unit has a three-way single socket or three sockets. The diffuser is often made of white glass.

Diffusers can be made of glass, metal, or fabric. Each has its advantages and disadvantages. Of the three, glass is possibly the best. It is easy to clean, supplies excellent diffusion, but, of course, if subject to breakage. Glass is also available in various tints, but the white type yields the most light.

Metal diffusers have the advantage of attractiveness. They can be made in many different styles, with ornamental metal trim. However, some modern glass diffusers are quite artistic, with white inner reflecting surfaces and ornamental outside colored surfaces. Some of the metal shades, particularly those with smooth burnished surfaces, are very easy to clean.

Fabric diffusers can be very luxurious; and because they are fabric, they fit in more easily with home decor. Cleaning may be a problem, however, and they may not have the life expectancy of glass or metal diffusers.

shade, generally made of metal, that reflects this diffused light downward.

Pulldown lamps have a number of advantages. You can set the height to chase shadows and to supply light from the best level. They are easier to reach for cleaning and bulb replacement. There are a few disadvantages, though. The shade is generally metal, and if it has bright finish ornamentation, you will find it turning black even-

BEDROOM DIFFUSERS

One of the more common, inexpensive types, is the surface-mounted ceiling fixture. Don't make the mistake of getting one that is too small. The fixture should have a minimum diameter of 12". For large bedrooms, get the type that has two or more sockets. If the fixture has three or possibly four sockets, this does not mean you must use them all. The advantage of having four, rather than two sockets, is that you can spread the light a bit more. Thus, instead of using two 100-watt bulbs, you would be able to substituxe four 50-watters. Also make sure the diffuser is shallow and wide. The reason for a shallow-type diffuser is that you want the light to enter the diffuser as quickly as possible. The greater the distance between the light and the diffuser, the less light will be available for the room. Also make sure the diffuser is wide, so that you are unable to see the bulbs it covers from any position in the bedroom.

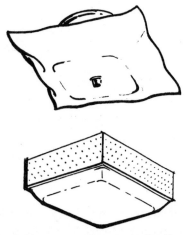

Bedroom diffusers: Unit at left is surface-mounted ceiling type held in place with single capped nut in center; unit in center drawing is similar to one at left. Diffuser can be plain or textured glass, or may be made of plastic. Ventilated ceiling fixture is at right. It has one or two sockets and is surface-mounted on ceiling.

An even simpler type of bedroom-ceiling fixture is the square-diffuser type. These are surface mounted, with plain or textured glass as the diffusing element. Some very low-cost diffusers for bedroom fixtures are made of plastic. The trouble with plastic is that it can discolor from heat, or else change its shape.

Still another bedroom fixture is the ventilated ceiling type. This kind of fixture is more utilitarian than beautiful. The light is boxed in on all four sides by rectangular metal strips with holes, and has a diffusing shade extending below this trim. This type of unit is surface mounted on the ceiling. It generally comes equipped with either one or two sockets.

BATHROOM DIFFUSERS

Bathrooms, particularly in newer homes, are often equipped with a center ceiling-type incandescent fixture, and tubular fluorescents around the medicine cabinet. The medicine cabinet may have overhead tubular only, side fluorescent only, or a combination of both. The tubular fluorescents are generally 24" types. The fluorescents may be bare, as in less expensive medicine cabinets, but a better type has a flat or curved glass or plastic diffuser. The diffuser may be plain or ornamented.

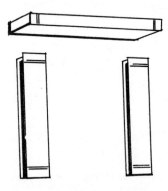

Medicine cabinets often come equipped with tubular fluorescents. The best type has shielded fluorescents. These are generally switch controlled at the fixture, with individual on-off switches for each. Cabinet may have overhead fluorescent, or side fluorescents, or both. Tubular fluorescents are 24" type. If there is no ceiling light in the bathroom (unusual, but it does happen) then medicine cabinet should have a tubular fluorescent above the mirror.

If the bathroom has a stall shower, it should be equipped with a vapor-proof ceiling fixture. The diffuser is a curved glass, white or frosted, to diffuse the light of an incandescent bulb, generally rated at 60 watts. Do not install a switch in the shower. The best place for the shower switch is immediately adjacent to the main light switch in the bathroom. Never turn bathroom lights on or off while wet or while standing with bare feet on floor. Make sure feet are dry, wear slippers, and stand on the bathroom rug for optimum safety when handling bathroom light or shower fixtures.

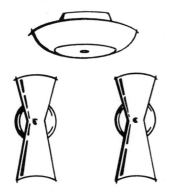

Vapor-proof ceiling fixture for stall shower: Use a 60-watt bulb. Do not install a light switch in the shower.

Side and overhead incandescent fixtures for bathroom: Note all are covered by diffusers. One- or two-socket fixtures can be put at sides of mirror to get greater amount of light. Mount side fixtures about 5' above floor level.

While bathrooms are generally smaller than other rooms in a home, they often require more light. Some bathrooms have side and overhead incandescent units. One or two socket fixtures are positioned at sides of the mirror and are usually located five feet above the floor. Various types of diffusers are used to reduce light-bulb glare.

UTILITY-ROOM DIFFUSERS

Fixtures in a utility room, a room that may hold the heating unit, or double as a "mud" room or laundry room, are often the less expensive types. Quite often the only light is supplied by a surface-mounted ceiling fixture. When installing one of these make sure the diffuser has a minimum diameter of 12". The unit may have one or two sockets. The two-socket type is preferable since it gives you more control over the total light. The diffuser is often held in place by a single cap screw.

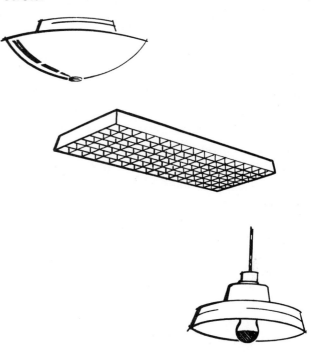

Representative utility-room fixtures: Unit at left is surface-mounted type with one or two sockets. Two-socket type is preferable. Minimum diameter of diffuser should be 12". Center drawing shows shielded fluorescent fixture. Two tubular fluorescents are generally sufficient. Drawing at right shows metal reflector and incandescent bulb with silvered reflector built into light bulb. Main reflector should be 12" in diameter, but 14" are better. Combination of reflector-type bulb and metal reflector reduces glare and spreads light.

A shielded fluorescent fixture is sometimes used in utility rooms. While four-tube fixtures are available, the two-tube type is often quite adequate since utility rooms are generally small, with unpapered walls having high reflectivity.

Some utility rooms have a metal reflector and a reflector-bowl bulb unit. A reflector-bowl bulb has a silver finish near the bottom section of the bulb. This works as a reflector in addition to the main reflector. Such bulbs are more expensive than the average incandescents. However, they do reduce glare and spread the light.

HALLWAY DIFFUSERS

Light fixtures and diffusers in hallways, like those in utility rooms, tend to be more utilitarian than beautiful. One type is the hanging-bowl fixture. These are available as round or oval. The oval type is better. Not only is it more attractive, but it spreads the light over a wider area of the hallway. A minimum size would be a hanging bowl having an 8″ diameter. You can use the same kind of fixture for lighting a hall with a high ceiling or a stairway. You can make the light fixture higher or lower by adjusting the number of links in the supporting chain. To remove a link, use a pair of gas pliers, open the link, and slide it out of its position. Some links are difficult to open, so it will take a bit of muscle.

Hallway diffusers: Unit at left is a hanging-bowl type, Oval type is preferable round. Length of supporting chain can be adjusted for optimum height. Unit at center is closed-globe type. White globe supplies maximum diffusion. Tinted globes also diffuse but can down on available light. Wall brackets, shown at right, are found mostly in older homes. When mounted on a wall on either side of a hall mirror they can add considerably to overall hall lighting, generally inadequate.

Another type of hallway diffuser is the closed-globe fixture. This is a first cousin to the similarly constructed closed-globe fixture for the kitchen. The globe can be colored or white. Unless the decor of the hallway demands otherwise, you

will find that a white glass globe is best for maximum diffusion of the light.

Some hallways, particularly in older homes, have wall-bracket fixtures. If you have a mirror in the hallway, you can take advantage of the high reflectivity of the mirror by mounting a pair of side wall-bracket fixtures, one on either side of the mirror. They supplement the general lighting in the hall. Since hallways ordinarily do not have access to windows, and hence have no outside lighting, fixtures are important. However, many hallways are dim because of too few fixtures, the wrong choice of fixtures, or bulbs with too low a wattage rating. If you must use a fixture with a tinted-glass diffuser, make up for the loss of light by using a light bulb (or bulbs) with a higher wattage rating.

TYPES OF DIFFUSERS

Any substance that covers an incandescent bulb or a fluorescent tube is a diffuser. This does not mean the diffuser must enclose the light source completely. Some diffusers, for example, are strips of glass or metal arranged so that the light can come out from between them. With such diffusers, light does not pass through the material itself but through the spaces. Some diffusers, such as those of metal, are completely opaque. Diffusers made of glass or plastic can enclose the light source completely, or may be open at the bottom, at the top, or in both areas. Diffusers can spread out the light, and be highly ornamental as well.

The drawing shows some of the more commonly available diffusers. There are, of course, many different kinds, but usually you will find them to be some variation of those shown in this illustration.

SWING-LAMP DIFFUSERS

Lamps can be moved up and down, as in pulldown types, or forward and back, or side to side, as in swing types. In the first the movement

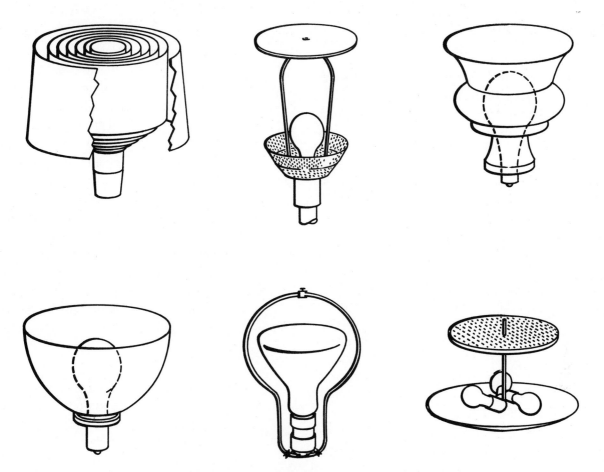

The diffuser at the upper left is a molded type with a louvered-top shield that prevents direct glare from the bulb. This diffuser is popular on study lamps giving a good spread of light over a desk area. The unit at the upper center has a prismatic refractor at the base of the bulb to help distribute light and reduce direct and reflected glare. The circular unit at the top of the lamp is a diffusing shield. A the upper right a glass diffuser shields the lamp from top viewing and still allows an efficient spread of light below the bulb. At the lower left the white glass bowl-shaped diffuser reduces direct glare from the bulb. This type of diffuser is popular on wall-mounted fixtures. Most of the light is directed upward toward the ceiling. Some bulbs behave as light sources and diffusers, such as the lamp shown in the lower center. The bulb is shaped differently from ordinary bulbs and gets away from the spot-source effect of most incandescent types. In the lower right a plastic or white glass diffusing disc at the bottom spreads light and reduces glare from the bulbs. The perforated disc at the top shields the bulbs from top viewing and redirects light downward.

is verticle, in the other horizontal. In either instance, there is great advantage in being able to position the light. The light can be adjusted to supply maximum illumination for a particular need, such as studying, playing the piano and reading music that may be difficult to see, or any other household activity. Some household chores, such as sewing, demand a more concentrated form of light, rather than the general illumination supplied by a ceiling fixture. For machine sewing, for example, it is helpful to mount a wall lamp about 14" above the working surface, 12" to the left of the needle of the machine and 7" from the wall. The bottom of the diffuser shade should be at eye level or slightly lower. The diffuser should be a type that allows light to escape from the top and bottom of the shade. Also, the diffuser should not be the type that changes the color of the light—that is, the light outside the diffuser should be white light, not red, or blue, or any other color. The swing-type lamp is not only helpful in supplying the right amount of light, but can be adjusted as needed for different work areas. Furthermore, when the work is finished, the light can be pushed back against the wall.

Swing lamps can be wall mounted, desk types, or floor lamps. For an activity such as playing the piano, center the shade of a swing-arm floor lamp 22" to the right or left of the middle of the keyboard and 13" in front of the center of the music rack. Note, however, as shown in the illustration, that the lower edge of the diffuser, a lampshade in this case, is substantially above eye leve. The purpose here is to allow the maximum light to fall on the printed sheet of music. However, there should be an additional diffuser, a circular type, going across the inside of the bottom of the lamp. The result will be diffused, instead of concentrated, light coming down onto the printed sheet. It also eliminates the possibility of eye fatigue caused by looking at unshielded elec-

Use a double swing-arm lamp for any household activity that requires intensive use of eyes. Sewing, for example, demands twice as much light as ordinary reading. To position the doulble swing-arm lamp, adjust it as shown in the drawings. The bottom of the shade must be positioned so that the person sewing cannot look directly into lighted bulbs.

tric-light bulbs, even though these will be frosted types.

Positioning of swing lamp for proper lighting of activity such as playing piano: Fixture should have a to kepp direct light out of sight of student at piano.

The double swing lamp permits light to be adjusted to user's best advantage.

184

CHECKPOINTS IN BUYING LIGHTING FIXTURES

There are two things to avoid when buying lighting fixtures—impulse buying and buying a fixture simply because it is beautiful. When you buy a fixture, keep in mind the basic principles of lighting: the quantity of light you need; its quality; its color; and the reflectance values of your ceiling and walls. Consider also that for part of the day lighting fixtures may be used to supplement natural lighting coming in through windows. You may also need more than one lighting fixture in a room, and so the two (or more) fixtures you get should complement each other, both from a viewpoint of attractiveness and light output.

Here are some points to keep in mind: The fixture you want to buy should be such that the light bulbs should be no closer than ¼" to the surface of the diffuser, whether that diffuser is glass, plastic, or metal. Remember, also, that light bulbs come in different sizes. Try the largest-size bulb you may possibly need in the light fixture, since a smaller size will always fit. If the fixture is a two- or three-bulb type, also make sure that larger-size bulbs will not interfere with each other physically.

Incandescent light bulbs produce large amounts of heat and so, if possible, select a fixture that supplies top and bottom ventilation. Completely enclosed globe types are used in kitchens, but the heat produced by the bulb in such fixtures has little chance to escape. This shortens the life of the bulb.

When using a diffuser with a lamp, you will get more light per dollar if the inside surface of the shade has high reflectibility. A smooth white surface will supply the most reflected light. A dull surface, or one that is rippled, will not yield as much light.

Some lamps are extremely attractive, but are poor sources of light. They may produce deep shadows, concentrate the light in very limited areas, or supply glare. The shape and dimension of a fixture should be such that it directs light uniformly and efficiently over the area to be lighted.

HOW TO IMPROVE YOUR LIGHTING

You can improve your lighting in a number of ways, but whether you will need to do some rewiring will depend on many factors. You may find, after redecorating, that the light in your home isn't as bright and sparkling as it once was. You may, for example, decide to wallpaper your ceiling or cover it with some fabric and so it is now a darker hue, instead of stardard white. White may not supply the most beautiful ceiling, but it does have much higher reflectance than a dark fabric, for example.

Whenever you redecorate, consider the effect the new color scheme will have on your lighting. Walls in a light-color paint or wallpaper will help give you more light. A flat paint makes light more comfortable. A gloss paint, or any paint haveing a shiny surface area will have higher reflectibility, and will produce more light in a room, but will tend to be unpleasant. Draperies and curatins that are dark and opaque not only cut down on natural light from windows, but absorb light in the sense that they have poor reflectibility. Just changing curtains and drapes alone will alter the lighting character of a room.

If you have any fixtures that use bare bulbs, replace them, unless they are located in seldom-visited areas, such as an attic. It is easy to get into an argument, pro and con, about the number of light bulbs to put in a fixture. Using a number of smaller-wattage-rating bulbs instead of one large one does spread the light more and give better diffusion. However, the cost of a number of small bulbs will be much more than the price of a single large one. Further, when a number of bulbs are used in a fixture, the very human tendency when one of the bulbs burns out is to ignore it, relying on the light supplied by the remaining bulbs. Thus, a room will gradually grow dimmer in time, with the change generally noted by visitors, not by the occupants.

A small bulb does not supply as much light as a larger one. Thus, a 100-watt bulb yields more than twice the light of two 50-watt bulbs. As far as your electric bill is concerned, it will cost you just as much to use a single 100-watt bulb as two 50-watts, but that's not the point. The point is that a single bulb supplies more light per dollar. A 100-watt bulb, as a further example, gives as much light as six 25-watt bulbs. Since 6 x 25 equals 150, you might assume that the six 25-watt bulbs would give you the equivalent light of a 150-watt bulb, but such is not the case. A 100-watt bulb uses only about two-thirds as much current as six 50-watt bulbs.

If you want more light, there are a number of things you can do: You can replace your present fixture with one that is more efficient in terms of distributing light. You can make sure the bulb (or bulbs) and diffuser are sparkling clean. You can replace your present lower wattage bulb with one having a higher wattage rating. Your fixture has a wattage rating and this is something you should ask about when you buy a new one. Make sure you use a bulb that does not exceed the wattage rating of the fixture. If you use a number of bulbs in the fixture, add the wattages of the individual bulbs to get the total wattage. Usually, you can consider a 150-watt bulb for a single lamp socket.

The same amount of light isn't needed for all occasions. You have two choices: You can use a three-way lamp or a dimmer. The dimmer is better since you can get all sorts of light output, ranging from completely off to completely bright.

Fluorescent lights give more light per dollar. However, if you decide you want a higher-wattage fluorescent, you will need to change the fixture as well. You can also use a dimmer with a fluorescent, but installing one is not as simple as with incandescent bulbs.

If you depend on floor lamps for much of your lighting, remember to make sure that the lamp cords are positioned so no one trips over them; and that lamp cords are not concealed beneath rugs. The distance from a floor or table lamp to the nearest outlet should be as short as possible. Cube taps make it easy to overload a convenience outlet. A cube tap is an electrical part with a pair of prongs that fit into an outlet. The surface areas of the tap have provision for inserting two or three plugs. To make matters worse, some home owners plug one cube tap into another, practically a guarantee that the convenience outlet will be overloaded.

You can add a surface wiring strip along a baseboard or counter top. These strips provide from three to six or more additional convenience outlets. They perform the same function as cube taps, and so once again you must make sure you do not overload the outlet to which the surface wiring strip is connected.

If the bulb in a lamp, such as a desk type or table type, is too high, you may not get enough light. In that case you can lift the shade with a riser. You can buy lamp risers in electrical shops. They are available in half-inch sizes or in multiples of a half inch. Unscrew the shade from the lamp, insert the riser, and then put the shade back on again. A bulb (or bulbs) inside a shade should be somewhere near the center of the shade. If the bulb is too low, it may shine into the eyes of the user. Similarly, if it is too high, it may also shine into the eyes of someone standing near the lamp.

If the bulb is much too low in the lamp, either replace the lamp or buy a deeper shade. If the lamp never seems to be the right height for the work you are doing, put the lamp on a support that will raise it: a small block of marble, ceramic, metal, or wood.

WATCHING TELEVISION

Some people watch television in a darkened room, and for a number of reasons. As a picture tube gets older it produces an image that is less bright. But the brightness of the picture must compete with the light produced by electric fixtures; and so, to get maximum viewing, the electric lights are turned off. A television picture viewed in a completely darkened room also supplies maximum contrast.

However, watching television is a strain on the eyes, for the viewer is looking directly at a light. Furthermore, this is a light that keeps changing. The best way to look at television is with a small amount of light in the room. Position the light (or lights) so there is no reflection from the picture-tube screen. The ideal arrangement is to have the light controlled by a dimmer, with the lights positioned so they do not shine directly on the face of the picture tube.

INCANDESCENT VS. FLUORESCENT LIGHTING

Incandescent and fluorescent lights do not compete with each other, but rather are supplementary. Some fixtures have a combination of incandescent and fluorescent bulbs. But there will be times when you will need to make a decision as to whether you should use an incandescent fixture or one that has fluorescents. The chart that follows supplies the pros and cons of both of these light sources.

STRUCTURAL LIGHTING

Most lighting in the home comes within one or more of several well-defined categories. There are ceiling lights, desk lamps, table and floor lamps. But while these are the main, most commonly used forms, there are several variations. An electric range, for example, may come equipped with a built-in light, or it may have a hood enclosing an incandescent or fluorescent bulb. A fish tank may be illuminated, or you may have lighting that is

purely decorative, such as lights that appear at the ends of tiny, flexible plastic rods.

There is also lighting that is used to make a room look more dramatic, to emphasize draperies or possibly a picture. An oil painting, for example, may have a small light mounted across its top to cover the surface of the picture with light. With lighting of this kind, the effect of illumination on overall room lighting is incidental. In these instances lighting is used for effect.

Pros and Cons of Light Sources

Incandescent Bulbs	*Fluorescent Tubes*
Can be concentrated over a limited area or spread over a wide area.	Provide more diffused lighting—a line of light, not a spot.
Initial cost less than fluorescent tubes.	Higher initial cost, but greater light efficiency—three to four times as much light per watt of electricity.
Designed to operate at high temperature.	Cool operating temperature. Generally about one-fifth as hot as incandescent bulbs.
Have average life of 750 to 1,000 hours.	Operate seven to ten times longer than incandescent bulbs.
Wattages range from 15 to 300 watts.	Wattages for home use range from 14 watts (15 inches long) to 40 watts (48 inches long).
Amount of light can be increased or decreased by changing to bulbs of different wattage because most bulbs have same size base.	Cannot be replaced by higher or lower wattage tubes.
Require no ballast or starter.	Require ballasts, and in some cases, starters.
Do not interfere with radio reception.	May cause noise interference with radio reception within 10 feet of the tube location.
Suitable for use in less expensive fixtures.	Adaptable to and commonly used in custom-designed installations and in surface-mounted and recessed fixtures.
Available in colors to enliven decor and accessories. Colored bulbs are 25 to 50 percent less efficient than white bulbs.	Available in many colors (plus deluxe cool white, CWX, and deluxe warm white), WWX, at much higher light output than colored incandescents.
Gain flexibility by use of three-way bulbs and multiple-switch controls or dimmer controls designed for incandescent bulbs.	Gain flexibility by use of dimming ballasts combined with dimmer controls designed for fluorescent tubes.

VALANCE LIGHTING

A valance (also known as a valence) is a board mounted horizontally across draperies. When they are wired for light, they can bring out colors in the draperies suspended below them and accentuate the beauty and color of the fabric.

Because incandescent bulbs tend to produce a "spot" effect, it is better to use fluorescent tubes for this purpose. Setting up a lighted valance is no great problem. Mount the fluorescent fixture so

CORNICE LIGHTING

If you have a particular wall you want to emphasize, you can use cornice lighting. Note the difference between valance and cornice lighting. With cornice lighting, all the light is reflected downward and the fluorescent fixture is much closer to the ceiling. With valance lighting, some of the light from the fluorescent is direct upward to the ceiling and is then reflected down from there. But some of the light also moves downward directly from the fluorescent.

An example of valance lighting, with construction details given in the drawing at the right: Use fluorescent fixtures without diffusers. You will need several such fixtures, the number depending on the length of the valance.

that the tube is at least 4½" away from the back wall, 2" from the valance board, and at least 10" from the ceiling. You might also consider using a dimmer control although they are considerably more expensive than dimmers for incandescent bulbs.

The switching for valance lighting should be independent of switching for all other lights in the room.

One of the advantages of cornice lighting is that it gives an illusion of height in a room having a low ceiling. Note, also, that in cornice lighting, the fluorescent fixture is mounted on the rear of the cornice faceboard. In valance lighting, the lighting fixture is fastened to a wood blocking attached to the rear wall. The reason for putting the fluorescent fixture on the faceboard in cornice lighting is that unless you do so, not all of the light will reach the entire wall-surface area and you may

Example of cornice lighting: Drawing at right supplies construction details.
Cornice may have draperies at ends.

have some shadows, particularly down at the lower end of the wall. You may need to experiment with the positioning of the fluorescent fixture to get complete light coverage of the wall.

In both valance and cornice lighting, remember that sooner or later you will need to replace the fluorescent tubes and so allow enough finger room to let you get in and change the tubes. With cornice lighting, the entire illuminated wall acts as a light reflector, and so the amount of light you are going to get depends directly on the kind of wall you are going to have. A white wall, possibly made of real or simulated brick, will have high reflectivity. A somber wall, covered with a dark fabric, will not supply as much reflected light.

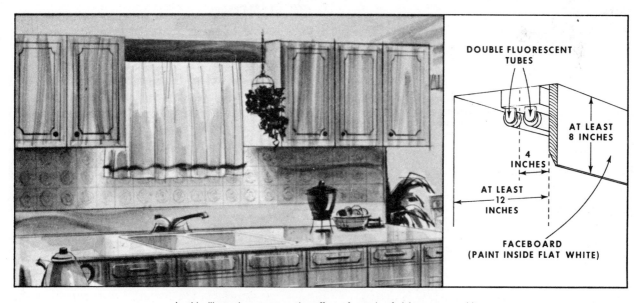

In this illustration you see the effect of a pair of deluxe warm white fluorescents recessed in a soffit above a kitchen sink. Construction details are given in the drawing at the right.

189

SOFFIT

By definition, a soffit is the under part of an overhanging cornice. In structural lighting, a soffit is recessed lighting. As an example, the drawing shows a pair of 30- or 40-watt tubular fluorescents recessed in a soffit above a kitchen sink. To make the fixture, use a faceboard that will extend at least 8″ down from the ceiling and mount it between a pair of kitchen cabinets. The board shown here is straight, but you can buy a piece that has elaborate curves and is more attractive; or, you can make your own if you are handy with a jig saw.

The advantage of having recessed lights in an above-the-sink soffit is that it supplies a warm light for easy vision at a work area that is often used. For fluorescents, try deluxe warm white types, using a pair of them. Because the distance between the kitchen cabinets is quite small, you could also use incandescent bulbs, possibly 75-watt bulbs, spaced about 15″ apart, suspended from the ceiling behind the faceboard or mounted directly on it. You might also consider such recessed lighting in other areas, such as along dressing counters in bathrooms.

BRACKET

A lighted bracket is somewhat like a valance, except that a valance is generally placed over a window. With a valance you would probably want draw drapes. A bracket is located over a wall, instead of windows. Placed above a sofa, as shown in the drawing, it supplements the light supplied by a pair of table lamps. Brackets are also suitable for mounting over work counters, snack bars, pictures, and wall hangings. You might even consider using one as a bed lamp. For reading in bed, put the bottom edge of the bracket faceboard 30″ above the top of the mattress. For general lighting, mount the bracket so that its bottom edge is at least 65″ above the floor. For local lighting, mount the unit so that the bottom edge of the bracket is about 55″ from the floor.

The faceboard of the valance, cornice, soffit, or bracket affects the amount of reflected light. Naturally, it is to your advantage to get as much reflected light as you can, so paint the inside of the faceboard with flat white. The way in which you decorate the outside of the faceboard will depend on what you personally want in the way of complementing your furniture.

A lighted bracket is located on a wall instead of over windows. Drawing at left shows one possible arrangement. Diagram at right supplies construction details.

190

LUMINOUS CEILINGS

One way of getting soft and widely spread lighting is by installing a luminous ceiling. These are used extensively for office lighting but are also suitable for some home areas, particularly kitchens. You can buy aluminum supports that are suspended by straps from the ceiling. The supports hold large sheets of milky plastic, sufficiently translucent to let light come through. Fluorescent fixtures can be mounted above the panels to supply light. The idea here is similar to that used for suspended ceilings, except that see-through panels are used instead of opaque ceiling tiles. With a setup of this kind, an entire kitchen area can be uniformly lighted.

LIGHTING MAINTENANCE

You have no doubt noted the many suggestions for lighting maintenance scattered throughout this chapter. These are repeated here, with a few more, in a sort of summary.

Dust on lighting fixtures causes a drop in lighting efficiency. Not only must bulbs be kept clean, but reflecting surfaces require care also. This includes ceilings since these are usually part of the lighting system. Ceilings should be painted regularly, particularly if a latex-type paint is used. Some latex paints do not yield their dirt readily and washing ceilings can be a difficult chore. Clean all lighting equipment at least four to six times a year. A good idea is to set up an every-other-month schedule. If you have bowl-type portable lamps, give them the clean-up treatment once a month.

Wash glass and plastic diffusers and shields in a detergent solution. You can use the same detergent powder that you put in your washing machine. Detergent is better than soap powders since detergents will dossolve dirt better and not leave a film. After washing, rinse in clear warm water, and dry. Don't replace diffusers and light-shields while they are wet and expect them to air dry. They will do so, of course, but may streak. An old bath towel, but one that is absolutely clean, is ideal for such a job.

Wipe incandescent bulbs, fluorescent tubes, and circle fluorescents with a cloth soaked in a detergent solution. Then wipe with a cloth soaked in clear warm (not hot) water. Finally, dry thoroughly with a clean bath towel. Never replace incandescent bulbs and fluorescent tubes while they are wet. Never turn on a bulb or fluorescent while it is wet.

Dust wood and metal lamp bases with a soft cloth and apply a thin coat of wax. You can wash glass, pottery, marble, chrome, and onyx lamp bases with a damp cloth soaked in detergent. After the base is as clean as possible, dry it thoroughly and then wax it. Rub the wax with a clean cloth to get a uniform coating and to bring out the highlights of the base.

You can clean lampshades with a vacuum cleaner if it has a soft brush attachment for that purpose. If your shades are made of silk or rayon and are handsewn to the frame, and have no glued trimmings, you can wash them in a detergent liquid. Rinse after cleaning in clear lukewarm water. Dry quickly and thoroughly to prevent rusting of the frame.

To dry lampshades that have just been washed, shake the frame vigorously to get rid of as much excess water as possible. Then pat (do not rub) the frame with an absorbent, clean bath towel. Get as much water off the frame as possible. Finally, hold the lampshade in front of a fan and let the blade of the fan air dry the lampshade. These sound like a lot of precautions, but once a lampshade frame gets rusty, part of the rust will come off on the lampshade and the shade will then have to be discarded.

Some lampshades are parchment types. Do not use water on these. Instead, clean them with a dry cloth.

When you buy a new lampshade you may find it covered with a plastic wrapping. Since the plastic wrapping will obviously help keep the shade from getting dirty, the normal tendency is to let the wrapping remain. Wrappings, though, create glare. When subject to the heat of a lamp, they may shrink, warp the frame, and wrinkle the fabric of the shade. Furthermore, some plastic wrappings are fire hazards. They can be ignited by the heat from incandescent bulbs.

A bulb can become defective in two ways. It can burn out, in which case the only option is to replace it. However, the filament of the bulb can burn off material that is then deposited around the inner surface of the glass, darkening it. The loss of material from the filament weakens it, giving the filament a very short life expectancy. The darkened areas cut down on available light, by as much as 25 percent to 50 percent, but despite that fact, it still takes the same operating power from the line and you still pay as much for using that bulb as you always did.

You can tell when a fluorescent is reaching the end of its days when it starts to flicker or develop darkened ends. If a fluorescent takes longer than usual to light, putting in a new starter may help. If you hear a humming sound from your fluorescent fixture, it is quite possible that one of the laminations of the ballast transformer has worked its way loose and is vibrating at a rate of 60 times a second. The core of the ballast transformer is iron, not solid, but made of thin sheets or slices called laminations. To get at the ballast transformer, you will need to remove the entire fixture since the transformer is mounted inside it. If the transformer is held together by long machine screws and nuts, all that is needed is to tighten these. If the transformer is potted—that is, covered with some sort of insulating pitch—it will be practically impossible to make the repair. Your choice, then, is to replace the transformer, or to install a new fixture.

LIGHTING CONTROL IN THE HOME

There are various ways to determine if your lighting system is correctly arranged. You should, for example, be able to light your way as you go from room to room. If you turn off the light in one room and must walk through darkness to get to the next light switch, then you may need to consider some rewiring. You should also be able to switch lights from each doorway in rooms with two or more doorways.

If your house has steps, then you should be able to turn on the lights for the step area either from downstairs or upstairs. As you enter your home, you should have a light switch at your left. The hinges of the door will be to your right and you will be opening the door with your right hand. If the switch is on the right side, you will have to walk into a dark hall or foyer and fumble for the switch. If there is no hall or foyer switch, you should install one.

If your house has a garage or carport, you should be able to control the lighting for either from inside the house. Otherwise you will find yourself walking into a dark area, groping for a switch. Now a lot of this might sound like common sense, but that's a misnomer anyway, since such sense isn't as common as you might think. Most accidents happen in the home, but what isn't generally known is that poor lighting or no lighting is a probable cause.

If you have small children, they may find it comforting to have a small light. You can get a 7-watt plug-in type that will fit into a baseboard convenience outlet. These come with an adjustable shade to allow you to direct the small amount of light onto the floor. Children who have some fear of the dark, and it is quite natural for them to have such a fear, do not necessarily want a lot of light. A 7-watt baseboard outlet type is adequate.

Chapter 9

MISCELLANEOUS ELECTRICAL WORK

AROUND THE HOUSE

Just because a person becomes sick is no reason to make an immediate phone call to a physician. Quite often a simple home remedy or an aspirin is all that is required. There will be times, of course, when the services of a doctor will be imperative.

The same rule applies to home wiring, lighting, electrical repairs, and maintenance. You do not call in an electrical contractor when you need to replace a fuse or change the plug at the end of a line cord. If you do not have the tools, or experience, however, for an elaborate behind-the-wall series of branches that must run back to the fuse or breaker box, or if you want to replace such boxes, then calling in an electrical contractor is in order.

There are numerous jobs you can do around your home to maintain or to improve your existing system. The reason for doing your own work, whenever possible, is that while the price of electrical parts is quite low, the cost of labor can be substantial. But you must use judgment, make sure that you do not violate your local electrical codes, and take care that you do not put your home and your life in jeopardy.

HOW TO INSTALL A DOORBELL

At one time doorbells were not at all associated with home electric wiring, but worked from one or more independent batteries. Battery replacement was not only a problem, but a nuisance, and so today a doorbell system uses a transformer.

A bell transformer is very simple. It has two coils of wire, not connected to each other, with both coils wound around an iron core. One of these coils is called the primary winding, or just the primary, and is permanently connected to your 117-volt AC line. Since there is no switch in this primary circuit, a current flows from the power line through the primary winding at all times. This current, known as an energizing current, is very small and the power consumed is negligible. The secondary winding of the transformer, sometimes just called the secondary, is connected to a pair of terminals on a bell. There are two wires that connect the bell to the secondary of the transformer. One of these wires, either one, is opened and a switch is inserted. The switch is a SPST type, generally of the pushbutton variety, and is mounted on the front-door jamb. When the push-

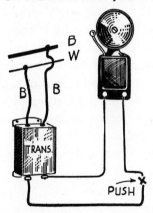

Setup for a single pushbutton doorbell: It makes no difference how the primary leads of the transformer are connected to the AC line. The secondary leads, similarly, can be connected to either post on the bell. The switch can be inserted in either one of the secondary leads. Some transformers have binding posts, but more modern types simply have the primary and secondary leads extending from the transformer. The primary and secondary windings can be identified by wording stamped on the transformer case.

button is depressed, a current flows through the secondary winding of the transformer and also through the doorbell, causing it to ring. It will continue to ring as long as you keep your finger on the pushbutton.

The transformer used in the bell warning circuit is a stepdown type. The voltage input to the primary is the line voltage, 117 volts AC. The voltage across the secondary winding is just a few volts AC, generally about 6 volts. There are some bell transformers that have split secondary windings. You will be able to identify these since they will have three secondary terminals. Thus, the voltage between terminals #1 and #2 will be 6 volts AC; between #2 and #3, about 12 volts AC; and about 18 volts between #1 and #3. The reason for this arrangement is that not all door-bells require the same operating voltage. Some are 6-unit types, others 12-volt, while a few require 18 volts. Thus, a single bell transformer can be used for any one of these.

The amount of current flowing through the primary winding is very small, but increases when the pushbutton in the secondary circuit is depressed. Since the primary is connected to the AC line, it should be handled in the same way as any other AC connection. Generally this wiring is run along a basement beam to the nearest convenient AC connecting point—that is, it is tapped onto the first available AC branch. The bell-ringing circuit doesn't have a separate fuse, but depends on the fuse of the branch to which it is connected. The primary wiring can be no. 16 or no. 18 two-wire sheathed cable. The same wire can be used for the secondary connection to the bell and pushbutton, although bell wire (from which it gets its name) is sometimes used.

The transformer may have binding posts to which you can connect your wires, although more modern transformers simply have wires coming out of the unit: a pair for the primary, and another pair for the secondary. In that case just splice your connections and cover with vinyl tape. You can

mount the transformer on any basement beam. In some installations, the transformer is placed right on the outside cover plate of the electric box to which it is connected.

In homes, and in some apartments equipped with both front and rear entrances, a combination bell and buzzer may be used. There are two pushbuttons, as shown in the drawing. One pushbutton is mounted on the rear-door jamb, the other on the front-door jamb. Depressing the front-door pushbutton activates the bell; pushing the rear-door button turns on the buzzer. The reason for using the buzzer instead of two bells is that this helps the occupant know at once which button is being pushed, front or rear. If you will trace the circuit, you will see that both the bell and buzzer are wired in parallel, and that both are open circuits until their respective switches are closed.

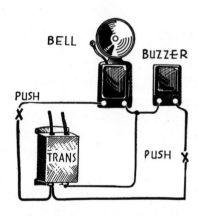

Combination doorbell and buzzer circuit.

While the drawing shows a separate bell and buzzer, you can get units that are combinations of both. While you would logically expect such a combination to have four connections, if you will examine the preceding drawing showing a separate bell and buzzer, you will see that these two components have one connection in common. This is the wire that joins the bell to the buzzer and then returns to the secondary of the transformer.

CHIMES

In new homes and in some older ones, you will find chimes in use instead of bells and buzzers. These may be two-tone types for the front door and a single-tone for the rear. Some chimes play tunes and some are combinations of electric clocks and chimes. But no matter how elaborate they become, they are wired and installed in the same way as doorbells. Chimes, though, may require a different operating voltage from that of a doorbell, often 10 volts AC, and so you may need to get a chime transformer. When you buy a set of chimes, then, determine the voltage requirement and find out whether you can use your existing doorbell transformer. If you do have a doorbell/buzzer setup, you will not need to change the wiring or pushbuttons, but you may have to change the transformer.

TROUBLE IN THE DOORBELL SYSTEM

Most often (but not always) trouble in an electrical system is due to the mechanical section, not the electrical. A doorbell/buzzer or chime arrangement is an electromechanical setup—that is, part of the system is electrical and part of it is mechanical, consisting of moving elements. The moving element in a doorbell or chime may be the pushbutton or the bell or chime. Quite often, when these signal systems stop working or do so intermittently, the fault is in the front-door pushbutton. Some of these are inexpensive types and fail after a short period of use.

Some doorbell pushbuttons come equipped with a small built-in light. These are helpful in helping locate the doorbell immediately. They are low-voltage types and are connected directly to the secondary winding of the bell transformer. As long as the light remains on, you know that the primary leads and the transformer are functioning. Ultimately, however, the light will wear out and will need to be replaced, but its useful life should be at least a year.

DOOR OPENER

A door opener is a device that works the same as a doorbell or chime arrangement. When a pushbutton, often located in the kitchen, is depressed, it closes a circuit permitting a small current to run through a catcher device that is part of the front-door lock. The current releases the latch, allowing the door to be opened. At the same time the noise produced by the vibrating latch is an indication that the door is ready to be opened.

HOW TO INSTALL AN ELECTRIC BOX

Most homes do not have enough convenience outlets and so you will see a proliferation of cube taps, or extension-type outlets, or even small extension cords. A better technique is to install more convenience outlets. The same thinking applies to switches, for you may want to switch control one or more convenience outlets, or have an extra switch so that you need not grope in the dark when coming into a room. In many new homes, for example, there are no ceiling lights for rooms such as the living room. Instead, you must depend on floor lamps only, and so the usual result is that you must always walk into a dark room, groping for the nearest floor lamp.

You can install electric boxes for convenience outlets and switches by following the same procedure for both. Locate the convenience outlets near the baseboard; and the switches, about 45" above the floor.

When you decide to install a box in an existing wall, you must position it between studs. There are several ways in which you can find the studs. One method is to knock on the wall at various spots. An in-between-stud space will sound hollow, but a stud will produce a "solid" sound. You can, if you prefer, buy a stud finder. This is nothing more than a compass that swings strongly when brought near a stud, since studs have nails in them. Still another way is to drill holes in the wall, using a 1/6" drill. Do this near the floor (remove the baseboard first) so that the holes will not show.

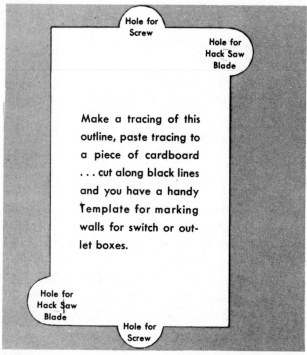

Hole for Screw

Hole for Hack Saw Blade

Make a tracing of this outline, paste tracing to a piece of cardboard . . . cut along black lines and you have a handy Template for marking walls for switch or outlet boxes.

Hole for Hack Saw Blade

Hole for Screw

Template for cutout for electric box for switch or convenience outlet. (Courtesy, Sears.)

Once you have located the studs, use the template shown in the drawing and make a tracing of the template outline on your wall. You do not need to tear the template out of this book or copy it. Instead put a sheet of carbon paper against the wall, with the carbon side facing the wall. Since you will trace with one hand, and with the other, hold the book, fasten the carbon paper to the wall with a bit of cellophane tape. After you have completed the outline, remove the carbon paper. Now drill ½" holes in the four circular areas shown by the template. Two of these are toward the upper right and two are at the lower left.

When the holes are finished, take a hacksaw blade and hold it so that the teeth are toward you. Put some vinyl tape around the end nearest you and then insert the blade in the top hole at the right and start cutting downward. Note that in this operation the teeth of the blade are opposite their normal position in a hacksaw. You will also find it

helpful to hold a small bit of wood against the area being cut out. As you cut, try not to twist the blade, or it will snap. Of course, it's a good idea to wear safety goggles.

When you reach the bottom of the cut, do not try to go around the corner by bending the blade. You'll only break it if you do. Instead, remove the blade and insert it in the other holes and start cutting. In this way you will be able to cut completely around.

Now take your electric box and make a decision as to which knockout you are going to use. Obviously, if you are planning to run BX or conduit downward, you will use one of the bottom knockouts.

Measure the length of BX or conduit you are going to use; and also, at this point in your work, make sure that it will reach the source of AC power. This might be another outlet or it could be a junction box. If you are using conduit, connect it to the box. If you are using BX, strip the BX as previously explained, and connect it to the box. In all cases make certain that you also bring in the grounding wire.

Installing an electric box for a switch or outlet can be easy or a nuisance, depending on how your home is constructed. As mentioned earlier, newer homes use sheetrock nailed against studs, but have no lath. Older homes made extensive use of plaster and lath and so you may have to chip away

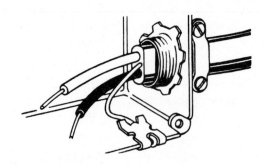

Method for connecting non-metallic cable to an electric box. The third wire in the cable is a grounding wire and must be connected to a grounding clip or screw inside the box. (Courtesy, Sears.)

quite a bit of plaster and cut through lath to get your box mounted. If you have lath, do not cut away two full lath strips. Instead, cut away one and half each of the others. This will supply a stronger mounting for the box.

The easiest cable to use is plastic sheathed. It is much easier to cut away the plastic than to hacksaw BX, and it is also not as much work as conduit. You can get hardware specifically made for fastening nonmetallic cable to an electric box. It consists of a threaded connector that fits over the cable and is fastened to it by a two-screw clamp on the outside. The threaded portion fits through the knockout hole in the box. The fastening is then held in place with a locknut, as shown in the drawing.

Whenever you add a convenience outlet, always use a ground wire. You can get a grounding clip that fastens onto the electric box. There are various ways of attaching the grounding wire to the box. The only important requirement is that you make a good, tight connection.

HOW TO UPDATE YOUR GARAGE ELECTRICALLY

If you have a garage, you have two minimum electrical components—a light and a switch. If you do not have a convenience outlet, you should have. The outlet will let you use power tools for working on your car, will let you connect a "drop light" so that you can spotlight any part of your car engine when you work on it, and will also let you connect a battery charger in the event your car battery needs such attention.

1. Sound for studs

2. Outline Template

3. Drill ½ inch Holes

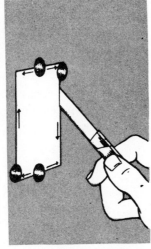
4. Cut with Blade

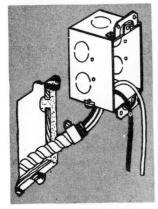
5. Draw wires into box

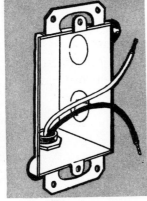
6. Anchor box to wall

Steps in the installation of an electric box. (Courtesy, Sears.)

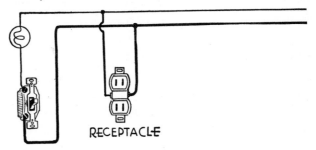

RECEPTACLE

Wiring arrangement for a convenience receptacle in a garage.

All you need do is install a wall-type electric box to hold a convenience outlet, following the procedures outlined earlier. Inside the house it is customary to mount convenience outlets right above the baseboard. In the garage, you should mount it about 46" to 50" above the floor. From a wiring point of view, it may even be desirable to put the outlet fairly close to the existing switch.

When you wire in a convenience outlet, you actually shunt it across the power line. This means that one terminal of the outlet goes to the black wire; and the other terminal of the outlet to the white wire. In the drawing you will see two parallel lines. The thicker line, the lower line, represents the hot lead. The upper, thinner line, represents the cold or ground wire. Connect to the two wires bringing power in to the switch and light.

HOW TO CONNECT AN OUTLET TO A SWITCH

Basically, whenever you wire in a new convenience outlet, all you are doing is connecting the two terminals of the outlet to the hot and cold wires of the power line. That's the electrical concept. But the actual work in wiring can be tedious and drawn out, or fairly simple, depending on how you approach the job. You can, for example, run the wires from the new outlet all the way back to the nearest available junction, in which case you may be making a lot of work for yourself; or you can connect the outlet to the nearest available switch. What you do depends entirely on how your particular house is wired. The junction box, conceivably, might be closer to the proposed new outlet than the switch, in which case it would make more sense to connect to the junction box.

To be able to connect to the light switch, there must be a ground wire inside the switch box. This will be in the form of a white wire connected to another white wire, with the two joined and covered by a solderless connector. Connect one

wire, the black wire, to the dark-colored terminal at the receptacle (it may also be brass colored); and the other wire, the white wire, to the light-colored terminal (it will probably be nickel-plated). Attach the white wire of the connecting cable to the white wires inside the switch box and the black wire to one of the black wire terminals right on the switch itself.

Now here is where you must be careful. One of the black wires on the switch will be going off to a light bulb somewhere. The other black wire will be connected to the corresponding black wire of a branch circuit. If you connect to the wrong terminal, you will now have what is called a switched outlet—that is, you will only get power at the outlet when the switch is turned on. You may not want this, since this action will also turn on the light. To get an unswitched outlet, transfer the black lead from the receptacle to the other "hot" terminal of the switch.

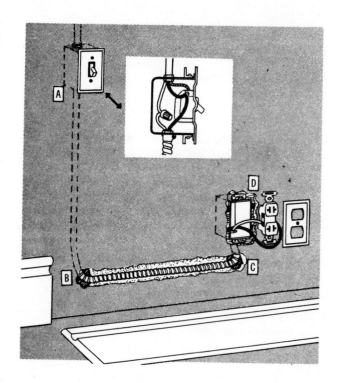

How to connect a new convenience outlet to an existing switch (A): Bend connecting cable gently at B and C. New unit shown at D. (Courtesy, Sears.)

In the drawing, the letter A represents the light switch, and B the connecting cable. BX is used in this example, but you may find it easier to use plastic-sheathed cable instead. The letter C indicates the entry of the BX into the baseboard receptacle box while D shows the position of the box. For an inside-the-home application you would want the new outlet near the baseboard.

Whichever cable you use, it should have a separate ground wire. Make sure it connects to a grounding terminal on the switch and also on a similar terminal in the electric box housing the new receptacle.

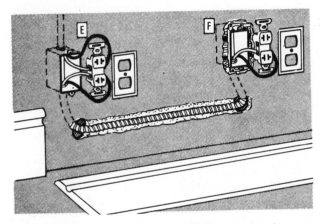

How to add new outlet (F) to existing outlet, (E). (Courtesy, Sears.)

advertisements to potential buyers that your home is inadequately wired. Built-in outlets add to the value of a house; cube taps and outlet strips lower it.

It is easy to add another outlet, as shown in the illustration. Use BX, conduit, or plastic-coated cable to make the connections. The letter E in the drawing indicates the existing box; the letter F the new one. Naturally, you should shut off power to the outlet box while working on it. Black wires go to brass terminals; white wires to chrome terminals. That's how easy it is. Use the template discussed earlier and put in an electric box for the new outlet, following the procedures that have been described.

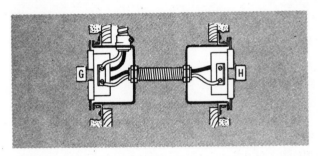

Connecting outlets back to back is an easy way of adding to existing wiring. Old outlet shown at G; new one at H. Boxes are joined by hollow-type, threaded nipple. Thread wires through nipple, fasten nipple in place with locknuts. (Courtesy, Sears.)

HOW TO ADD ONE OR MORE NEW OUTLETS

It is possible to get additional outlets in a number of ways. One method is to use a cube tap. Another is to buy an outlet box or strip. This latter unit consists of four or more receptacles in one housing connected to a wire that ends in a plug to be inserted into a receptacle. Look on these as temporary expedients, not as permanent installations. Cube taps are unsightly and are easily pulled out of their outlets. They may or may not make good contact with the outlet into which they are plugged. Outlet boxes and outlet strips are subject to the same criticism. Further, if you own your own home, cube taps and outlet strips are

HOW TO INSTALL OUTLETS BACK TO BACK

One of the easiest ways to get more outlets in your home is to install them back to back. You do not even need to tap the walls to find studs or use a stud locater. The presence of an existing outlet indicates there are no studs. Cut through the wall on the opposite side, using the template previously discussed. Because of the closeness of the two boxes, you will not need to use conduit, BX, or sheathed cable. Instead, use a threaded nipple and run the three wires; one black, the other white, and the third a bare ground wire, through the nipple. Connect the wires, tighten the nuts holding the threaded nipple, and that's it.

In all instances, whenever installing new convenience outlets, be sure to select grounding types. These will have three holes: two for the active prongs of the male plug, and one for the grounding prong. Also make sure that you connect the ground wire to the terminal of the outlet.

HOW TO REPAIR TABLE AND FLOOR LAMPS

Modern lamp cord generally uses some form of plastic insulation, but you can also get rubber-covered types as well. Older floor and desk lamps, however, were made with natural-rubber-covered wire. Natural rubber is a vegetable product, and even though anti-aging compounds are mixed in with it, the rubber eventually dries and crumbles. If, as you flax such wire, the insulation cracks, replace it. Don't try cutting away a section and patching. Such a repair will not look good, and the rest of the wire will soon need attention, anyway. Replace the entire wire. You can do this by disassembling the lamp, noting how the wire is connected, and then substituting a new cable. You can buy wire with a molded-on-rubber or plastic male plug, so you will actually need to make only two connections at the lamp switch.

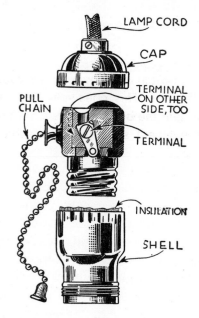

LAMP CORD

CAP

PULL CHAIN

TERMINAL ON OTHER SIDE, TOO

TERMINAL

INSULATION

SHELL

Pull-chain socket assembly of table and floor lamps.

Pull-chain type lamps are constructed using a socket as shown in the drawing. To remove existing wire, separate the socket into its component parts. Adjacent to the pull chain you will find two terminals to which you can connect the exposed ends of the new lamp cord. The cord will probably consist of stranded wire. No soldering is necessary. Strip about ½" from the ends of the two wires and try not to cut through any of the strands. After the strands are exposed, twirl them between your fingers, always in the same direction, to give the effect of a single continuous wire. Wrap this wire around the terminal screw in a clockwise direction and tighten the screw. Cut away any excess wire with a pair of diagonal cutters. Now do the same by connecting the other wire to the other screw. Push the three parts of the lamp socket together again and the wiring job will be done. Make sure that the insulation on the inside of the shell covers the wiring you have just completed. The top edge of the shell is ridged and so is the bottom edge of the socket cap. These two parts will snap together when you push them against each other.

HOW TO POSITION A RECEPTACLE PROPERLY

Sometimes, when replacing an electrical outlet you will learn for the first time that the electric box in which the original outlet was mounted is at some angle inside the wall. The box may be so securely in position that it may be difficult or impossible for you to straighten it. However, the holes at the top and bottom of the electric box are usually elongated to make allowance for such conditions. Be sure to mount the outlet so that it is vertical. The box housing the outlet cannot be seen, so that doesn't really matter, but the outlet itself is visible and should be straight, just as a matter of aesthetics.

Sometimes a receptacle will be pushed rather deeply into a wall, making it difficult for the outlet to be flush with the wall. In that case use flat washers behind the receptacle-mounting screws.

Use several such washers until the receptacle is in its proper position.

Even if the electric box is mounted at an angle, the receptacle itself should be straight.

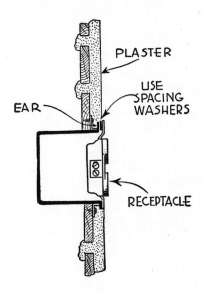

If the electric box is too deeply recessed, you can bring the receptacle (or switch) forward by using spacing washers. This drawing shows an installation in an older home using plaster walls. The same situation can arise in a new home using sheetrock.

If the electric box is too deep and you are going to use it for a switch, the result will be that the toggle of the switch will barely extend from its covering plate. It will not only look bad, but it will make the switch difficult to operate. Again, use washers behind the switch-mounting screws until the switch is in its proper position. In both cases, outlet or switch, you can check by putting on the face plate. The receptacle should protrude slightly in front of its face plate, while a switch should have the toggle out as far in front of the face plate as possible.

GARAGE LIGHT AND POWER CONTROL

In some homes the garage is completely detached, thereby presenting a lighting problem. It means that entry is always made into a darkened garage, and if the control switch is at the end opposite to the door, then walking into or out of the garage can be a process of fumbling through the dark.

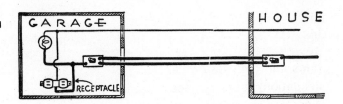

Circuit for controlling garage light from the house: You will need a pair of three-way switches. This circuit controls power to garage lamp and receptacle simultaneously. One cannot go on without the other.

If the garage has an existing light, and it undoubtedly has, then it must have a light switch. Replace this light switch with a three-way type. Locate the branch circuit that feeds the garage. Now this branch may come into your house from the basement, making a connection at some junction box. In that case, run a cable between the branch and a new box. You will need to put the three-way switch in series with the cable before it enters the box. This does not mean the switch must be near the box. You can run a branch up to some convenient spot and insert the three-way switch there.

The drawing shows one possible arrangement. However, with this setup, both the garage light and the receptacle are controlled by the switch. Thus, when you turn off the garage light either in the garage or your home, you also turn off the outlet. However, you might want that outlet to be "live" at all times. For example, you might have a charger connected to it because you intend to leave the charger on all night. Or, you might want to operate a small heater to keep the temperature in your garage from dropping too low.

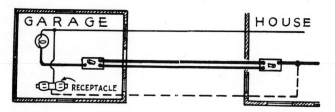

This is a better remote-control arrangement using a pair of three-way switches. Now the receptacle in the garage is independent of the switch.

You can make the outlet in the garage independent of the light by including another wire, which is shown as a dashed line in the drawing. Note this is a "hot" lead. But how can you tell, just by looking at a drawing, which is the hot lead? Simply look at the switches and at the wiring. Ground leads are never interrupted, and so the line across the top of the drawing is a ground lead. In both drawings, the heavy lines across the bottom are hot leads. The dashed line indicates that a connection is made between the hot terminal on the in-house branch and that this hot lead is brought over to one side of the receptacle. The other side of the receptacle is wired to the ground lead. This arrangement makes the outlet independent of the light switch in the garage.

While this description is for a garage, presumably separated from a house, it is applicable to many other situations. You can also use it to control the light in a separate utility building or a toolshed located away from the main house. You can use it as a setup for turning a light on in a dim section of a large basement before you walk down the stairs. In some cases you might want to install this circuit in the bedroom of an infant, so that you can turn a light on before you enter the room.

SWITCHED VS. UNSWITCHED OUTLETS

Most convenience outlets in the home are unswitched types. Power is always available at the outlet and all you need do is plug in a lamp or appliance. In some instances, though, you might want the outlet controlled by a switch. This would require a switch in series with the black or hot wire going to the receptacle. Do this by following the wiring techniques described earlier. A receptacle so controlled is called a switched outlet. Always remember, though, that outlets have power ratings. This is governd by the size of the wire running from the outlet back to the fuse or breaker box. It is always better to "underload" an outlet. If a pair of wires forming a branch to an outlet are capable of carrying 15 amperes, then you can calculate the approximate wattage capability by multiplying the maximum current by the line voltage, usually 117: 117 times 15 equals 1755 watts. As a matter of safety, keep the load on that outlet at 1,000 watts (1 kilowatt) or less. The outlet itself must also have this wattage rating.

HOW TO CONNECT A PULL-CHAIN FIXTURE

You can add a pull-chain fixture to any junction box you have in your basement, whether that box is mounted horizontally or vertically. This type of lighting addition requires no extra cable, and is simply a matter of connecting a pair of wires.

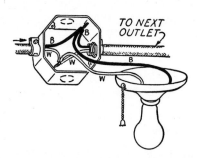

Method of connecting a pull-chain fixture to an existing junction box.

A pull-chain fixture has a number of advantages. It not only gives you additional light in dark areas, but you can also unscrew the bulb and insert a threaded plug, thus converting the fixture to a temporary convenience outlet. The pull chain is a switch, built into the fixture. If the chain is short and the fixture is rather high up, just add a string to the chain. Attach a small weight of some kind to the end of the string to keep it taut.

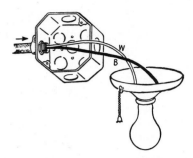

You can put in a new box and get the convenience of a pull-chain fixture. The pull-chain fixture can be equipped with a mounting plate and held to the box with just two machine screws.

If you do not have a junction box, or if the junction box you do have isn't conveniently located, you can run a length of plastic-sheathed cable and install a new box. Just make sure that you use three-wire cable (one of the wires will be a ground wire). The advantage of putting in a new box is that you can locate it exactly where you wish.

HOW TO INSTALL A JUNCTION BOX

Whenever you decide to install additional outlets and switches in your home, you will usually tap off an existing branch. The other alternative is to have a run directly back to the fuse or breaker box.

Whenever you break into an existing branch, you may not simply locate a cable somewhere, open it, cut into it, and join some extra wires to it. Wherever you join wires carrying power, you must have an electric box.

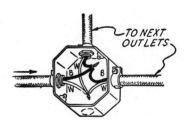

How to add a junction box: Ground wire isn't shown in this picture, but make sure this wire is connected to the new box.

The illustration shows a box inserted into cable running horizontally. Since you must install a box, do so where it is accessible. You may want to add a pull-chain fixture right on top of the box, or you may want to tap another branch off that box at some future date. Wiring is always simple in these installations: White wire always connects to white wire; black to black. After making the joints, cover all wires with solderless connectors. Also make sure you put a metal cover plate over the junction box. But before you do so, make sure the bare grounding wire from the new cable is fastened to a grounding clip on the new box.

ALTERNATIVE WIRING APPROACHES

Sometimes it is very easy to connect to existing wires in a box; at other times it may be difficult. It all depends on the size of the box and the number of wires in it. In some areas, local electrical codes determine the amount of wiring connections per box volume. Cramming a lot of connections into a small box increases the shorting hazard possibility, and also makes it more difficult to work with "add-ons."

If you need to connect an outlet to a box, you will have two ways of making the connections. You can run wires from the outlet to the box, as shown in the illustration at the left. As an alternative, you can open the wires coming into the box and connect them directly to the terminals on the receptacle, as indicated in the drawing at the right. The technique shown in the drawing at the right produces a less crowded wiring situation in the box. The whole idea in electric wiring is to select a wiring arrangement that is the simplest, with the least crowding of wires, and using the minimum run of wire. However, that isn't always possible and so sometimes you will need to make compromises.

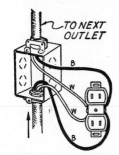

Two methods of wiring a receptacle to a box.

switch is connected directly to the ground or cold wire of the branch, and so must be marked W.

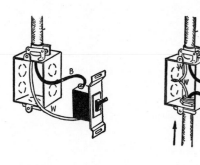

Switch at left has connections to black wire (B) and white wire (W); switch at right connects to a pair of black wires.

SWITCH WIRING

Sometimes you will need to remove a switch to replace it. When you remove the face plate and examine the switch wiring, you may see a pair of black wires connected to the switch, or a white wire and a black wire. This does not mean the wiring is incorrect, simply that different circuit arrangements were used.

The pictorial at the left shows a switch with a black and a white wire connected to it, while the drawing at the right is a similar switch, but attached to a pair of black wires.

To understand how this is possible, consider the two circuit diagrams. The only difference between the two is in the positioning of the switch and the lamp. In the upper diagram the switch precedes the lamp; in the other it follows it. Consider the upper diagram first. Coming in at the left we have a hot wire, a black wire, and this wire is connected to the switch. When the switch is closed, both sides of the switch, labeled B, will be joined, and it will be as though the black wire continues uninterrupted to the lamp. Hence, both wires to the switch are black.

Now examine the lower diagram. The hot wire, still labelled B, is connected to one side of the lamp. We can consider the lamp filament an extension of the hot wire, and so the wire on the other side of the lamp is also marked B. But this wire continues right on to the switch, hence we have marked this as B also. The other side of the

THE PROBLEM OF COLOR CODING

In the electrical industry, white is the standard color for a neutral or ground wire, while black and red are used for the hot leads. The advantage of this is that you should be able to open any box and know immediately which is the ground and which is the hot wire. If you have any doubt, you can always check with a test lamp. Clip one end of the test lamp to the metal frame of the junction box. This is ground. Then touch the other clip of the test lamp, in turn, to the various wires in the box. Naturally, you will need to remove the solderless connectors first, and power must be on. At any time the lamp turns on, you are touching a hot wire. If the lamp does not go on, the wire is a ground. Run the test with the switch turned off.

One of the problems concerning color coding of wires is that both BX and plastic-sheathed cable are available only with wires already in position. Now go back to the preceding illustration showing diagrams of switches and lamps. Usually, the lamp will be at some distance from the switch, as in the case of a ceiling fixture and a wall switch. The upper diagram presents no problem, for we have a white wire and a black wire connecting to the lamp.

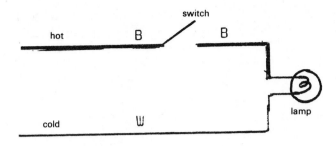

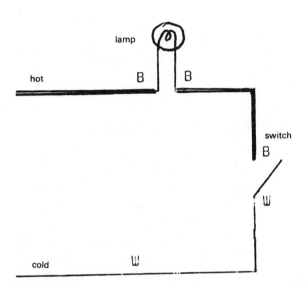

Two possible circuit arrangements for switches: Letters B and W refer to black and white wires.

CONTROLLED AND NON-CONTROLLED OUTLETS

You may have a branch coming from your fuse or breaker box to a junction box, with branches running in several directions from the junction box. These branches will ordinarily lead to various outlets in different parts of the house. You can install a switch in this junction box to control any one of the outlets you wish. All you must be careful about is to select the right black wire to break into. Usually you can trace the wiring by observing the direction in which the branches go after they leave the junction box. If you aren't sure, connect test lamps to the outlet. Disconnect wires, one at a time, until the test lamp in the outlet to be controlled goes out. Now, you certainly aren't going to be disconnecting wires with power on, so you will need to find the fuse or breaker controlling the junction box you are working on. It also means you will be running back and forth between the junction box and the fuse or breaker box, turning power off and on, so in a situation of this kind it is helpful to have someone stationed at the fuse or breaker box to help you.

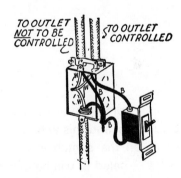

You can use a switch to control one outlet, and leave the other outlet (or outlets) uncontrolled.

Now examine the lower diagram. We have a pair of black wires going into the lamp, but that pair of black wires will be supplied by a cable of some kind. If you are using conduit you can fish a pair of black wires through it and you have no problem. But what about BX and plastic-sheathed cable? They always have a white and a black wire. Thus, if you do use such cable for wiring a lamp as per the lower circuit diagram, you will run into a color-coding conflict. The way to get around this is to take some black paint and daub the insulation of the white wire with some of it. This means that at some later date, if you need to examine the switch wiring, you will realize that both wires are hot, and not one hot and one cold.

This job isn't as difficult as it sounds since you will be ignoring any white wires in the junction box. All you need do is find the correct black wire, open it, and then connect the open ends to your switch. You will, of course, need to make a run between the junction box and the switch and mount the switch in its own box. The drawing shows the switch adjacent to the junction box.

This is seldom the case. Thus, the junction box may be in your basement, but the switch might be located in an upper floor.

HOW TO INSTALL A BOX HANGER

The easiest way to mount an electric box is by using wood screws to fasten it to a solid, wood support. This isn't always possible since the place you want to install an electric box may be plaster or sheetrock. Wood screws will not hold in these materials. However, you can use a box hanger instead, as shown in the two drawings.

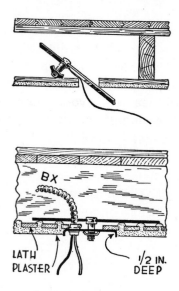

You can use a box hanger to anchor an electric box to a sheetrock wall. It may also be necessary to use a box hanger in older houses where the lath is weak or split. Drawing at left shows how to slip hanger into open space; drawing at right indicates how stud holds box against wall, with hanger providing support. Use a string or flexible wire to help position the hanger. Remove this aid after the hanger is in place.

After you have located the spot where you want to mount an electric box (you may want it as a junction box, receptacle, or switch box), make a small opening. The hanger will have a threaded stud at its center. Connect a bit of string or flexible wire to the stud, and then push the hanger into the open space, as shown in the drawing at the left. Manipulate the hanger with the string until the stud is in a downward position. Make sure the hanger is located so that it is flat against the sheet rock or lath.

Knock out holes as required in the box. If you are using BX, slip a threaded connector over it and tighten it to the BX with the screw in the connector. Now bring the wires of the BX into the box. Move the box up against the stud so that the stud protrudes into the box. Put a locknut on the stud and it will now hold the box loosely in position. At this time you will want to use an insulated bushing on the BX, or if you are using plastic-sheathed cable, you will want to tighten its connector. Finally, tighten the locknut on the stud and the box will be firmly in position.

HOW TO FISH WIRES

One of the more difficult jobs in electrical wiring is to install hidden wiring in completed houses. As long as walls are not up, putting conduit into position, or using BX or plastic-sheathed cable isn't difficult. You must first locate a section of the wall that has an open space. Once you find it, you will know that the space extends from floor to ceiling, but is shut off at both those areas. This means you must drill holes at sections where there is usually no room for anything to pass through. One spot is joint B as shown in the drawing.

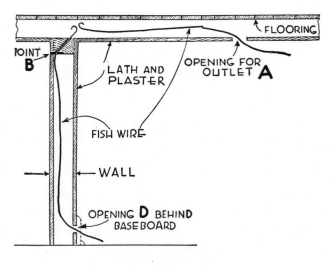

Method of fishing wires through walls.

In the room, remove the baseboard. The baseboard is usually held in by nails to the wall, so you should be able to pry it off. Once the baseboard is removed, you can cut an opening in it (point D in the drawing). You will also need to cut an opening at point A. This would be the ceiling. The only problem remaining would be to drill through at joint B. Assuming you have done this, get two lengths of fish wire, and form loops at each end. Work the wires up and across and try to get the two hook ends to engage. No, it isn't easy and takes lots of patience. Also, it isn't a one-man job. It takes two people, and furthermore, the two should be able to work together.

Fishing wires through a wall isn't easy for a professional electrician and much less so for the amateur. If at all possible, get a structural plan of the house. This will show you, at least, where you might possibly run into some interference.

The most serious problem in this wiring installation is getting the wire through joint B. The next drawing at the left has an upward arrow (#1) and a horizontal arrow (#2). When you fish through hole #1, the wire will have a tendency to stay out of the wall, and so you may need hole #2 to give you access to the wire to keep it in place.

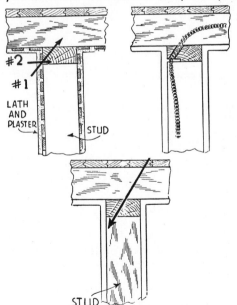

Drawing at left shows holes to be drilled trough joist to supply a passageway for fish wire. Center drawing shows fish wire pulled through into position. Drawing at right shows how you can drill downward to supply through hole for fish wire.

The center drawing shows the wire fished into place, while the drawing at the right supplies an alternative drilling method. You can drill down from above. Drilling upward is much more difficult and so you may prefer the technique at the right.

There is still one more way, the easiest of all, and that is to drill a hole through the floor. If you can select an inconspicuous spot, or possibly one that is always covered, you can make the work much simpler.

HOW TO BORE CHANNELS

To drill holes to supply a channel for fish wire and then cable calls for a long bit and a wood drill. The drawing at the left shows how to do this. Do not drill straight upward, but at an angle. Your problem will be to avoid drilling into a wall-supporting stud. If you do, your only option will be to move over a few inches and drill once again.

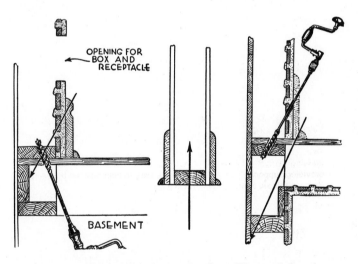

To supply a channel from basement to first floor, drill upward through basement ceiling at an angle (drawing at left). In some homes you may be able to drill straight up (center drawing). Drawing at right shows how to drill downward to supply a channel from an upper floor to a lower one.

In some homes, as shown in the center drawing, you can drill straight upward. And if you want to bring a cable down from an upper to a lower floor, start at some position behind the baseboard (remove the baseboard first) and then drill downward at an angle.

In all instances, when you use a wood drill and bit, you will be able to tell when the bit reaches the open space in the wall. It will turn much easier.

HOW TO AVOID DRILLING

If you must run cable from floor to floor, there is just no way to avoid drilling unless you can somehow take advantage of an existing channel. Floor-to-floor wiring, or vertical wiring, takes planning and lots of effort. However, if you want to wire horizontally, you may find it less difficult to do. One of the problems with horizontal wiring is that the studs or joists of the house are in the way. They represent the framing of the house and are supports for the walls. However, if you want to install an outlet or an outlet and a switch, and you can manage to make a run to the junction of a branch, then the work isn't that difficult. You can cut a groove in the wallboard, sheetrock or plaster. Hold the cable in place with staples. After the cable is in position and all electrical connections have been made and have been tested, you can plaster in over the groove.

HOW TO INSTALL CABLE

There is always the possibility that you may add another room to your house, or remove walls to install a new wall. As long as the wall interior is exposed, you have an excellent opportunity to install new wiring. You may, for example, decide to put in a ceiling light where none had existed before, or you may want to add more outlets or switches.

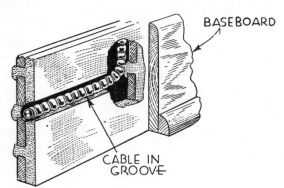

Cable can be made to fit into groove cut into wall.

One of the problems in electrical wiring is the presence of studs; the wood supports that form the frame of the house and are used for holding walls. The drawing shows two possible ways of connecting electrical parts. Note that both require drilling through the studs.

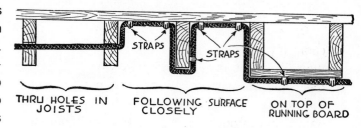

THRU HOLES IN JOISTS   FOLLOWING SURFACE CLOSELY   ON TOP OF RUNNING BOARD

Three ways of running non-metallic cable in a basement. You can drill holes through the joists. This is a method favored by some electricians since the wire is supported without straps. It also uses the least amount of wire, making a run as short as possible. The next method is to follow the surface of the wood as closely as possible. Some electricians prefer installing a running board. This is a board nailed across the beams and then used for supporting the wire cable.

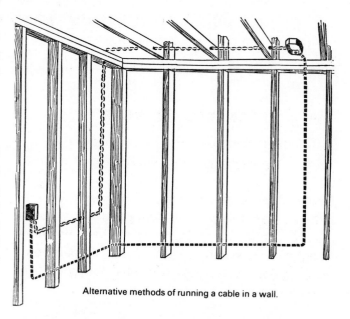

Alternative methods of running a cable in a wall.

Since both do the same job, and both are equally effective, you may well ask what difference cable positioning could possibly make. Yet, there is a difference. The lower cable will be in the wall, behind the wallboard or sheetrock forming the wall. This part of the wall will be covered by the baseboard. This means that the cable is always accessible without spoiling the appearance of the wall, possibly requiring repainting or repapering. To get at the lower wire, remove the baseboard. You can then cut the wallboard reach the cable, and do whatever work you require.

If you decide to position the cable higher, you can still get at it, but note that you will need to make repairs to the wall after you are finished.

There is still another advantage to the lower cable. If you will trace it, you will see that it avoids the ceiling. The result is that if you want to get at this cable you will not, at any time, need to touch the ceiling. Ceiling work is difficult—not that it is hard to cut through the ceiling, but you must have your head and neck in an extremely awkward position. Furthermore, unless you wear safety goggles, you can easily get plaster in your eyes. The upper cable travels through a large portion of the ceiling.

Thus, there is more to putting in a cable than just getting it into the wall and out of the way. If you plan for the future in your wiring, then the future will be much easier for you when it arrives.

HOW TO CONCEAL THE WORK

Cutting into an existing wall is always a problem. If the wall is painted, the section of wall that has been removed can be replastered and then painted once again. However, it isn't easy to match paints since paint, although it carries the same identification number on the can, may differ slightly from batch to batch. Also, old paint on a wall gradually oxidizes and changes color. The solution may be to paint the entire wall.

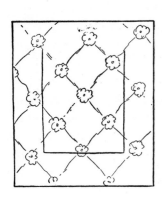
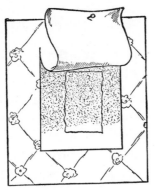

Working with wallpaper-covered walls may be a bit easier. Draw a light pencil line (do not use ink or a marking pen) and then use a sharp, single-edge blade to make the cut (do not cut freehand; use a ruler). The reason for making a pencil outline is that pencil can be erased. Use a new blade since a new blade is sharp; an old blade may make a ragged cut. Make two vertical cuts and one horizontal cut. The paper will then be in the form of a flap that can be lifted. If the paper tends to adhere to the wall, you may be able to use water to help, but it does get to be a bit tricky. After you have made your electrical installation, fill in the opening with plaster, make sure it is as smooth as possible, paste the wallpaper flap, and then drop it back into position. If the cuts you made were sharp, then the joined edges of the paper should be barely noticeable.

Whenever you paint or wallpaper a wall, don't throw away the leftovers. They will be most helpful when (not if) you must cut into a wall to make a change in your electrical wiring.

HOW TO INSTALL A CEILING OUTLET

Before you can mount a ceiling fixture, you must have a ceiling electric box. Not only does this box supply physical support for the ceiling fixture, but the wiring as well. Mounting the electric box in a ceiling is the same as mounting it in a wall. You can use an electric box strap, or if there is a wooden ceiling support, or lath, you can hold the box in position with wood screws. The cover plate for the box can have a threaded stud mounted in its center. To this stud you can fasten a threaded nipple, and once this is done you have the mechanical means for supporting the fixture.

You will have a pair of wires, coming into the ceiling box, one white and one black, connected to a branch AC line. You will need to insert a switch in the black lead so as to be able to turn the light on and off.

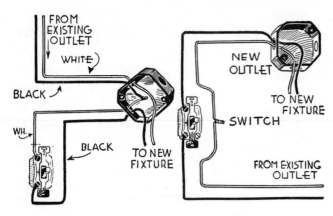

Alternative methods of wiring ceiling electric boxes.

Examine the drawing at the left. Near the top of the drawing we have two wires coming from an existing AC voltage source, possibly an outlet; and coming from the switch we have another pair of wires in a cable, one of which is white and the other black. Remember, however, that the switch is in series with the hot line and that we never switch the cold or ground line. Thus, the white wire coming from the switch should really be a black wire. At the switch dab a bit of black paint on this wire to remind you at some future date that this is indeed a hot wire. Also touch a bit of paint to the end of this white wire where it comes into the electric box on the ceiling, again to remind you that the wire is hot. You will need to do this, since BX and plastic-sheathed cable come equipped with black and white wires. With conduit you can use a pair of black wires from the switch to the ceiling electric box, so identifying wires with paint will not be necessary.

Now look at the white lead coming from the existing outlet. It goes directly into the electric box and is then available for the new fixture. We could call this box a terminal box, since ground ends at this point.

The drawing at the right shows an alternative wiring approach. Assume that you have plastic-sheathed cable in this installation. Power is obtained from some existing branch, possibly an existing outlet. The cable is brought into the electric box containing the switch and is then cut. One end of the black wire is connected to a brass screw on the switch. The other end of the black wire is attached to the other brass screw. The white wire is connected to a nickel or chrome screw. Immediately adjacent to this screw and connected to it by a small metal strap is another nickel or chrome screw. A white wire goes from this screw to the ceiling electric box. In the drawing the white wire is shown as being spliced, near the switch. While you could splice the white wire, it is easier to attach to the screws. Another technique would be to ignore the ground screws altogether, and to let the white wire continue, unbroken, through the electric box housing the switch. With the technique shown in the second drawing, the one at the right, there is no need to paint wires since black is used as the hot lead throughout.

MOTORS

Rarious appliances in your home use motors. Your kitchen electric clock is motor driven; so is your refrigerator and washing machine, your sewing machine, your washer, and your vacuum cleaner. The ventilating fan in your attic has a motor, and so does your air-conditioning unit. Your electric typewriter has a motor and so does your hand-held hair dryer. An astonishing number of motors are used in the home, but their presence is usually not known since they are ordinarily covered and operated directly by a switch on the appliance. But when a motor decides not to work, it also makes the decision for the appliance.

WHAT YOU SHOULD KNOW ABOUT MO- TORS

Every motor has a pair of poles. The earth has a pair of poles, one north and the other south. Every magnet also has a pair of poles, similarly designated. A motor, however, can have one pair of poles, two pairs, and so on.

Motors used around the home are generally AC types, designed, like all the other appliances you have, to work from 117 volts AC. This voltage changes its polarity, or reverses its polarity, 60 times a second. This frequency of change is known as the cycle per second or Hertz, and so for most homes the line frequency is 60 cycles per second, abbreviated as 60 cps, and more recently also designated as 60 Hertz or 60 Hz. When you buy an electric clock, or a similar motor-operated unit for home use, you will probably find a label or tag on it somewhere indicating it is designed to work from 117 VAC, 60 Hz.

If it is of any interest to you, you can calculate the speed of any of your AC motors by dividing the number of poles into 3,600, which is the frequency of the AC line in minutes, instead of seconds. There are 60 seconds in one minute, and if the frequency is 60 cycles per second, then in one minute, 60 times 60 equals 3,600 cycles per minute. Divide 3,600 by the number of poles in the motor and you will learn its speed in RPM (revolutions per minute). A 2-pole motor, for example, is 3,600/2 equals 1,800 RPM. This motor will complete 1,800 revolutions in one minute.

If the motor has 8 poles, its speed will be 3,600/8 equals 450 RPM. Thus, a high-speed motor will have fewer poles than a slow-speed motor. Usually, the greater the number of poles not only results in a slower speed but also in a heavier motor.

MOTORS AND HEAT

If you have a motor-operated appliance that seems to get very hot after being used for awhile, regard it as normal. You may find a metal tag on the motor stating, "40 degrees C. continuous." The letter C. refers to degrees centigrade or Celsius. Centigrade and Celsius are the same, but don't confuse them with degrees Fahrenheit (F^0). Forty degrees C. continuous is an indication that the temperature of the motor will not increase by more than this amount. Forty degrees C. is the

same as 72° F. Assume the temperature in your living room is 70° F., as it may very well be. If you decide to vacuum your rugs, and keep the cleaner on for quite awhile, its temperature may rise by 72° F. But your house is already at 70° F., and so the temperature of the motor can go up as high as 70° plus 72° equals 142° F. That is very hot and for this reason the motor is generally housed where you cannot get at it and touch it very readily. 142° F., by the way, is the maximum temperature, and the motor would be on for quite a long time before getting that hot.

There are two basic parts in a motor: the rotor and the stator. The rotor is the part that turns or rotates; the stator is the section of the motor that is fixed in position. Like transformers, the stator and rotor are made of thin sheets of steel, known as laminations. These are punched out to hold coils of wire. A motor is really a first cousin to a transformer, except that in a transformer both windings, primary and secondary (corresponding to rotor and stator), are fixed in position.

MOTOR ROTORS

The rotor, the turning part of a motor, can be one of two basic types. One of these is the wound type, consisting of laminations of thin steel, cut out along the edges to accommodate insulated copper wire. The laminations are arranged so that they have slots across the surface into which the wire may be pushed.

The other type of rotor is called a squirrel cage. In this rotor the laminations have holes punched near their edges with coppers bars inserted. No wire is used.

In a transformer, the primary and secondary windings have no physical connection. Even if the secondary is wound directly on the primary winding, they are still separated by insulating material. The same is true in a motor. The rotor and stator must be separated, although the distance between them is often very small. Generally, the stator is wound so that it forms a housing around the rotor. The rotor is mounted on a shaft and is fastened to it. This shaft, usually a cylindrical rod made of steel, protrudes from the rotor and turns with it. It is this rotating shaft that supplies the torque or turning power for gears, levers, cams, or other mechanical arrangements.

UNIVERSAL MOTORS

All motors, no matter how small or how large, or how they are designed or used, come under the general heading of transducers. A transducer is a device that changes energy from one form to another. A microphone is a transducer: It changes sound energy to electrical energy. A battery is a transducer: It changes chemical energy to electrical energy. A motor is a transducer: It changes electrical energy to mechanical energy. Transducers are important since they let us change one form of energy to another.

The electrical-energy input to a motor can be AC or DC. The AC can be supplied by power lines inside your home. DC is usually furnished by batteries. Some motors run on AC only; others on DC only. A universal motor will work from alternating or direct current; hence its name. Like people, motors have characteristics of their own. The universal type of motor runs at very high speeds when it is not loaded—that is, when it is turning, but not working or driving a load. The speed of such a motor can be as high as 20,000 revolutions per minute (20,000 RPM) but this very high speed can drop to as little as 1,000 RPM when the motor is put to work.

Despite this characteristic, the universal motor is used for working conditions when the load is applied immediately and remains constant. Since the motor is not allowed to idle, it cannot reach the very high speeds that could destroy it. An electric fan is one such example. The fan blades are always fastened to the rotor and so the load

(the blades) remains constant. Universal motors are also used for vacuum cleaners.

SPLIT-PHASE MOTORS

Your washing machine may have a motor of this type. The rotor is a squirrel-cage type and there are two stator windings. One of these is connected to the power line at all times when the appliance is turned on; the other is used as an auxiliary winding, and works from the time the motor starts until it reaches working speed. Compare this motor to a car. When an auto starts, it requires a large amount of energy to go from a stopped to a moving position. Once the car is in motion, it can continue with much less energy demands. A motor needs more starting than running energy; hence two stators. Once the motor is running, then the extra torque supplied by the second stator is no longer needed. The second stator is automatically disconnected by a centrifugal-type switch on the rotor. As the rotor turns, a lever on the switch is pushed by the motion in an outward direction. When it reaches a certain position after the rotor has achieved operating speed, it will open a switch, cutting off the flow of current through the windings of the second stator.

Split-phase motors require a large starting current, a current that can be as much as six times the running current. A ¼ horsepower motor may demand as much as 35 amperes starting current, but this current will gradually decrease as the rotor reaches full operating speed.

YOUR WASHING MACHINE

If your washing machine uses a split-phase motor, then you should realize the disadvantages of overloading the unit. With very heavy loads, the motor draws a high current and will continue to do so until it reaches its working speed. But if it takes the motor a long time to do so, the windings may burn out. A winding on a motor may be designed to carry a current, such as 35 amperes, for a reasonably short time. This large current, however, heats the coil windings of the motor, and this in turn may cause the insulation to char. The charred material will fly off as the motor rotor turns and so the adjacent turns of exposed copper may touch and short against each other. This increases the current drain to the windings, which get even hotter, and cause still more insulation to char. The process is a cumulative one and finally the winding takes so much current from the power line that the fuse or breaker opens.

The fault is not in the motor, but is due to overloading. The split-phase motor works on AC only and usually has a maximum rating of ⅓ horsepower.

THE MEANING OF HORSEPOWER

Horses came before machines and so, in the early days of the steam engine, some comparison was needed between the amount of work a horse could do and machines. The term, horsepower, a somewhat ridiculous yardstick, is still used in connection with motors. One horsepower, abbreviated as HP, is equivalent to 746 watts. A quarter HP motor is 746/3 watts and a half HP motor is 746/2 watts. You will find the HP rating of a motor on a metal plate fastened to the outside surface of the motor. More useful bits of information on this plate would be the line voltage, frequency, power (in watts), and current requirements.

CONDENSER MOTORS

The word condenser, although still widely used, is gradually being replaced by the word capacitor. The condenser motor is so called since it has a capacitor that helps limit the starting current to a smaller amount. This type of motor has a number of advantages over the split-phase type. While it can only be used on AC voltage, it has a higher starting torque, and will not burn out as quickly. Torque means turning power. When a load is very heavy, high starting torque means that the current

demands of the motor will be reduced more quickly. The load is the object being set in motion by the motor. If used in connection with a washing machine, the load is the tub to be rotated full of laundry. Your refrigerator quite possibly uses a condenser-type motor.

REPULSION-INDUCTION MOTOR

This is a heavy-duty type, works only on AC, and is available in ratings up to about 10 horsepower. The unit has a wound rotor, and in some models a short-circuiting device converts the motor into the equivalent of a squirrel-cage type. Because of its high starting torque, it is used with machinery that is difficult to start.

SYNCHRONOUS MOTOR

This motor is socalled since its speed is synchronized to some multiple of the power-line frequency. It maintains its speed except when it is heavily overloaded, and so it is regarded as a constant-speed motor.

Synchronous motors are usually quite large and in this form are designed for industrial use. They can also be built quite small, in fractional horsepower types. There are either large or small but no in-between, moderate horsepower types.

The electric clock in your home is probably a synchronous-motor type. Since the frequency of your alternating current is 60 cycles per second (or 60 Hz), it is easy to gear the clock so this is translated into terms of 60 seconds per minute. Clock motors often have a permanent magnet rotor made in the form of a wheel with teeth.

There is a modification of the synchronous motor into a form known as the hysteresis synchronous or simply hysteresis type. Its advantage over the synchronous motor is that it is self-starting. If, for some reason, power to your home is interrupted, this type of motor will start again as soon as power is restored.

Older-type electric clocks that used a synchronous motor had to be started by twirling a small metal knob on the back of the clock. More modern clocks, using hysteresis synchronous motors, are independent of such starting devices and begin turning automatically as soon as power is applied. Hysteresis synchronous motors are also used in record players and record changers, both because of their self-starting feature and because of their ability to maintain a constant speed, whether loaded or unloaded.

HOW TO TAKE CARE OF MOTORS

About the only care a motor might require would be an occasional drop of oil. However, motors used in modern home appliances are "self-oiling" types, and since they are usually put in some sort of housing, may even be difficult to reach.

A motor is a moving device and like all moving devices will ultimately wear out. Unless you have the correct tools and experience in motor repair, it is better not to try to fix it. Even an electrician or an appliance-repair expert will not try to repair a motor on your premises. They will remove the old motor and either put in a new one, or a rebuilt type.

Motors are also used in a number of kitchen devices such as mixers and grinders. Current is brought into motors through a pair of wires, following the same technique used for supplying current to an electric-light bulb. Inside the motor housing are a pair of brushes, generally made of carbon. One of the more common troubles in motors is that these carbon brushes wear away. When they do, the only solution is to replace them. With home appliances you may find the brushes (there are two) held in place by a chrome-plated screw. Remove the screw and pull out the brush. You can then take the brush or mail it to any company that services this type of appliance. However, you must also supply the part

number of the brush. If you received manufacturer's literature with the appliance, you should be able to find the number on the parts list. Failing that, your only alternative is to return the kitchen appliance to an authorized service station for that particular unit.

MANUFACTURERS' LITERATURE

Whenever you buy a household appliance, no matter how small or large that appliance may be, you will get an instruction manual and a warranty registration card. Fill in the warranty with your name and address, plus any other information required, and mail it back to the manufacturer. Keep your copy of the warranty and a copy of your sales slip together in a safe place. If your appliance becomes defective within the warranty period, you may be able to save money on parts, labor, or both. The manufacturer's literature not only describes the appliance, but explains its use, and also supplies an inventory list of all the parts, together with part numbers.

LINE CORDS FOR MOTORS

Lamp cord is not generally used for home motors except when those motors are quite small. Motors in this category would include clock motors and motors for electric shavers. A good rule of thumb is never to make the connecting line cord any longer than possible. Yes, there are certain appliances that do demand a long line cord. A vacuum cleaner is a notable example, but here the problem is that the unit must be moved. If you have a work surface in a kitchen that holds a number of appliances—a toaster, mixer, broiler, and the like—and if these remain in one position, the connecting cord can be made shorter, even if these cords have molded male plugs at their ends. Cut off the plug and a portion of the wire and then connect the wire to a new plug.

MULTI-INPUT MOTORS

Some motors are designed only for use on a 110-volt line, others for 220-volts only, while some can have their wiring rearranged to take advantage of both. It is always better to operate a motor at a higher voltage, if this is possible, since it reduces the motor's current requirements by 50 percent.

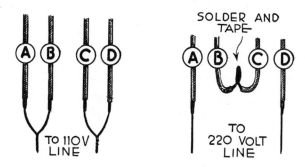

Motor connections for 110-volt AC line (left), and 220-volt AC line (right).

The drawing shows four wires, in two pairs, identified as A and B, C and D, connected to a motor. The drawing at the left shows how these are joined for 110-volt use. When wires B and C are joined, wires A and D can be used with a 220-volt line. These are just generalized instructions, of course, but the information will be contained in the operating manual accompanying the motor. The motor leads, for example, may be color coded. Some motors come equipped with a built-in switch to permit an easy changeover from 110 to 220 volts.

Whenever you buy a motor and that motor is easily accessible, always read the plate mounted on the motor frame. The plate may read "50 Hz/60 Hz," indicating that the line frequency may be either 50 cycles per second or 60. The plate may also read "single phase." Since all homes use single phase AC power, this need not concern you. Single phase means a single voltage. Three phase means three voltages, out of step with each other. The plate on the motor may also specify "volts 110/220; amps 20/10." This means that the motor can work from either 110 or 220 volts, depending on how you make connections to the motor's wires; and that for 110 volts the current will be 20 amperes, while for 220 volts it will be

10 amperes. The chart shown below indicates the current demands of a motor and the minimum wire size you should use for connecting such motors to the power line. But while the table indicates a minimum size, it is satisfactory to use a larger-size wire if you want to do so. Remember, also, that the larger the current demand of the motor, the more advisable it is to make the connecting power cord just as short as possible.

Amperage of Motor	Minimum Size Wire Required
1 to 12	14
13 to 16	12
17 to 24	10
26 to 32	8
34 to 44	6

Amperage of Motor	Minimum Size Wire Required
46 to 56	4
58 to 64	3
66 to 76	2
78 to 88	1
90 to 100	0

FUSES FOR MOTORS

Since the starting current of some motors is substantially higher than the running current, using an ordinary fuse will produce problems. If the starting current of a motor is 20 amperes and the running current is 3 amperes, a logical choice would be to use a 5-ampere fuse to protect the motor while in operation. Yet, the 20-ampere starting current will "blow" the fuse. For this purpose it is better to use the time-lag type of fuses. These will permit a high starting current, but will open if the motor draws excessive current while working.

The drop in current of a motor from its start to running position is due to the electric behavior of the motor. Motors and electric generators are quite alike and, as a matter of fact, while a motor is running it behaves like a generator and produces a voltage. This motor-produced voltage, sometimes called a counter electromotive force or a counter EMF, is a voltage in opposition to the line voltage; and because it opposes the line voltage, the current for the motor is reduced. However, if a motor should jam, or if for any reason the rotor stops turning, the counter EMF disappears and the motor behaves as though in the start position. With the loss of the counter EMF, maximum current flows into the motor. This current can damage the motor windings quickly, possibly starting a fire inside the motor by igniting the wire insulation, or at least causing it to carbonize. The following chart indicates motor running current and maximum fuse sizes to use:

Motor Amperes	Maximum Fuse Size
1 to 5	15
6	20
7 to 8	25
9 to 10	30
11	35
12 to 13	40
14 to 15	45

Motor Amperes	Maximum Fuse Size
16	50
17 to 20	60
22	70
24 to 26	80
28 to 30	90
32	100
34 to 36	110

MOTOR BRANCH CIRCUITS

If a motor requires a large amount of current, supplying that current can sometimes be a problem. There are two factors involved. One of these is the size of the wire you plan to use. The other is the distance from the service entrance to the motor. For most homes this distance will be less than 130'. However, you must divide this number by a factor of 2 since the current must not only flow to the motor but back to the service entrance: 130 ÷ 2 equals 65'.

The following table indicates the various horse-power ratings of motors and the size of wire to use for either 115-volt or 230-volt service:

The distances given in the chart are one-way. Divide each number by 2. As an example, assume you have a ¼ HP motor located 100' from your service entrance, and that you intend connecting

Hp.	Volts	No. 14	No. 12	No. 10	No. 8	No. 6	No. 4	No. 2	No. 0
¼	115	140	220	350	560	890	1,400	2,300	3,600
⅓		110	170	260	420	660	1,100	1,700	2,700
½		90	140	220	350	560	890	1,400	2,200
¾		60	100	160	250	400	640	1,000	1,600
1			80	130	200	320	450	800	1,300
¼	230	560	890	1,400	2,250	3,600	5,700	9,000	8,900
⅓		420	660	1,050	1,670	2,600	4,200	6,700	6,500
½		350	550	880	1,400	2,200	3,500	5,600	5,100
¾		250	400	640	1,010	1,600	2,600	4,200	3,600
1		200	320	500	800	1,300	2,000	3,200	2,800
1½		140	220	350	560	900	1,400	2,300	1,900
2		110	170	270	430	690	1,100	1,800	1,200
3				190	310	480	860	1,200	820
5					190	290	470	740	
7½						210	320	520	

ONE-WAY DISTANCE TO MOTOR

The figures in the table above shows the maximum ONE-WAY distance in feet that each size of wire will carry the amperage required for motors of various sizes, with 3% voltage drop. If the motor is overloaded, the drop will be greater. If you expect full power from your motor, do not skimp on wire size.

this motor to the 115-volt line. Locate ¼ HP in the column at the left. A horizontal line separates 115-volt from 230-volt ratings, so examine the listings above this line. The first column is for no. 14 wire. If you will look directly below the designation no. 14, you will see 140. This means 140'. Divide this by 2 and the result is 70'. But since the motor is 100' away, move to the next column. Under a heading of No. 12, you will see 220. Divide 220 by 2 and the result will be 110. Because the distance involved is only 100', you can safely use no. 12 wire. The wire referred to in this table is copper wire. The voltage drop or loss along the line connecting the motor to the fuse or breaker box will be about 3 percent. If the line voltage is 117, then 3 percent of 117 is 0.03 times 117 equals 3.5 volts approximately. The voltage appearing at the input terminals of the motor will then be 117 less 3.5 equals 113.5 volts. Wire size becomes increasingly critical for motors having a higher horsepower rating.

HOW TO HOOK UP AN ELECTRIC RANGE OR DRIER

The voltage used by an electric range will be either 115 volts or 230 volts, depending on the setting of its controls. When a range is put in its self-cleaning cycle, or is used for roasting and similar applications, high heat is needed and so the range will use 230 volts. The top burners will use either 115 or 230 volts, depending on the setting of the controls. For low heat it will be 115 volts.

Unlike other appliances in your home, your electric range will not share its branch line. You will probably have a separate branch running directly from the fuse or breaker box, using a three-wire cable of no. 6 wire.

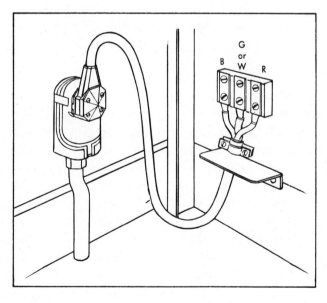

Method of connecting an electric range or drier to a heavy-duty wall receptacle. (Courtesy, Sears.)

You will find coming out of the back of the range a terminal for connecting three wires. The terminal at the left is for a black wire; that on the right is for a red wire. Both are "hot" and each measures 115 volts to the center terminal. The voltage from the black wire to the red wire is 230 volts. The center terminal, marked G or W, is for the neutral or ground wire. With some appliances this center wire will be coded in some other color, such as green. It is still a neutral or ground wire, however.

One end of the power cord coming out of the appliance is a special three-prong plug. The use of a plug permits the appliance to be disconnected easily from the power line. The metal frame of the appliance should be connected to the center ground terminal. The wiring shown in the drawing is suitable for either an electric range or dryer. However, this does not mean they operate from the same branch.

Like the electric range, the drier uses 230 volts and 115 volts, depending on the setting of its controls. When using a wall receptacle for plugging in the drier (and this applies to the range as well), get a special heavy-duty wall receptacle. These come in various sizes, so get one having a wattage rating that is at least equal to (or preferably greater than) the highest rating of the appliance. Regular electric dryers may be rated at about 4200 watts, while special high-speed dryers are about 8500 watts. As in the case of the electric range, the metal housing of the dryer must be grounded.

Whenever you plan to install very high power appliances, such as the 8500-watt high-speed drier, check with your local power utility first. They may need to install special power lines to take care of your requirements. For appliances such as electric ranges and driers, it is advisable to check your local electrical codes to make sure you conform to their requirements. In some areas, wiring for such appliances may need to be done by or supervised by a licensed electrician.

WATER-HEATER INSTALLATION

There are two basic types of water heaters: those having a single heating element and those having two. The advantage of the double-element type is that it permits a more constant supply of hot water where there is a great demand for heated water, usually in large families. The current flow is governed by thermostats, one for each element. When the water drops below a pre-designated temperature, the thermostat turns on the current to the heating element. When the water reaches its required temperature, th ther-mostat triggers a circuit that turns the current off. As in the case of an electric range and drier, it is essential to double check with your local power company.

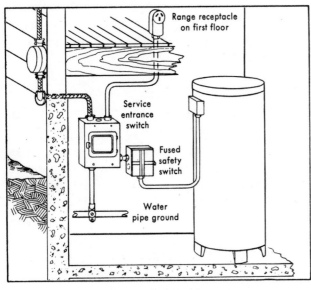

Electric water-heater installation. (Courtesy, Sears.)

PROTECTING YOUR INVESTMENT

For most people the purchase of a home is their largest single investment, so it is just ordinary common sense to protect that investment as much as possible. Protecting it, though, is not enough, for you want that investment to grow.

One way of making it grow is house maintenance, with electric wiring an important part of that maintenance.

There is no such thing as permanently adequate wiring. A house wired ten years ago may be below standard today. If you rewire your home, you can be fairly sure that a few years from now it may require further attention.

There is some electrical work you can do around your home by yourself, easily and quickly. But if you do plan on using heavy current motors or appliances, there are five steps you should take:

1. Prepare a plan of what you intend to do. Measure the distance between the service entrance and the location of the appliance. All of the fuses and breakers in the box may be fully occupied and so you may require a supplementary box.

2. Consult your local power company. Show them your plans. They will need to know the kind of appliances you intend to install and their maximum current rating. They will probably check your records to learn your average power use.

3. You may need a permit for your proposed wiring. Ask your power company to let you consult a book called *The National Electrical Code.* Some utilities will supply you with this without charge.

4. Your local municipal government may have special laws about wiring. These laws may demand the services of a master electrician or may require an electrician to be on the premises during wiring. You may need to obtain a permit before going ahead with the wiring. Finally, you may require a certificate of inspection after the wiring is done.

5. Check with your insurance company to learn if "do-it-yourself" wiring violates any provision of your home-owner's policy or fire-insurance policy. Don't rely on a verbal reply—get it in writing.